DESIGNING SACRE

Sacred spaces exemplify some of the most exciting and challenging architecture today. *Designing Sacred Spaces* tells the inside story of seven architecture firms and their approaches to designing churches, mosques, synagogues and temples, monasteries and retreats. Twenty beautifully illustrated case studies located in Asia, Europe, and North America are showcased alongside discussions with the designers into concept and design development, materiality, and spatial analysis. Complementing these are essays on the cultural, historical, and theoretical meaning and importance of sacred spaces. By exploring the way we see religion and how we understand secular and sacred space, *Designing Sacred Spaces* reveals how we see ourselves and how we see others. A *tour de force* of first-person narratives, research, and illustrations, this book is a vital desk reference.

Sherin Wing received her PhD in the Humanities from UCLA, USA. In addition to being a published scholar, she also writes for several publications including *Architecture Magazine*, ArchDaily.com, *The Huffington Post*, and *Metropolis Magazine* on a wide range of issues surrounding the cultural, economic, and social aspects of architecture.

DESIGNING SACRED SPACES

Sherin Wing

Routledge
Taylor & Francis Group
New York London

First published 2016
by Routledge

711 Third Avenue, New York, NY 10017
2 Park Square, Milton Park, Abingdon, Oxfordshire OX14 4RN

Routledge is an imprint of the Taylor & Francis Group, an informa business

First issued in paperback 2018

Library of Congress Cataloguing in Publication Data
Wing, Sherin.
Designing sacred spaces / Sherin Wing.
pages cm
Includes bibliographical references and index.
1. Religious architecture—Case studies. I. Title.
NA4600.W56 2016
726—dc23 2015013021

ISBN: 978-0-415-74500-0 (hbk)
ISBN: 978-0-367-02831-2 (pbk)

Acquisition Editor: Wendy Fuller
Editorial Assistant: Grace Harrison
Production Editor: Hannah Champney

Typeset in Fairfield and Avenir
by Keystroke, Station Road, Codsall, Wolverhampton

DEDICATION

For Guy

"Equal parts fascinating history-theory, illuminating design diary and dialog, and feast for the eyes and soul, Wing's *Designing Sacred Spaces* is a compelling and beautifully structured book that teaches us, not only about religion and culture, but about design process, perception, and the power of space to be transcendent. It's a fascinating read with multiple voices and points of view. A welcome addition to anyone's library, certainly not just those of architects."

– Alice Kimm, JFAK Architects and Adjunct Associate Professor, USC School of Architecture, USA

"Sherin Wing is changing the architectural dialog for the better. In this rigorously researched, thoughtful, well-written book she argues against the European/American centric examination of our built environment, and opens the discourse by including sacred spaces around the globe. She argues and proves that architecture is at its best when it represents unique and complex cultures, a specific locality as well as its policies and beliefs. What better place to start human habitation than in the spiritual realm?"

– Susan S. Szenasy, Publisher and Editor in Chief, *Metropolis*, USA

"An inspiring book that is as thorough and insightful as it is beautiful. An excellent reminder of the heights that contemporary architects can achieve."

– Sam Lubell, Contributing Editor, *The Architect's Newspaper*, USA

CONTENTS

PART 1

INTRODUCTION

Chapter 1

Introduction

The genesis of this book is simple. My husband was working on a project with a colleague to design a Shaolin temple in California. The design needed to include a workout space, a sitting (meditation) space, an altar, some changing rooms, and a small store. His colleague, unfamiliar with the traditions of Buddhism, was nevertheless certain that his own religious faith would ensure a respectful design. Except that it didn't. The altar was put to the side of the interior to make way for other programmatic elements.

You can't put Buddha in a corner: the altar must be in alignment with the North–South axis. It was a mistake that anyone might make. Especially if an architect relied solely on instinct to accommodate the necessary symbolic and practical aspects of a religious space: worship, socializing, educating.

In secular spaces, plans and circulation frequently rely on practical considerations since components are often of similar or equal importance. Religious spaces are different. Planning religious program requires not only design skill but also cultural knowledge. For architects who deal primarily with secular spaces, this can be a challenge.

For one, many religions involve a hierarchy of spatial necessities that must be maintained. These necessities cannot be moved simply because a programmatic element might be more conveniently placed in one location over another.

Even more bewildering is that the hierarchy of programmatic elements differs widely from religion to religion, depending not just on doctrine combined with individual interpretation, but also on a given community's specific needs.

So I began to investigate. How are sacred spaces produced? How do you design a space if the culture is unfamiliar but nevertheless requires a skilled approach to symbolism, tradition, iconography, and rituals? How do you address the larger metaphysical issues materially? And is religious space created during the design process by an architect or designer? Or is it determined by its users, including the people who commission them? What programmatic elements *must* be present in order to designate a space sacred? Is it necessary to research the historical meanings of symbolic ritual objects and program?

Builders and architects have grappled with these issues for millennia and their responses have been unique and varied. Over the years, clients and donors have become more culturally and intellectually sophisticated. They require designs that evoke religious symbolism while reflecting the plurality of intellectual and design possibilities. Shifting conditions in social, economic, and political spheres[1] has created "new relationships between. . .people and objects used for their. . .religious identities."[2] Rather than rely on intermediaries as they did in the past, practitioners now emphasize "direct access to the sacred through ritual mediations with objects and in spaces that engage the senses."[3]

To explore these issues, this book examines the sacred space portfolios of seven architecture firms. Under three major sections that include churches, mosques, synagogues, and temples, monasteries, and retreats, each chapter examines a single firm's work within that category. Firms within each typology are organized alphabetically.

We will find that every project differently combines the way and to what degree secular and religious symbols, values, and practicalities manifest. Investigating how each firm approaches these variables—client needs and agendas, religious doctrine, spatial necessities, and materials—and combines them with their own enduring aesthetic sensibilities and design philosophies will reveal how unique this process is.

Doing so exposes how the values that define us interact on individual and institutional levels to produce religious spaces. We will discover that sacred and secular spaces are neither empty containers nor inherently vested sites. Rather space becomes activated through human interaction.[4] All spaces are culturally constructed arenas that are constantly (re)produced.[5] In other words, one way to express individual and institutional values is through built space. And as the projects in this book demonstrate, there are different secular and religious ways to establish spatial relationships.[6]

While the narratives provided by the architects themselves are enlightening, it is equally important to contextualize the projects and their narratives culturally, historically, and theoretically. Many of the old architecture historiogaphies are limited by discourses that are essentializing. Too often, they reiterate erroneous opinions that have become authoritative merely through years of repetition. Worse, many today will rely on opinion pieces found on the web, mistaking the proliferation of opinion-based information with true knowledge, and even more elusive, wisdom. Foregrounding individual narratives with larger intellectual constructs advances better insight into the cultural and spatial implications of their projects.

To provide a better insight, each of the sections is interspersed with essays on culture, epistemology, history, religions, and space. Each academic discourse contains a "specialized discourse[s] represented in discussions among scholars. . .[that] foreground themes overlooked by research steeped in [other scholarly] agendas."[7] In anthropological terms, historians must illustrate what they represent as much as how they represent it.[8]

However, each discipline privileges certain methodologies and stances that are based on an accepted canon of "authoritative" narratives and works. These in turn canonize certain concepts and terms. Their authority often rests merely on a willingness to accept them *as* authoritative.[9]

It is important to "employ methods and theories suited to study collectivities and suprapersonal patterns of meaning" that encompass societies, economies, polities, and structures.[10] New methodologies will uncover new insights. I therefore examine multiple perspectives and disciplines to correct the elisions inherent in using only one or two analytical methodologies.

The designer narratives, together with the essays, will advance a fundamental epistemological shift on how sacred spaces function materially and symbolically. These intellectual examinations are interspersed throughout the book, imparting a deeper understanding of the issues raised. Epistemology provides the cornerstone that anchors these insights into the meanings and functions of sacred spaces.

What remains is the exchange between constancy and flux. Fluidity in design coexists alongside necessary, fixed symbolic elements. Moreover, underlying the heterogeneous nature of these projects are non-religious themes that also remain fixed, including each architect's design principles that work with necessary programmatic elements which are dictated by religious doctrine. All these factors become activated and adjust as they interact with client needs, principles, and ideals.

Notes

1 Paul Eli Ivey. Review, *Gothic Arches, Latin Crosses: Anti-Catholicism and American Church Designs in the Nineteenth Century* by Ryan K. Smith; *American Sanctuary: Understanding Sacred Spaces* by Louis P. Nelson, *Journal of the Society of Architectural Historians*, Vol. 67, No. 3 (September, 2008): 456.

2 Ivey, 2008: 454.

3 Ivey, 2008: 455.

4 Michael J. Walsh, "Efficacious Surroundings: Temple Space and Buddhist Well-being," *Journal of Religion and Health*, Vol. 46, No. 4 (Dec., 2007): 475.

5 Walsh, 2007: 476.

6 Marilyn E. Heldman, "Architectural Symbolism, Sacred Geography and the Ethiopian Church," *Journal of Religion in Africa*, Vol. 22, Fasc. 3 (August, 1992): 223.

7 John Corrigan, "Spatiality and Religion," in *The Spatial Turn: Interdisciplinary Perspectives*, edited by Barney Warf and Santa Arias (New York: Routledge, 2009): 159.

8 While Hackett examines how the study of religion itself must remain aware of its methodologies in the collection and presentation of concepts and facts, the insight is heuristically useful here (Rosalind I.J. Hackett, "Anthropology of Religion," in *The Routledge Companion to the Study of Religion*, edited by John R. Hinnells [London and New York: Routledge, 2005]: 155).

9 There is no prediscursive authority as such. Instead, what is "accepted" is often mere replication and thoughtless repetition of earlier conclusions, conclusions that contain unacknowledged, political, *interested*, agendas. See, for example, James G. Crossley and Christian Karner, "Introduction: Writing History, Constructing Religion," in *Writing History, Constructing Religion*, edited by James G. Crossley and Christian Karner (Burlington and Hampshire: Ashgate, 2005): 3; see also Edward Said, *Culture and Imperialism* (New York: Random House, 1994): 77.

10 Robert M. Gimello, "Chang Shang-ying on Wu-t'ai Shan," in *Pilgrims and Sacred Sites in China*, edited by Susan Naquin and Chün-fang Yü (Berkeley and California: University of California Press, 1992): 89.

Chapter 2

New Terms

Simply put, words have history. And with that history comes power. To use a linguistic distinction, words are signifiers that point to an entire context. The context—the meaning of words, as well as that of concepts, objects, and spaces—are all created through the action and interaction of people. Meaning, then, is achieved through re-assertion and re-inscription.[1]

That said, certain words and meanings become privileged over time through constant repetition and usage. In fact, authors will often use a term simply because they read it elsewhere and assume it must be prediscursively authoritative. After all, writing tends to confer an unquestionable authority and over time, repetition cements that authority.

One example is the terms "sacred" and "profane." Many are familiar with these terms, made popular by Mircea Eliade's book, *The Sacred and the Profane: the Nature of Religion*. Even if they are not familiar with his work, for most academics and even the general populace, the sacred/profane dichotomy is authoritative and prediscursive.

However, a closer examination of these two terms reveals several problems. In Eliade's view, sacrality and its opposite, profanity, are permanent. They embody inherent, qualitative characteristics which may even appear self-explanatory: sacred is associated with religious, transformative activity, and profane encompasses the rest of people's activity and the environs they occur in.[2]

More important is the context that produced these static definitions. Eliade used a very Eurocentric interpretation of cultural traditions for his anthropological study. Unlike early Enlightenment enthusiasts, he actually traveled to distant lands, watched people, and then made observations based on those observations.[3] That seems acceptable, but there is a catch: he failed to research the histories, cultures, and traditions of the peoples he examined *prior* to encountering them in person. Without a proper cultural or historical context to frame what he saw, he instead relied on his own Eurocentric biases about "others" and how their religions functioned.[4] In other words, Eliade projected a Eurocentric framework of what religion means and how it functions onto non-European peoples. For those things he could not explain in European terms, he made biased assumptions about the "other."

What Eliade did amounts to a universalization, one that privileges a European definition of how people use and interact with religion. It is problematic precisely because cultural generalities rapidly devolve into monolithic oversimplifications.[5] Cross-cultural is not interchangeable with universal.[6] What's more, it is not, as critics of cultural studies assert, endlessly relative. It is merely *different* from what they know.

Euro/American scholars would never consider advancing such sweeping generalities on their own history—just think of all the ink scholars and dilettantes have spent on the complexities of the American Civil War. Then consider how these same people will condense all of Liberia's history, for example, into a few short sentences or even words.

The dichotomy "sacred vs. profane" also relies on a Eurocentric ontology. The terms purport a single narrative based on Eurocentric and Christian definitions. As one example, "profane" contains negative Eurocentric and Christian connotations: the word oftentimes extends to "impious" or "disrespectful," or, even "idolatrous," all meanings which clearly privilege Euro-Christian renderings of cosmology. Yet despite reflecting a Eurocentric, rather narrow meaning, their constant use over time promotes "sacred vs. profane" in unquestionable, transhistorically authoritative terms. That produces discourses that resist changes or additions to the discussion, in turn adversely restricting discourses on sacrality and space.

As the projects within these pages exemplify, religions conceptualize sacred and secular differently, spatially and doctrinally. To use the old "sacred vs. profane" terminology instantly conjures a Eurocentric narrative that is inapplicable and often inaccurate.

By using the words "secular" and "mundane," we eschew the history and power associated with "profane." Both avoid the preconceptions about profanity and what that means. In doing so, it is my hope the reader will be able to view these projects and, equally importantly, the words each architect uses to explain them to gain a new vision of what religious architecture in the contemporary world is.

Space vs. place has undergone similar shifts in definition. Early scholarship characterized them in a dichotomous relationship that resembled the old "East vs. West," "traditional vs. modern" dichotomy. In this configuration, place was old and traditional while space was new and modern.[7] More recently, Lefebvre reimagined space as a "place" that was a specific locale upon which people impart particular meanings through their actions. Other scholars prefer to use the term "place" to draw a distinction between the particularity of a locale that contains specific activities and meanings.[8] Given, however, that this book is also about architecture as it creates these locales, I have chosen to use the term "space."

In the end, words, like the relationships and objects they signify, are not fixed. Sacrality, secularity, and space itself are neither inherent nor fixed. Each is fluid and produced through engagement and interaction. This is not to argue that there are not certain words or concepts that are objectively bad—for example, torture and murder are most certainly amongst them. The point is that context is of paramount importance in understanding how one defines concepts and cultural traditions, particularly religious cultures.

Notes

1 Keith D. Lilley, "Cities of God? Medieval Urban Forms and Their Christian Symbolism," *Transactions of the Institute of British Geographers*, Vol. 29, No. 3 (Sept., 2004): 297.

2 Mircea Eliade, *The Sacred and the Profane* (New York: Narcourt, 1957, 1987): 17, 20.

3 Says Payden, "comparativism. . .can make superficial parallels, false analogies, misleading associations," (William E. Paden, "Comparative Religion," in *The Routledge Companion to the Study of Religion*, edited by John R. Hinnells [London and New York: Routledge, 2005]: 216).

4 Paden, 2005: 216.

5 Paden, 2005: 216.

6 Paden, 2005: 219.

7 Patrick A. Desplat, "Introduction: Representations of Space, Place-making and Urban Life in Muslim Societies," in *Prayer in the City: The Making of Muslim Sacred Places and Urban Life*, edited by Patrick A. Desplat and Dorothea E. Shulz (Bielefeld: Transcript Verlag, 2012): 18–19.

8 See, for example, Desplat (2012), and Edward Casey (1997).

Chapter 3

Architectural History and Historiography

Architecture is the inscription and *re*inscription of space. As such, it occupies the intersection of social, political, religious, and cultural needs and values. These operate on multiple levels to accommodate different groups simultaneously.[1] By reflecting current institutional forces, architecture either maintains or overthrows the social power of specific social groups based on gender, economics, and politics, to the detriment of competing groups.[2]

Historical chronicles, both general and scholarly, supply useful tools in understanding these forces. However, these narratives are only as useful as their parameters. They must be clearly defined and adhered to. Too often, architecture history deploys vague definitions. In addition, most studies privilege European projects which posit Western-centric projects at the apex of architecture.[3] That process reiterates and re-authorizes Eurocentricity. These stagnant discourses reify what is considered "orthodox" in a way that elides aesthetic, Eurocentric agendas.[4] Although European and American (hereafter Euro/American)[5] models may be instructive in certain cases, their principles are not universal, nor should they be universally applied.

That means architecture originating in non-Euro/American regions cannot be evaluated by the contrastive "modern" (read: Euro/American) vs. "traditional" (read: everywhere else) dichotomy. Rather than relying on fixed definitions of "traditional" or "local" to explain what they see, writers must utilize terms that are more precise and less Western-privileging.[6] Nor is it sufficient to deploy an additive approach, supplementing taxonomies specifically conjured for non-Western European cultures onto a Euro/American model. Finally, terms like "folklore," "mythology," and "ceremonial" are biased and condescending, and do not actually explicate on the true condition of history and cultures of non-Euro/American peoples.

The Secular Frame

Because architecture endures beyond the generation in which it is built, buildings become "important repositories of cultural information."[7] Architectural projects signal contemporaneous cultural, political, and economic values. As time progresses, projects acclimate to people's changing social, economic, and political demands.[8] Secular and sacred spaces are not only defined by the social and political identities of those who built them, but are also fluid spaces that change over time.[9] The changes that occurred in the 1960s urban project by Lucio Costa and Oscar

Neimeyer documented by Iwan Baan provide a good example of an architectural social vision that has been fundamentally changed by people's real needs.[10]

To understand this phenomenon, architecture historians and practitioners cannot simply rely on popular structuralist theoretical distinctions between intent and interpreter. Structuralist interpretations of architecture forget that Structuralism was developed to study linguistics, and later texts. Significantly, texts and art cannot adapt to shifting political, cultural, social, and economic demands in the way that architecture can and does: it is only people's interpretations of texts and art that alter and assimilate. So while some argue that texts are "a practical set of actions involving the realities of power and authority," in reality, texts are often ideals and personal opinions and values.[11] Texts do not reflect an actual physical *practice* in the way architecture does.

Built spaces are not a representation of something else. They also do not serve a primarily aesthetic role, notwithstanding the political and social dimensions of literature and art. There is no reciprocal interaction between books/art and people, but interaction between people in buildings lies at architecture's heart. Therefore architecture cannot be a structuralist "reading" or a post-structuralist personal experience of "significance." Those who claim to "read" architecture should remember it is not a text nor can it be reduced to two dimensions.

Architecture is multi-dimensional and should be understood in those terms.[12] As a three-dimensional space, it organizes and hierarchizes human interaction.[13] To adequately comprehend its social, environmental, and symbolic components requires a complex methodology that incorporates not just the architect or an "interpreter" such as a historian, but also its users over time.[14] Built spaces combine "ecological (construction materials and methods, and climate), social organizational (household and community), and symbolic (cosmology and meaning)," elements.[15]

In other words, architecture contains and reflects political, technological, social, and cultural dimensions. These manifest physically, fostering interaction and exchange amongst and between people and spaces.[16] What's more, the spaces architecture creates are defined by discrete boundaries.[17] In fact, it is the boundaries created by architecture that promote, proscribe, and contain human interactions.[18] Designers and historians must remain aware of these multiple meanings, all of which stem not just from intent but function.[19]

Historiography of the Sacred Frame

Given architecture history's penchant for theoretical critiques, one might expect an insightful, deep narrative on the meaning and production of sacred space. Yet there are also significant limitations to current analyses. A study on investigating religions offers insight into how architectural narratives on religious space have become so entrenched. It identifies four positions a writer/historian can take: 1) the complete observer, 2) the observer as participant, 3) the participant as observer, and 4) the complete participant.[20]

Historians are frequently observers, but in architectural historiography, most fall into the third category. In other words, architecture historians are participants first, observers second. Because they are "insiders" or "participants as observers," their agendas include promoting and valorizing the typologies that they also favor as practitioners, typologies such as materials, lighting, and aesthetics. Another outcome of being an insider/observer is that architecture writers focus on iconic projects, as if these are representative of an entire typology. They are not. They are icons. Still other books are organized around single firms in elaborate coffee table tomes.

Privileging either single firms or iconic projects results from an educational system that reinforces cults of personality over skill at one's profession. Put differently, the conventionality of favoring firm identity over all other categories reflects an ingrained stance that values architecture stardom over the practicalities of how to produce effective, meaningful projects. Such books severely limit understanding of how sacred spaces function, are produced, and what comprises them.

A survey of these books shows they venture into typological analysis that favors aesthetics to the exclusion of all other constituents that shape building projects. Other narratives privilege geometry and the divine,[21] lighting,[22] nature,[23] and even phenomenology.[24] Each of these is advanced as a defining taxonomy for investigating sacred space.

Specific examples include one investigation that examines "contemplative" or "solemn" atmospheres through lighting.[25] Another defines sacred space in terms of communicating with another realm and shifting one's consciousness toward the sacred.[26] A third attempts to quantify projects through a survey on what makes sacred spaces unique using subjective descriptors: "Extraordinary Architectural Experiences. . .[are] defined as an 'encounter with a building or place that fundamentally alters one's normal state of being.'"[27] With the goal of seeking a fundamental "shift in physical, perceptual, emotional, intellectual, and/or spiritual appreciation of architecture" the conclusions are less than systematic. Unfortunately, most of these are subjective approaches that eschew replicable methodologies.

Such chronicles amount to opinions that contain little grounding in archaeological, cultural, doctrinal, geographical, historical or theoretical research. So while program, materials, and design are all meticulously analyzed, the cultural, historical, and symbolic meanings of sacred spaces might be summarized as, for example, hearkening ethereality. The disregard for peer-reviewed research and sources is an unfortunate casualty of the emphasis on aesthetics which begins in the educational system. And while aesthetics are an important component of architecture, there are other, equally vital forces at work. Rigor and specificity must be applied to all these areas, not only the aesthetic ones.

As a result, cultural, economic, political, and social forces that shape sacred projects are ignored. Instead, readers are lured by overwhelming eye candy in what amounts to visual catalogs, not informative research. Unsurprisingly, most visual catalogs that dominate Euro/American analysis also privilege Euro/American architects and their works.[28]

Sacred spaces are not permanently, fixedly sacred—they require constant *re*identification and reaffirmation by people, not theories.[29] A multi-disciplinary framework that incorporates epistemological, postcolonial analysis with archaeology, geography, and philosophy offers a more comprehensive, relevant perspective on architecture and sacred spaces.[30] The following pages will strive for just that. We will find that initially, secular architecture can be transformed into sacred architecture and the obverse is also true.

Notes

1 Denise L. Lawrence and Setha M. Low, "The Built Environment and Spatial Form," *Annual Review of Anthropology*, Vol. 19 (1990): 483.

2 Lawrence and Low, 1990: 486.

3 Julian Bermudez and Brandon Ro, "Extraordinary Architectural Experiences: Comparative Study of Three Paradigmatic Cases of Sacred Spaces, The Pantheon, the Chartres Cathedral and the Chapel of Ronchamp," 2nd International Congress on Ambiances (Montreal, 2012): 689–694.

4 Sherin Wing, "Gendering Buddhism: The Miaoshan Legend Reconsidered," *Journal of Feminist Studies in Religion*, Vol. 27, No. 1 (Spring, 2011): 5.

5 Euro/American in my rendering delineates European and American. This is distinct from Euro–American, which, like Chinese–American, is both a racial and an ethnic distinction.

6 Talal Asad, *Genealogies of Religion: Discipline and Reasons of Power in Christianity and Islam* (Baltimore: Johns Hopkins University Press, 1993): 12.

7 Lawrence and Low, 1990: 491–492.

8 Says Harkin, "places contain the concatenation of past events and ways of being. . .[they are] reminders of a past that is continuous with the present. . .all occurring in a defined space" (Michael E. Harkin, "Sacred Places, Scarred Spaces." *Wicazo Sa Review*, Vol. 15, No. 1 [2000]: 50).

9 Ivey, 2008: 456.

10 Iwan Baan, *Brasilia – Chadnigarh Living With Modernity* (Zurich: Lars Müller Publishers, 2010).

11 Catherine Bell, *Ritual Theory, Ritual Practice* (Oxford: Oxford University Press, 1992): 82.

12 William Whyte, "How do Buildings Mean? Some Issues of Interpretation in the History of Architecture," *History and Theory*, Vol. 45, No. 2 (May, 2006): 167.

13 Mark Rakatansky, "Identity and the Discourse of Politics in Contemporary Architecture," *Assemblage*, No. 27 (August 1995): 10.

14 Whyte, 2006: 168.

15 Lawrence and Low, 1990: 458.

16 Whyte, 2006: 163.

17 Amy Gazin-Schwartz, "Archaeology and Folklore of Material Culture, Ritual, and Everyday Life," *International Journal of Historical Archaeology*, Vol. 5, No. 4 (2001): 264.

18 Lawrence and Low, 1990: 454.

19 Whyte, 2006: 155.

20 Kim Knott, "Insider/Outsider Perspectives," in *The Routledge Companion to the Study of Religion*, edited by John R. Hinnells (London and New York: Routledge, 2005): 245.

21 Geoffrey Simmins, *Sacred Spaces and Sacred Places* (Saarbrücken: VDM Publishing, 2008): 53.

22 Andrezej Piotrowski, "Architecture and the Iconoclastic Controversy in Late Medieval Italian Cities," in *Medieval Practices of Space*, edited by Barbara A. Hanalwalt and Michal Kobialka (Berkeley and Los Angeles: University of California Press, 2000): 115; Simmins, 2008: 47; Barbara A. Weightman, "Sacred Landscapes and the Phenomenon of Light," *American Geographical Society*, Vol. 86, No. 1 (January, 1996): 59, 66.

23 Bell, 1992: 173; Ivey, 2008: 455; Susan Naquin and Chün-fang Yü, "Introduction," in *Pilgrims and Sacred Sites in China*, edited by Susan Naquin and Chün-fang Yü (Berkeley and California: University of California Press, 1992): 3.

24 Bell, 1992: 131; Bernard Faure, "Relics and Flesh Bodies: the Creation of Ch'an Pilgrimage Sites," in *Pilgrims and Sacred Sites in China*, edited by Naquin and Yü ,1992: 160; Walsh, 2007: 478.

25 Eva-Maria Kreuz, "Light in Sacred Buildings," *Design Manuals*, Part 5 (2008): 60–67.

26 Michelle Lee McGahan, "Architecture as Transition: Creating Sacred Space" (Master's thesis, University of Cincinnati, 2004): 3.

27 Bermudez and Ro, 2012: 689.

28 Richard A. Horsley, "Religion and Other Products of Empire," *Journal of the American Academy of Religion*, Vol. 71, No. 1 (March, 2003): 14.

29 Ivey, 2008: 456.

30 Caroline Walker Bynum, "The Mysticism and Ascetism of Medieval Women: Some Comments on the Typologies of Max Weber and Ernst Troeltsch," in *Fragmentation and Redeption: Essays on Gender and the Human Body in Medieval Religion* (New York: Urzone, Inc. 1992): 53.

Chapter 4

The Architectural Construction of Identity

Whether individual or collective, private or institutional, identity is a process. It is not a fixed entity, nor does it remain static over time. Identity contains physical, material, and theoretical elements which must all be constantly asserted. What's more, identity is a political process because it reflects specific interests, values, and beliefs.[1]

In other words, identity comprises individual and institutional ethics and priorities which can be deconstructed into intellectual, cultural, economic, material, and political components.[2] Together, they express and reflect principles and values in a positive sense—that is, those things we accept—and in negative sense—those things we reject. These principles and ethical standards are articulated through human interaction, negotiation, and even contestation.[3]

Architecture is one expression of individual and institutional identity.[4] Architectural program, plan, materials, and design aesthetics signify social, economic, and political values, ideals, and goals.[5] Given that, architecture can be an individual and/or institutional expression because it "organizes, hierarchizes, and systematizes activities, behaviors, orderings, visibilities, movements."[6]

If we accept this, then we must also accept that architecture is characterized by movement: contestation, negotiation, and reification comprising physical and theoretical orientations and concepts.[7] Put differently, architectural space is fluid: it is neither a container nor objective phenomena.[8]

Identity and Religious Spaces

These characteristics all apply to religious architecture, as well. Sacred spaces transcend "everyday intuitions about space ('extension,' 'containment,' 'boundedness')."[9] Like secular spaces, they are constantly redefined and reaffirmed through active, often ritualized engagement.[10] Note that ritual does not necessarily imply only *religious* behavior, but rather, repetitious behaviors that are meaningful.

What's more, as time progresses, the values and goals sacred spaces represent become redefined and may even change entirely, from primarily religious to primarily secular. Alternatively, they may exemplify a different set of religious traditions.

In terms of people's identities, religious spaces reinforce "the regimes of power that organize life outside [them]."[11] In them, "people can encounter a self-consciously constructed culture together" that is religious in nature.[12] Sacred spaces therefore reiterate collective and individual identity[13] but they are different from secular spaces because people construct both secular and religious relationships within their borders.[14] What's more, the human actions and interactions that occur within sacred spaces reaffirm social status,[15] thereby reiterating individual and collective identity.[16] In fact, religious spaces comprise an ideal arena for the dynamic and constant (re)production of identities precisely because the issues contained within their borders are so fiercely contested.[17]

People's identity, then, lies at the heart of religious architecture.[18] Sacred architecture defines and re-defines our *selves* and therefore our identities[19] by cultivating our behaviors and mindsets.[20] These interactions are further shaped and constrained by religious doctrine, secular values, and spatial limitations. Given all this, it is no wonder that "religious space is always polyvocative."[21]

If we accept these insights, we must reject any interpretation or chronicle of sacred spaces that depends solely on historical texts. Too often, history, religious studies and archaeology privilege the presumed orthodoxy and orthopraxy found in texts and the traditions they highlight.[22] While it is vital to understand historical narratives, they routinely propose a single, uninterrupted narrative, which results in the appearance of a single orthodoxy. Both assumptions are false. However, if taken as the sole source, one is apt to understand that each region, culture, or nation has a single narrative that progresses from the past to the present in an even sweep.

The truth is more complex and involves the vicissitudes and shifts produced by social, economic, political, and spatial forces. They, like the narratives they produce, privilege certain sources driven by underlying, often hidden, agendas. Using multiple academic sources including social history, doctrinal studies, and spatial theory as they reflect politics, economics, culture, and science will construct identity as it should be understood.[23]

Analyzing sacred spaces, like building them, is a dynamic process. Analysis reiterates values, principles, and goals.[24] Additionally, it is a form of self-expression in which "critical, analytical methods. . .informed by ideology, produc[e] interpretations. . .are subjective, 'interested' act[s] of ideological commitment."[25] In other words, the choice of subject matter, methodologies, and conclusions all reflect the self and in that way are also self-identifying. Research necessarily contains inclusions and exclusions which point to an agenda determined by one's values, ethics, and principles, which are by definition political: "all historians make research decisions and impose categories on the infinity of evidence and on the enormous variety of human stories embedded in their subjects."[26]

Notes

1 Steven Seidman, 1994: 10, as cited in Christian Karner, "Postmodernism and the Study of Religions," in Crossley and Karner, 2005: 37.

2 Horsley, 2003: 34.

3 David Howarth, "Space, Subjectivity, and Politics", *Alternatives: Global, Local, Political*, Vol. 31, No. 2 (April–June, 2006): 112; David Chidester and Edward T. Linenthal, "Introduction," in *American Sacred Space,* edited by David Chidester and Edward T. Linenthal (Bloomington and Indianapolis: Indiana University Press, 1995): 9.

4 Michael Awkward, "Race, Gender, and the Politics of Reading," *Black American Literature Forum*, Vol. 22: 1 (1988): 12.

5 Dolores Hayden, *The Power of Place: Urban Landscapes as Public History* (Cambridge: MIT Press, 1994): 30–33.

6 Mark Rakatansky, "Identity and the Discourse of Politics in Contemporary Architecture," *Assemblage,* No. 27 (August 1995): 10.

7 Chidester and Linenthal, 1995: 12.

8 Denis Cosgrove, "Landscape and Landschaft," *German Historical Institute Bulletin*, No. 35 (Fall, 2004): 2.

9 Howarth, 2006: 110.

10 Chidester and Linenthal, 1995: 8, 16; Walsh, 2007: 476–477.

11 Corrigan, 2009: 168.

12 Barrett, Mark, "The Monastery as Sacred Space," in *Sacred Space: Interdisciplinary Perspectives within Contemporary Contexts*, edited by Steve Brie, Jenny Daggers, and David Torevell (Newcastle upon Tyne: Cambridge Scholars Publishing, 2010): 11.

13 Selina Ching Chan, "Temple-Building and Heritage in China," *Ethnology*, Vol. 44, No. 1 (Winter, 2005): 65.

14 Edward S. Casey, *The Fate of Place: A Philosophical History* (Berkeley and Los Angeles: University of California Press, 1997): 310–312.

15 Hayden, 1994: 9.

16 Bernard Faure, "Space and Place in Chinese Religious Traditions," *History of Religions*, Vol. 26, No. 4 (May, 1987): 345.

17 Brigitta Hauser-Schäublin, "The Politics of Sacred Space: Using Conceptual Models of Space for Socio-Political Transformations in Bali," *Bijdragen tot de Taal-, Land-en Volkenkunde*, Vol. 160, No. 2/3 (2004): 298.

18 Burgess says, "Architecture *itself* assembles and re-assembles the constellation of possible positions," whether or not they are sited in places of conflict (J. Peter Burgess, "The Sacred Site in Civil Space: Meaning and Status of the Temple Mount/al-Haram al-Sharif," *Social Identities*, Vol. 10, No. 3 [2004]: 318).

19 Corrigan, 2009: 161.

20 Barrett, 2010: 17, 20.

21 Corrigan, 2009: 160.

22 Mark C. Horton, "Islam, Archaeology, and Swahili Identity," in *Changing Social Identity with the Spread of Islam: Archaeological Perspectives*, edited by Donald Whitcomb (Chicago: University of Chicago, 2004): 68.

23 John R. Hinnells, "Introduction," in *The Routledge Companion to the Study of Religion*, edited by John R. Hinnells (London and New York: Routledge, 2005): 1.

24 Chidester and Linenthal, 1995: 3.

25 Sherin Wing, "Re-Gendering Buddhism: Postcolonialism, Gender, and the Princess Miaoshan Legend" (PhD diss., University of California Los Angeles, 2010); Awkward, 1988: 12.

26 David W. Blight, *Race and Reunion: the Civil War in American History* (Cambridge, MA: Belknap Press of Harvard University Press, 2001): 13.

PART 2

CHURCHES, MOSQUES, AND SYNAGOGUES

Chapter 5

Arcari+Iovino Architects[1]

Mr. Edward Arcari, AIA, Founder and Principal

Mr. Anthony Iovino, AIA, LEED, Founder and Principal

PROJECTS

Korean Presbyterian Church, Oakland, New Jersey[2]

The project is located on a heavily wooded site alongside an existing school building. The sloped site takes advantage of natural light. Daylight illuminates the lower level, which consists of classrooms and bible study rooms.

The main level consists of a 350-person sanctuary and meeting spaces. The upper level consists of a mezzanine overlooking the sanctuary and gallery space.

Project is 36,000 square feet.

Completed in 2011.

Zichron Mordechai Synagogue, Teaneck, New Jersey[3]

Located in a residential neighborhood, this project was designed for a congregation of 100 persons.

The worship space occupies the upper floor, with separate entrances for men and women. The gathering space is at grade level. A small kitchen, storage room, and restrooms are also located on this level. The study space is located below grade and also functions as a play area for children.

The materials mimic those used in the surrounding neighborhood. The sloped, inverted roof offers both natural light and views of an old tree, while maintaining privacy from the street.

Materials include brick, stucco, and painted wood.

Completed in 2002.

Background

For Arcari+Iovino Architects, religious projects comprised their first commissions. "We got involved with the archdiocese of Newark and that was our first project in 1992," says Mr. Arcari. "Before that, we were doing some freelance work, like residential additions for a Jewish community in Munising, New York."

Mr. Iovino elaborates, "Having that commission gave us the motivation to formally branch out and give our own firm a shot. We started out because we thought we had nothing to lose and we could afford to make no money for a few years. Which is what we did!" he laughs. "But then that branched us into some more local, public architecture work."

He continues, "Looking at our competition at that time in 1993, the only people doing work were the people working in the public sector. We started with one thing and that led to another and then another. Eventually we did our first public library in that same town and that started an entire niche of public libraries. And then other civil work followed."

Designing for Religion

Clearly, religious practice also shapes design. "For example, with the Korean church, they didn't want too much glazing to distract people attending service," says Mr. Arcari. "So we had these little cuts to bring in the daylight, which also served as a buffer for the acoustical requirements. Your eyes are focused upward and the walls protect you from the outside world."

Interestingly, iconography did not significantly influence this project, nor has it had a large effect on a current project. Says Mr. Arcari, "The synagogue, the Syrian church that we're currently building, the Korean church, for each of them there really is no statuary, there's no strong iconography. They all requested that, to be really spare and sparse."

Mr. Iovino explains, "For the Syrian Orthodox Church, so much is about the form of the building. The other ones, we were free to do any form that we felt was right for the context." Mr. Arcari continues, "The Syrian Church had to face East. They wanted twelve windows for the disciples. They wanted a lot of arches, based on the architecture of Syria, Turkey, Lebanon. They were building forms we needed to deal with." The design solution was reached, Mr. Iovino says, through communication: "We communicate what we see in terms of the more pure forms and less frills."

Elements of both the religion itself and the religious community's practical needs exert their influence differently to shape each project. "The Korean church was interesting because it was all about their community," Mr. Arcari says. "This particular community goes not just to attend a Sunday service, they go for community and they'll spend the entire day there, from morning until evening. The place is designed with the worship area, but that space is also designed as a concert hall. Music is central not only in the service but for the community as well. So the way the walls and ceiling are designed, we worked with the sound so it's really a multipurpose space."

He continues, "Below that, in the basement area, it's all about education. They have a dozen or so bible study rooms. They have three kindergartens up through sixth grade classrooms. They have an indoor playroom and a gym. In the upper level, they have almost like an art gallery or a comfortable seating area that overlooks the basketball court. So there's something for everyone."

Mr. Iovino elaborates, "The basketball court space also works as a gathering space. So people file out from the church area itself into this space where you can have coffee, cake. So you can be in this gallery/café space. That gives you these intimate pockets all around the building that allow people to congregate after mass."

Clients and Community

Clients choose architects for very different reasons: budget, aesthetic vision, political and social goals, as well as numerous practical considerations and issues. For example, when the clients for the Teaneck Synagogue approached Arcari+Iovino Architects, their goal was to achieve something aesthetically different. Says Mr. Iovino, "For the Teaneck Synagogue, they hired these two Italian guys to design it and I think it benefits them as well as us. They're going to get something different because of our experiences and perspectives. In fact it would be hard for us to design a traditional Roman Catholic church now because of what I've seen all my life through my work."

Trust is fundamental to addressing the needs of their clients. That is achieved through good communication. Mr. Iovino emphasizes, "It's a matter of working with different groups so you gain their trust and they have confidence in what you're presenting them."

Mr. Arcari says, "Part of what we do to build trust is to attend whatever kind of services the groups have. I'll go to their masses. I'll go to the synagogue, I'll go to the Korean service and spend some time with them, whatever kind of celebration they have. And then eating with them afterwards or other things they do. That helps us and we develop their trust over time so that they know we're not just somebody coming in there and foisting a pretty picture on them. They understand that we're making the effort."

In fact, building trust through listening and communication lies at the heart of eventual success. Mr. Arcari explains, "We're working on a Syrian orthodox church right now and we reached out to the community through two or three focus groups during the design process. We would present our design, and his eminence, the head of the church, would give a little speech to see if they had any questions. After, we would all eat together. We did that three times."

Working with the entire community is fundamental to the process as well. Says Mr. Iovino: "It's about making the residents more comfortable with the neighbor. Especially if the neighbors aren't familiar with the religion. It's just good to make good neighbors by introducing them to our process and design, because these are sited in developed neighborhoods so how is it integrated with your design vision within the neighborhoods.

"It's just one more piece of the puzzle we consider early on," says Mr. Arcari. "We don't design a building in our heads. We fit it to the site, programmatically, whatever the religious requirements may be. I don't think we ever start a project with an idea already in our heads."

The community is not just limited to the neighbors or the religious community; it also includes the planning board. Mr. Iovino explains, "Of course before that you have the planning board approval process, so the community is less likely to come out against the project in a negative way. Because people who come out now who were going to be negative are now positive.

"In the end, it's inspirational going to church with these people, in all of these different religions that we've done projects for," says Mr. Arcari. "They devote so much of their lives to their church. It's really a community for them, whether it's spending all day or a weekend there. And they all contribute heavily to their church communities. It's inspiring to watch people come together because of their faith."

Site and Design

"Where we are right now, it's pretty well built out," says Mr. Arcari. "It's not like we have a church in the middle of nowhere that will be the focal point of a town. It's pretty much infill. For example, the Teaneck Synagogue is basically the size of a house. It occupies the footprint of what was previously there, in this very tight residential neighborhood. And they had to go through a planning board process to allow them to build there. For that project, we not only dealt with the planning board but also about 40 or 50 unhappy neighbors.

"What's unique about the Teaneck Synagogue is that it's a vertical solution," says Mr. Iovino. "The footprint is so small, it's essentially stacking three primary functions. It has a basement and two levels. So we had to understand what their needs were in terms of separation within these floors in the vertical space." In other words, "we had to understand their sacred and learning spaces and how they used them so that they could get the most out of each of the spaces."

He continues, "Given that it's in a tight suburban environment where your neighbors are twenty feet away or so, we still have a fair amount of glass, but it points out at the right direction and looks at certain things while still maintaining privacy. So we were trying to give them a treehouse of a space on the top floor, where you have a sense of privacy and a connection to the outdoors. Especially in that project, we were trying to make it feel bigger than it is."

Materials and Lighting

"No matter what the building is," says Mr. Iovino, "you want something that can be timeless and not trendy. Teaneck Synagogue was very interesting because the way the zoning was written for the town, they wanted us to use materials that were common in the neighborhood, which are brick and stucco. They also wanted sloped roofs. So we put the sloped roof and inverted it into a butterfly form and we used the brick and the stucco to really identify parts of the building."

This approach differed from the Korean church: "We were more free to do almost anything we wanted to. Generally, they wanted materials that were warm and timeless, which I think is common with these kinds of projects. For this community, they wanted some wood, a lot of brick." The palette, thus, was "staying with earth tones. We also used stucco on the fins of the sanctuary."

Another important factor? "How daylight comes in and how artificial light shines out of these buildings. I think the composition of the building in terms of how someone approaches the building and experiences it inside is important for the user in setting the tone in how someone arrives." Mr. Iovino continues, "You want to create a space that's inviting and also that will afford the privacy you want. In both of those projects, we have these vertical towers of light as markers to come inside. And at different times of the day, it's also a way of bringing the outside in." In fact, he says, "In Teaneck Synagogue during this time of the year in late Fall, it's wonderful, all of the colors of the trees just wash and paint the walls inside with color."

On Secular and Religious Projects

Residential projects share more with religious ones than one might initially expect. Mr. Iovino observes, "Residential work is closer to religious work from the owner's perspective. Public work and corporate work has a bit more distance. There, you deal with a board and you deal with a committee, but they don't feel it's their personal dollars."

What's more, "When dealing with a committee in a religious situation, that committee will defer to a smaller group or even an individual who has a lot of knowledge in construction or design. And then it comes to us."

Budget

For religious projects, says Mr. Iovino, "It's all about budget in terms of final design." This is because, as Mr. Arcari observes, "It comes from the parishioners. Everybody fundraises and in everyday life, these people rarely finance such projects. So everybody plays a more active role, as opposed to in a municipal project where they budget for something and then they bond for it."

That means that budget limitations can significantly shape design decisions. But as Mr. Iovino points out, this was fortunately not the case with their projects. "The designs we did with Teaneck Synagogue and the Korean church," says Mr. Iovino, "were really close to what we initially proposed. And the function of the building went hand in hand with the form of the building." Adds Mr. Arcari, "Nobody has ever really pushed back on our design vision. They might want to temper some of the cost issues like choosing one material over another. But I don't think we ever presented anything that was radically changed."

Notes

1 Edward Arcari and Anthony Iovino. Interview with Sherin Wing via Skype. Los Angeles, November 4, 2013.

2 "Korean Presbyterian Church." Accessed November 5, 2014. http://aiarchs.com/portfolio_5b.html.

3 "Zichron Mordechai Synagogue." Accessed November 5, 2014. http://aiarchs.com/portfolio_5a.html.

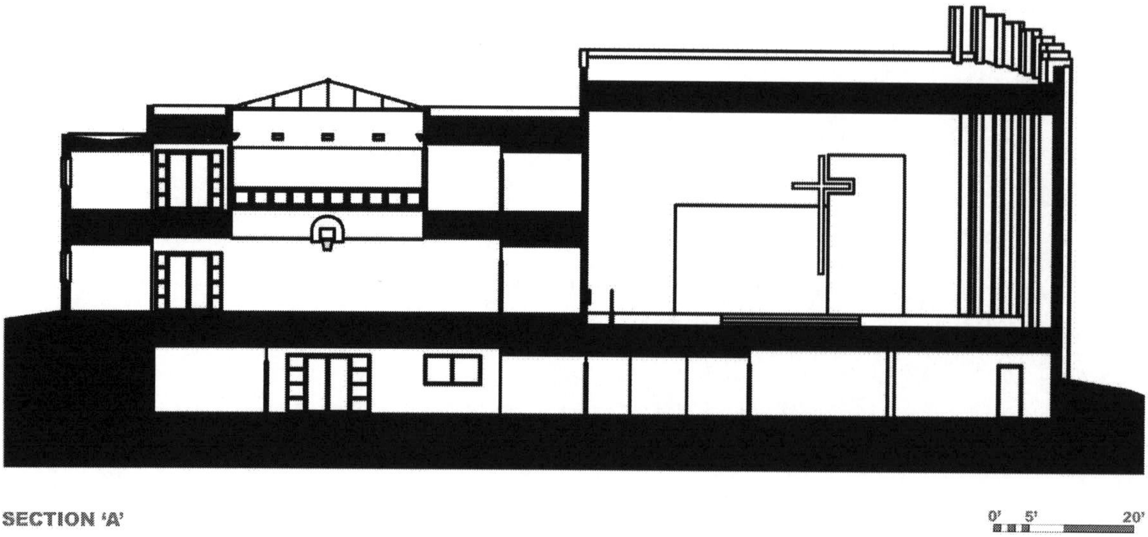
SECTION 'A'
0' 5' 20'

Korean Presbyterian Church Section A

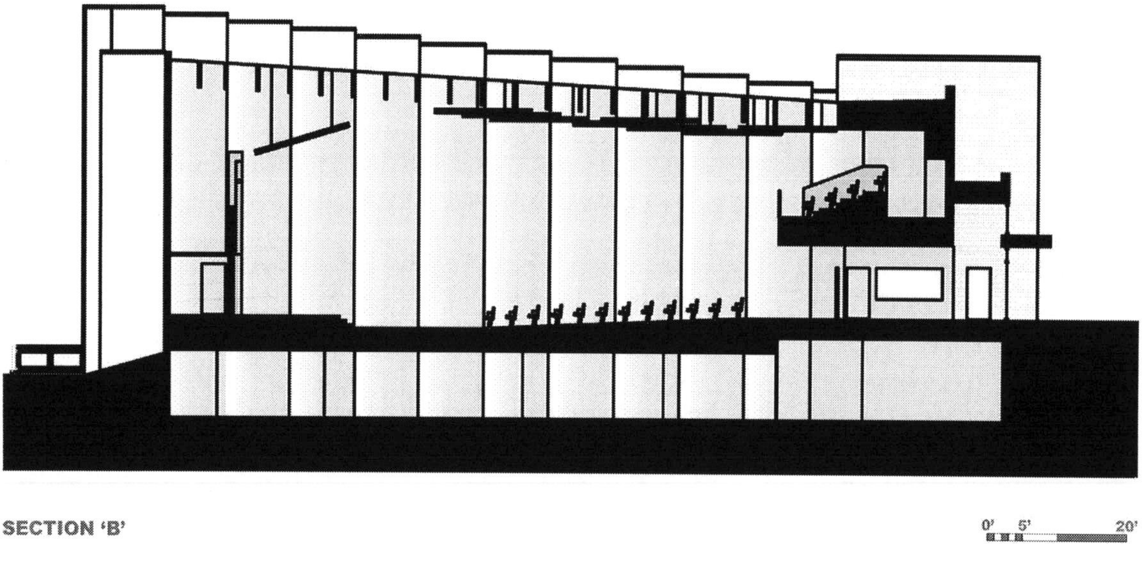
SECTION 'B'
0' 5' 20'

Korean Presbyterian Church Section B

Korean Presbyterian Church Plan 1

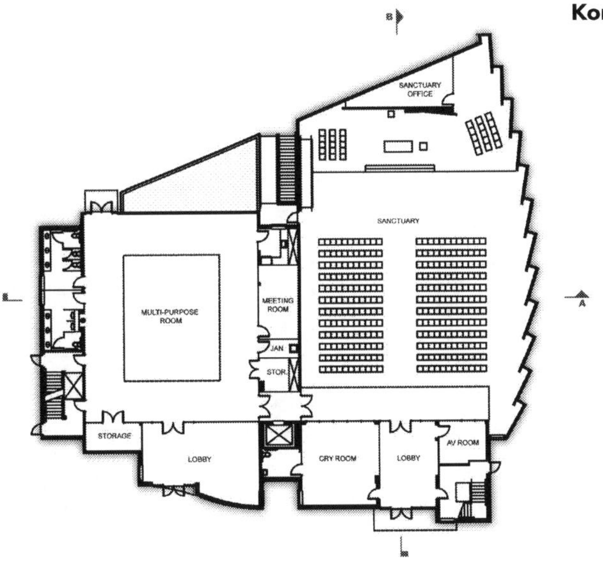
SANCTUARY OFFICE
SANCTUARY
MULTI-PURPOSE ROOM
MEETING ROOM
JAN
STOR.
STORAGE
LOBBY
CRY ROOM
LOBBY
AV ROOM

MAIN LEVEL PLAN

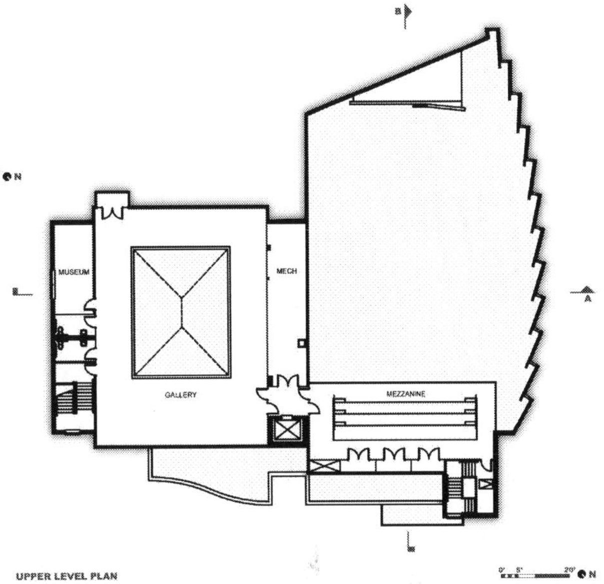
MUSEUM
MECH
GALLERY
MEZZANINE

UPPER LEVEL PLAN

Korean Presbyterian Church Plan 2

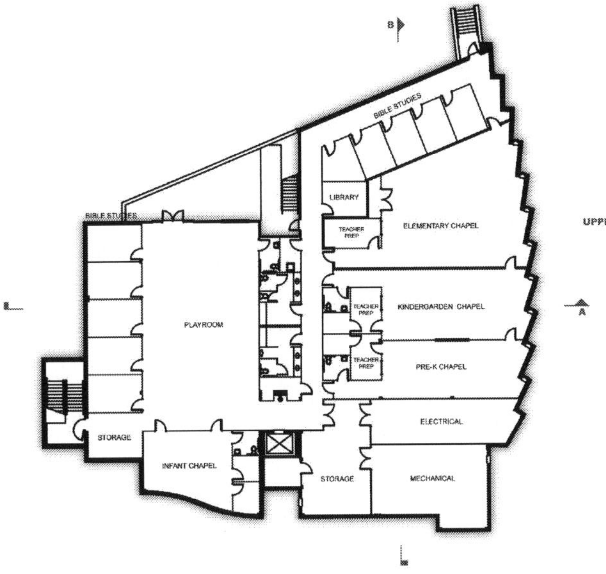
BIBLE STUDIES
LIBRARY
TEACHER PREP
ELEMENTARY CHAPEL
PLAYROOM
KINDERGARDEN CHAPEL
PRE-K CHAPEL
ELECTRICAL
STORAGE
INFANT CHAPEL
MECHANICAL

LOWER LEVEL PLAN

Korean Presbyterian Church Plan 3

Teaneck Synagogue exterior

Teaneck Synagogue exterior

Teaneck Synagogue interior

Teaneck Synagogue interior

Chapter 6

hMa (Hanrahan Meyers Architects)[1]

Ms. Victoria Meyers, M.Arch, Founder and Principal

PROJECTS

Infinity Chapel, Greenwich Village, NY[2]

The project for Tenth Church of Christ, Scientist, is a 4,000 square foot cubic sanctuary that incorporates sacred geometries in the form of squares, golden section rectangles, and spheres. The south, north and west walls curve inward to suggest a spherical shape of the chapel.

A large square opening in the west wall brings light into the sanctuary. The curved west wall is punctured by a large square opening to bring light to the sanctuary. The congregation faces the west curved wall, as well as the Garden Sanctuary, which is viewed through floor to ceiling glass openings behind the stage.

The glass façade entryway leads directly to the Christian Science Reading Room. Five light monitors illuminate the pathway east to west, from the Reading Room to the chapel. The three monitors in the Reading Room project light on the ceiling and also on the Sunday School below. The fourth monitor marks the rear edge of seating in the chapel, while the fifth is on the stage itself.

Below the ground level is the Sunday School, which also functions as a public meeting area.

Materials include white glass and concrete with large pieces of old-growth ash used in the Reading Room storefront window areas, the librarian's desk, two benches, and the chapel podium. Oak is also used for chapel benches, and the Reading Room casework is also oak.

Project is 8,000 square feet.

Completed in 2010.

Chapel of the Light, Queens Herald Church, Flushing, NY[3]

Project is a 4,800 square foot sanctuary with 24,000 square feet of renovation.

Completed in 2009.

Project Narratives

There are several different ways to describe architecture projects. One can discuss design development, materials, even client needs. Another way is to uncover the architect's own design intent. For Infinity Chapel, Ms. Meyers begins simply: "Infinity Chapel is about circulation and infinity. Disappearing edges. It was achieved by creating these cuts in the floor slab, of which there are five. They walk you through the space. They appear in seemingly random locations but actually are key locations which go hand in hand with how we furnished the space. So there's one where the seating area is which acts almost like a coffee table with chairs. There's another one that is integrated as part of a bookcase."

From there, "You enter into the chapel, which is separated from the Reading Room by a wall of clear glass. And the next one is embedded in the first set of pews. And the last one is embedded in the space where the pulpit is. And the next is looking at the garden which is outside the chapel."

For the Chapel of the Light, it was, as Ms. Meyers says, "about this notion of recreating that sense of being on a floor slab which was floating. So that you didn't know where your edges were again. But you were disconnected again. So you didn't know if the floor was actually structured to the wall or if you were just unhinged from the wall."

Developing Design

With these foundational concepts in mind, Ms. Meyers details the design process: "For the Chapel of the Light, they bought this building which was a very interesting 60s building in which the architect was obviously fascinated with architects like Saarinen and had made this fake, folded plate roof. It wasn't really a folded plate, but he made it look like a folded plate. Which I loved. It had these edges which came down to the structure on the side and it had all these windows that had been ply-wooded over.

"I thought, open all the windows on your edges. Put translucent glass on them so you don't have distractions outside. I also wanted to carve out a trough in the floor to put an edge of light in the floor. Where the congregation was seated could therefore begin to take on the characteristics like the seating area in Ronchamp, because the seating area is raised about ten to twelve inches off the floor."

She continues, "There is also this series of light wells and sound wells that connect the upper space of the Chapel of the Light with the lower space so they're virtually connected."

Ms.Meyers explains yet another way sound provides connection: "There are also these panels that can be opened so you can hear sound through them or they can be closed and they close very tightly so there is a complete separation of sound." This design allows for "The opportunity to have chamber musicians in the basement playing or singing and then you can hear it in the chapel. So you know it's live but you have no idea where it's coming from. It was this effect of being at the theater or the ballet and having the orchestra in the pit. In a way, through sound, it breaks down the edges of the space."

However, good design is not just a single gesture; rather, it invokes multiple intents and strategies: "We also broke down the edges of the space with different surfaces of glass. So when you're looking at the rear wall of the chapel, it looks as though there is clear glass at the bottom and there's all this other glass above which is translucent but has natural light streaming through it as well." She adds, "There is also natural light coming from above where there's a mezzanine and there's natural light. But none of the light is natural except that which comes from the clear glass. It's all a fake. But again, it's a way of creating an illusion."

For Ms. Meyers, good design also motivates people by generating interest beyond just the building itself: "In the case of Infinity Chapel, they felt they had a gradually reducing membership. So they talked to us and asked my opinion. I said that when I had seen Christian Science churches as I drive around the countryside, they're generally tiny little storefronts that have books in them that advertise them as a bookshop. And the church is in there somewhere, but it's kind of scary to go in there because you have no idea what you're getting yourself in to."

Ms. Meyers suggestion was to pique the curiosity of the unattached passer-by: "If you had a completely glass front that looks like a Starbucks and people walk past, they can see right in to the whole thing. That way, they can see the book-store and beyond that, they can see the chapel. And even beyond that, they can see a garden," she says, "So they're going to want to come in because they want to see what you did. They're going to feel very safe about coming in because it's a beautiful, enjoyable space.

"It really worked out for them," says Ms. Meyers, "their membership has something like quadrupled, which is good! When we were working with them they had only 40 members. So they have done really well with their membership. And I went to an AIA discussion in the south, and someone from the Christian Science organization said that this project has become the prototype for Christian Science organizations throughout the country. So that was helpful for their future projects.

Graphic design was another integral element: "They always like to put a particular saying from Mary Baker Eddy as a focal point, which in this case was frosted glass. We spent some time with a graphic design signage person. We did a couple of tests of different levels of transparency or translucency to the text, both in the glass which is where the Mary Baker Eddy piece was, or simply put on the wall in typeface. It worked out well. At first the client wondered why do we have to make this difficult. I told them if we're not careful, the way we put the text up can destroy the sense of the surface we're putting it on. So we have to put it up carefully so that the wall supports the text but the text also supports the wall. So that took a month or two to test ideas before we actually put it up."

Clients

Developing a good relationship with the client requires several different skills and strategies. "As an architect you have to look at a client, if they're not supporting your program, you have to look at them a certain way and say you know what, if you really want this other program, there are other architects out there who will give it to you. You should not be working with me, you should be working with one of those people. Clients may not necessarily want to hear that but it's about being a good fit."

"The experience is very much like going on a date," says Ms. Meyers, "because if they hire you, it is like getting married. The relationship sometimes lasts longer than many marriages in Hollywood. Even a small project takes five years from start to finish."

She explains, "For many architects starting out, they have no concept that they're not done until they hand the clients the Certificate of Occupancy, which takes a long time to get a hold of. That's especially true if you're doing a church because a church is a public assembly building. And public assembly means you have a much more rigorous process of sign-off than you have with other types of buildings." She adds, "When you have public assembly, you probably have more than 75 people congregating in a space. So if there's an emergency, they have to be able to get out of that building quickly and safely. So that affects the way you look at public sign-off and that is key to getting the certificate of occupancy. And your client is not going to give you your final payment until you get the certificate of occupancy sign-off. Nor should they because they don't have a legal space they can use yet."

That said, the opportunity to build a strong relationship and produce an interesting project that serves the practical and aesthetic requirements for the client is unique to religious projects. How? Ms. Meyers finds that, "What's really interesting about doing sacred spaces is that a lot of times those clients seek out more interesting architects. Because they want something more than just an off-the-shelf approach to the way they their program is achieved." This was certainly true for Ms. Meyers' firm, hMa, which got its first religious project after the publication of her book: "The first project we got was the people from the Christian Science organization. And it happened because my book, *Designing With Light* was coming out and they read about it online. When they saw the book, they felt that I was addressing concepts that were key to the kinds of experiences they were seeking in their church. Then they called us. So it was really helpful that I had that book, but it was also just a circumstantial thing."

Cost

For projects that rely on community fundraising, maintaining a budget can be challenging for both client and architect. Says Ms. Meyers, "These things do cost quite a bit to achieve. When you look at Infinity Chapel, that curved wall that cantilevers out towards the congregation is really expensive. That curved wall probably added $250k at least. It was something the client asked for. They came to us because they saw my book, but they also said we want curves. To which we answered, we do curves, that's fine. Then they left the office and we made this model with all these curves, and really the only expensive curve was the one that cantilevered. All the others, if they're just vertical curves and they're just curves in plan, it doesn't cost that much. It's really easy to handle. But a cantilever shape like that, which you need to do at least in one place when you're doing those curves or it gets kind of icky, then you're looking at money. But it's a very beautiful effect."

She elaborates, "There is a function to cantilevering it the way we did. There is a huge air conditioning duct that came up the one side where it's flat and then bent over and came across at the top. That thing is four feet by eight feet in section. And that's supplying all the HVAC in that room, which it does very successfully. And you never see where the air comes out from behind the curve. So that for me was very useful because the worst thing you can have is to come into your space and see these horrible grills. It's like seeing a theater set where the theater designer didn't get it quite right and there's this annoying thing that keeps distracting you from the play.

Materials

Understanding the potential of different materials, their properties and how these can be used to enhance a project is fundamental. Says Ms. Meyers. "Materials and the love of them are basic to being a good architect. I think that because we've done a lot of smaller projects and projects that are built in upstate New York and in the metropolitan area, we've gotten quite involved with wood framing, though not in New York of course.

"Wood is a material I really love," confesses Ms. Meyers. "Michael Greene talked about making skyscrapers out of wood, which I don't think we'll ever see in our lifetimes. But wood is amazing as a finished surface in addition to framing. Both inside and outside. I think it's one of those basic materials that makes us feel at home because it reminds us of trees. And different species of trees. And that relationship is a very primal relationship and it makes people feel really comfortable.

"Concrete is fantastic because again, it's a very primary material. It's masonry. It's something which gives us the ability to make a very plastic, elastic surface. Meaning that we can make surfaces that are curved and curvilinear with concrete."

Ms. Meyers sees part of her job as sharing her love of materials with clients. That requires communication. "This is something that younger architects and all students don't really understand. Sometimes I show the clients books but a lot of times when I have a client who is having a hard time getting into the process of design, I grab my Lautner book and I can pull that person in because they see the way that Lautner uses wood and they relax. And they feel that, 'I can go there, I love this.'"

It extends beyond books, however: "I like to get big pieces of each material we use," she continues, "as a part of the preparation for meetings with clients. When I have the client come over and we talk about the materials and the drawings, I will spend a full day before that meeting arranging that room. Because that room is like setting a table for a big dinner party. It's like setting the table and I want it to be an experience for the clients when they walk in."

Ms. Meyers sets the scene: "I get big chunks of my materials like a big piece of steel, glass, concrete, stone. I always get my wood from this person who worked with Nakashima and has a shop in New York City. I always get huge pieces of wood from him, either walnut, ash, or maple. I pick these big pieces that are three or four inches thick and three or four feet long by two feet wide. These are pieces you can handle and get a sense. He doesn't put any finish on them except wax and they're all hand-planed. So they're perfectly smooth.

"I also like to have the glass but it's not off-the-shelf. It's been hand-cut and framed by pieces of steel that have been put together by a master craftsman. So the way they're handling and framing the glass is unique and definitely a work of art."

These large sample pieces are integral to engaging the client in the design process: "It's important to have these objects available so clients can understand the magic the architect can perform. I lay it out very artfully like a painting, like a Mondrian on the table. When clients walk in, they see the table is arranged with all these pieces of materials. Then they see the model of the project sitting next to the big samples of materials. The clients will often go over and start picking up the materials and feeling them and looking at them. And I find it becomes very real for them. It mixes the architectural experience of the meeting with the concept of shopping. Which is a low-brow way of thinking about things, but we do live in a consumer society. It's a way of keeping the conversation going. It makes the client feel comfortable and it keeps the conversation going."

Large samples of materials are also a fundamental part of Ms. Meyer's own design process. In fact, she says that, "I often will not draw a project unless I have those materials sitting at my desk because I find those materials to be a very powerful intellectual reminder of what I'm doing. So you don't even discuss materials until you've got something more concrete to share with clients."

Models

For Ms. Meyers, engaging a client also entails model-making: "Another thing we do," she says, "is we'll make the model of the building or the room, or series of rooms, showing the client what it is. And then we'll choose a room we're going to show for perspective and we'll build it huge. Like we'll build it 3 x 4 x 3 feet out of foam core and it'll be completely blank. But it will have apertures where we have light coming in. Then we very carefully light it and we shoot it. We'll shoot maybe two hundred shots of different lighting conditions. Then pick maybe three or four of those shots. After that we'll Photoshop the room into it, which creates very powerful images which are also pretty thrilling for people to look at.

"This is something I recommend to my students, to create big blank boxes and shoot light into it and photograph it. It's a great tool for investigating space and understanding where you're bringing light into a room. And how you're going to do that and what the effect will be. Because suddenly you can see the space and your clients can see the space. If you don't do that you can't see the space and your clients can't see the space.

"We can throw that together, the model and shoot it, in two days and one day Photoshopping. Whereas if that was a professional rendering, it would take three to four months."

On Architecture

"As an architect, you can either present stuff as an actor, or you can present your stuff as a magician," says Ms. Meyers. "I believe strongly in creating my work as a magician. There are tricks that I do. I don't let people see behind the screen when they're walking through the space, but they are surprised when these things happen." For the Infinity Chapel project, she says, "Suddenly they begin to question where the edges are because they don't know where they are located in the space. And I think that dislocation is part of why we call the Chapel the Infinity Chapel. It's meant to be about the dislocation you have in time."

Architecture can use many devices and strategies to create different effects. She says, "There are many different architectural devices the architect can use to trick a person's mind into being in a place that they wouldn't ordinarily go to. It is like setting a scene so something can happen in a spiritual or psychological way."

For example, Ms. Meyers explains that in the Chapel of the Light, "When you sit in the seating area, the surface of the seating is slightly tilted; you're meant to feel like you're in a ship on the water and the rest of the church is the water. So that sense of flotation allows you to be in a meditative space where you enter into whatever is happening in the church. That was why I wanted the floor to be disembodied. So you would come into the space where you were unhinged from the structure of the building and you were floating. And I think it works really well."

In fact, says Ms. Meyers, if architecture is done well, it can create this effect repeatedly. She explains further, "I think that is the level at which really good architecture works. You walk into a good architectural space where the architect has unhinged you from your everyday existence and puts you in a confrontation or in a discussion with this other way of being. The space therefore puts you in conversation with yourself and your history of the way you understand things."

Ms. Meyers explains further, "That is one of the reasons spiritual space is interesting, because it sets up the perfect excuse for architects to generate that kind of form. When you're working on a house or corporate office, it's hard to convince the client that they need to make really interesting, therefore more expensive spaces that are very engaging and spiritual. When it's a church or a mosque or a Buddhist meditation hall, it's part of the program, so the program is really interesting." After all, she observes, "Le Corbusier was an atheist but he certainly made great churches."

Notes

1 Victoria Meyers. Interview with Sherin Wing via Skype. Los Angeles, March 3, 2014.

2 "Infinity Chapel." Accessed November 14, 2014. www.hanrahanmeyers.com/sacred_infinity.html.

3 "Chapel of the Light." Accessed November 14, 2014. www.hanrahanmeyers.com/sac_chapel.html.

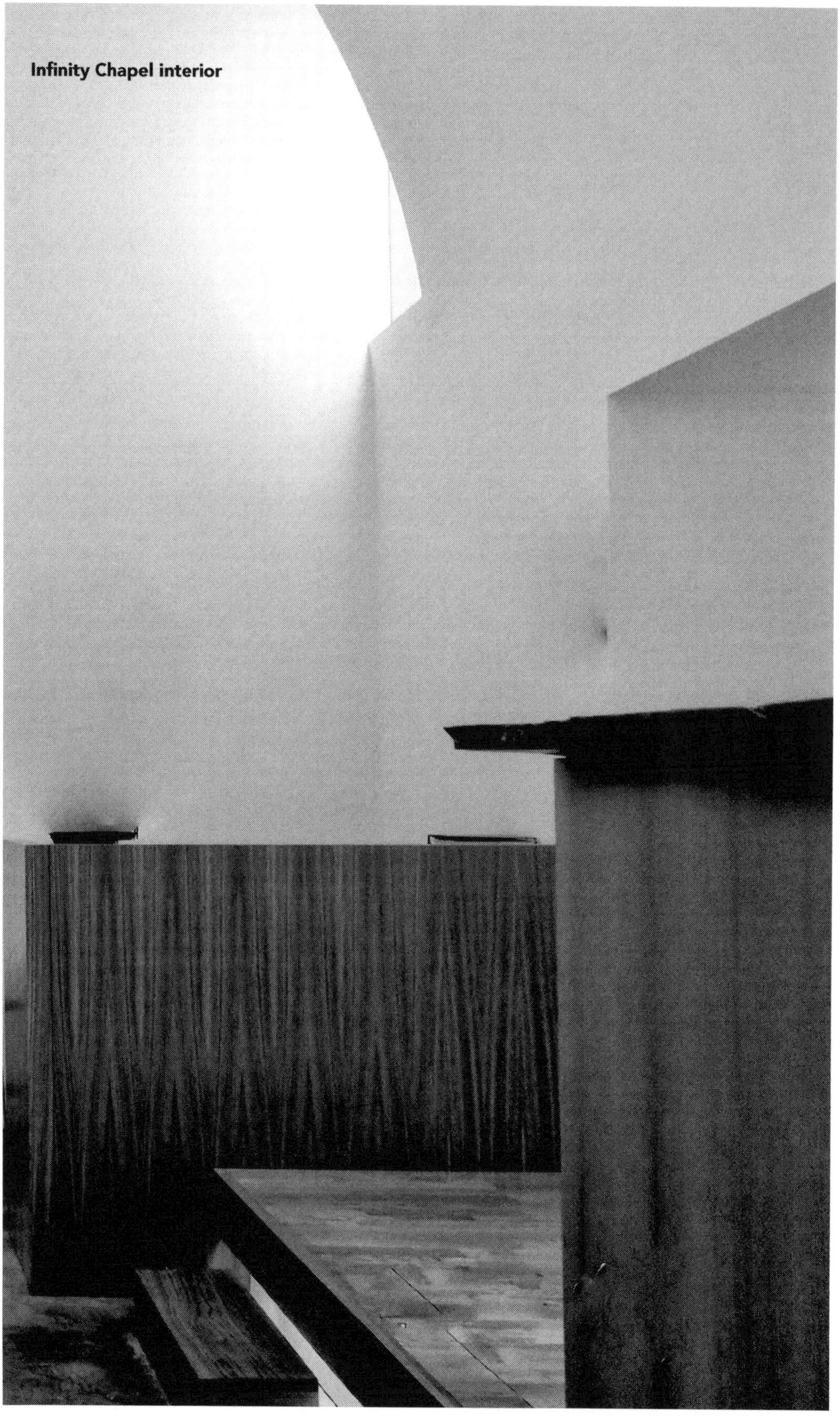

Infinity Chapel interior

Infinity Chapel interior

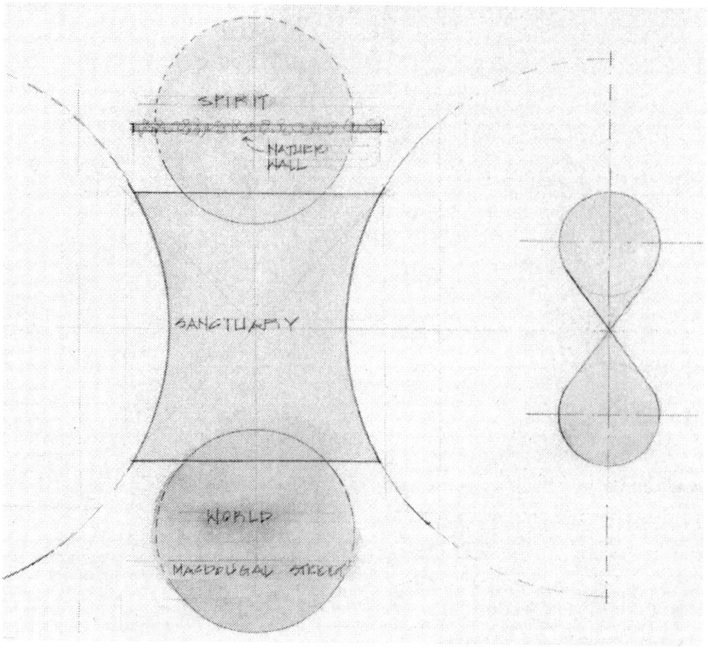
SPIRIT
SANCTUARY
WORLD

Infinity shapes diagram

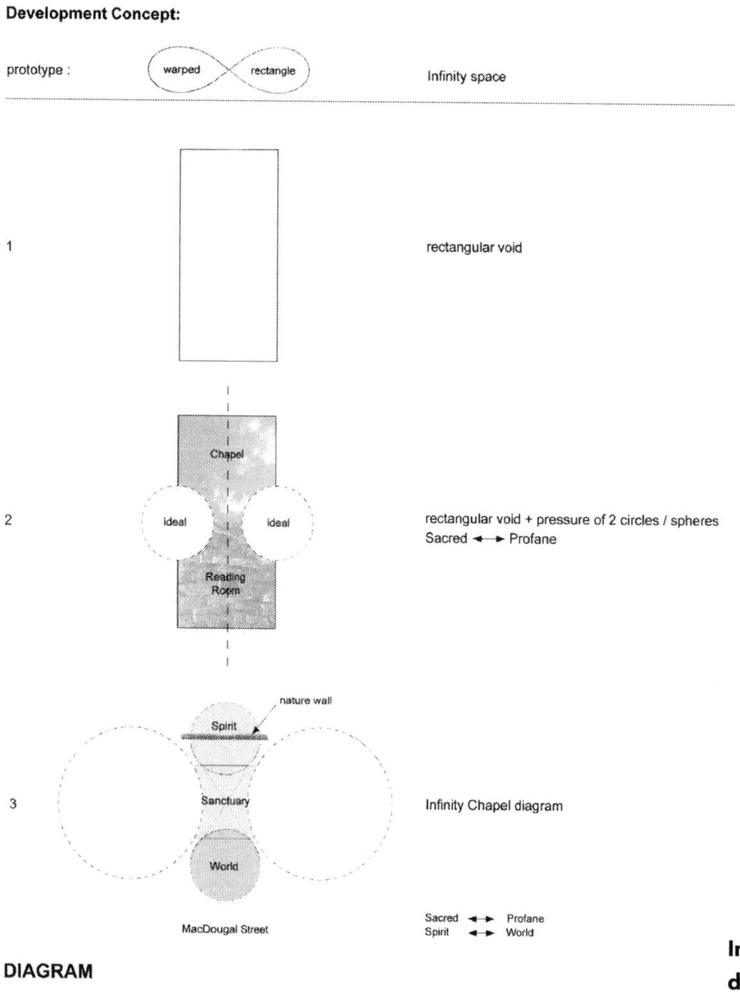
Development Concept:
prototype :
warped
rectangle
Infinity space
1
rectangular void
2
Chapel
ideal
ideal
Reading Room
rectangular void + pressure of 2 circles / spheres
Sacred ↔ Profane
3
nature wall
Spirit
Sanctuary
World
MacDougal Street
Infinity Chapel diagram
Sacred ↔ Profane
Spirit ↔ World
DIAGRAM

Infinity Chapel development diagram

Development Concept :

Infinity light sequence diagram

<u>Sequence of Light</u>

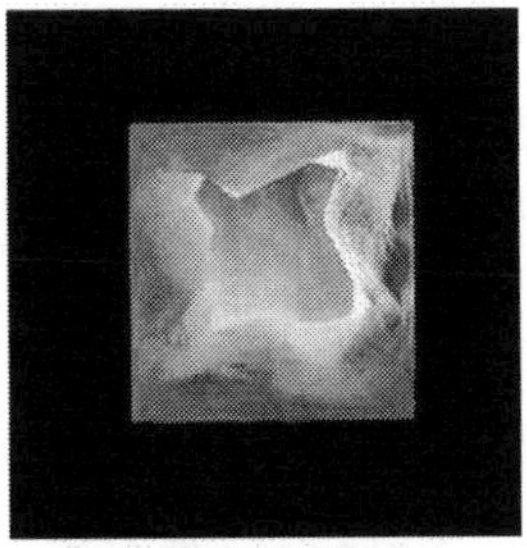

monitor #1 : Reading Room / Sunday School

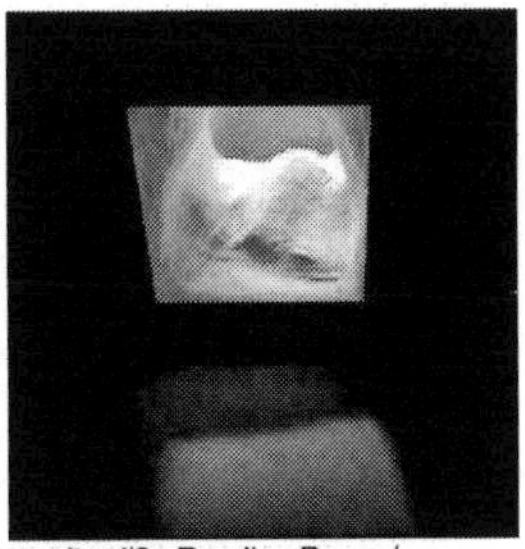

monitor #2 : Reading Room / Sunday School

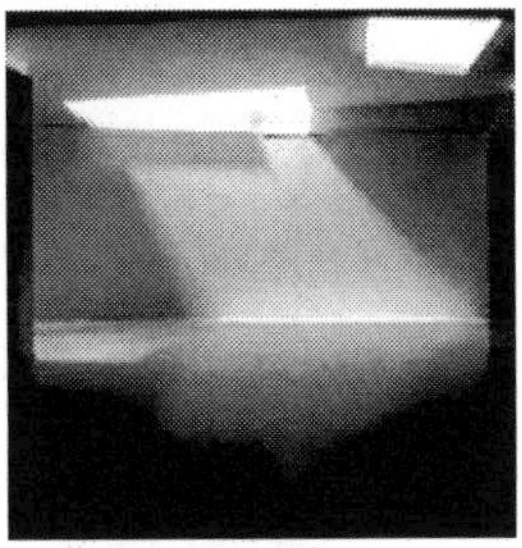

monitor concept model

light monitors from Sunday School

monitor concept model

light monitors from Chapel

DIAGRAM

Development Concept :

<u>Light Paths:</u> Light wells ←→ World to Spirit // Reading Room ←→ Chapel

Light wells ←→ Innocence to Wisdom // Sunday School ←→ Chapel

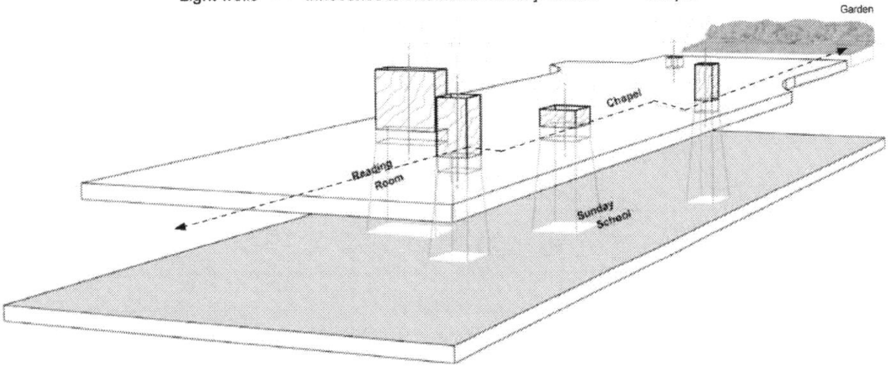
Garden
Chapel
Reading Room
Sunday School

Infinity light sequence diagram

Sequence of light : street to garden

Infinity Chapel interior

Infinity Chapel interior

Chapel of the Light stage rendering

Chapel of the Light side wall rendering

Chapel of the Light stage

Chapel of the Light interior

Chapel of the Light exterior

Chapter 7

Kris Yao Artech[1]

Mr. Kris Yao, FAIA, Founder and Principal

PROJECT

Peitao Catholic Church, Tapei, Taiwan[2]

Built to commemorate the induction of a Chinese saint, the project incorporates a 50-meter high circular form merged within the church to serve as a focal point. The temple itself is located on the third floor of the church, which, in conjunction with the banyan trees outside as a background, creates a floating effect.

Religious design references include the banyan tree for the tree of life. The passage leading to the temple is lined with saints as well.

Skylights provide illumination during the day, while night-time lighting is powered by PV panels.

Materials for the project include reinforced concrete, PV panels, and marble stone cladding.

Project is 14,598 square meters.

Completed in 2001.

Research and Design

How does one design a religious space? Where does one begin? For Mr. Yao, it begins with studying the religion's philosophy: "By studying their philosophy, I am able to gain better understanding of different religions. For example, when I was asked to give a proposal for the Catholic church, I did have to study what they did because I was unfamiliar with their religion and practice.

"I started by talking to the practicing Catholics in my office to point me in the right direction of where to begin researching more deeply, especially in the ceremonial and ritual aspects of the religion. That was important because those practices are quite specific and they have more rituals that other Christian sects." This gave Mr. Yao and his team a starting point to research the architectural necessities of the religion more deeply.

For another Christian church project, Mr. Yao says, "I was also asked to enter a competition for a church that was not Catholic. It was more abstract and it was more about an expression of space as it relates to the divine." In this case, he says, "It took less study and more consultation with those sponsoring the competition. But I still had to know what people do, for example during a mass, as well as the functions of the other rituals.

"All projects have their agendas and their goals. Architects have to think whether the goals are first attainable and achievable," he says.

Site

For Mr. Yao, the process begins very simply, with a visit to the site: "I always have to go to the site. I don't want to sound abstract, but architects have to go to the place to feel the unspeakable feeling that you can only get from being there.

"Nowadays people use Google maps and all kinds of 3D stuff. There are other things they also teach in school, like traffic, sun angles, wind, which are important." But, he says, "That only helps us to understand a little bit. Because every place has a special thing and we have to go there to feel it. You have to be in the site to know. In fact, you have to go to the site many times. Even after your schematics are done, you should go there again and imagine or visualize how it will be. I think that's very important. And this is not specific to religious projects—all projects should start this way."

Developing Design

"I always visit other churches and temples. If we build temples according to Buddhist philosophy, then we should not stick to a particular kind of a form because the purpose of a Buddhist temple or a monastery is to remind us of mindfulness. That's what Buddha taught, that everything we practice or do as a Buddhist is to remind us of mindfulness. Either reading sūtras or meditation or going on pilgrimages. That is the core that we should not forget."

How this philosophy actually shapes a design, however, is very different from project to project. "One of the first modern temples I designed was the Luminous Buddhist Center. At that time, most of the temples in Taiwan were in the imperial roof style. But this group was different. They said they had a very small building and they hoped I didn't mind but they insisted on a modern building. I was very happy to accept it! And after that building was done, people responded very positively. So it sort of opened up a door. People realized that temples didn't have to be in the old imperial style."

While a modern approach is appealing, Mr. Yao warns, "There is also the issue of trends, where people start doing all these kinds of supposed 'Zen-like' spaces. These are very simple, minimal, modern type buildings and people think that this is the only thing to do.

"I understand things differently. For example, in Tibetan temples, they paint all the walls and the ceilings in all different colors. As if that isn't enough, they hang a lot of colorful banners along with other things and it's so busy. But can you say that this kind of temple is wrong? No, its purpose is again to remind us of mindfulness."

Clients

All projects share the architect's and the client's values as they reflect their unique relations: "The client's goal, their purpose in developing each and every project, is clearly very important. For a commercial project, for example, a client will have a set of things they're looking for. For public housing, there's another set of values they cherish. And for religious projects, it's very different. Some may want to achieve a more meditative place like the Water Moon Monastery I did. But I've also encountered some projects where they may just want to impress the public."

How an architecture firm achieves these goals as a firm while simultaneously advancing the client's goals depends on the type of firm one is discussing. Mr. Yao explains, "Generally, there are two kinds of architects. One is more interested in expressing who they are, their style, their philosophy, their outlook as represented by the architecture. There's a strong personal style. You don't go beyond style or personal outlook."

But, he says, there is, "A different kind of architect who is less interested in a so-called signature of their own rather than fulfilling the project's needs. I'm not the first type. My interest is to fulfill what the project needs. The reason is every project has a different cause and condition, a different story and different site. So it's difficult for me if every project has to come out the same. It doesn't logically make sense for me."

He observes, "When one is designing for Buddhist clients, there is no one who actually has the final say. Religious groups normally are composed of a lot of people. Either they are monks and nuns or they are patrons. So when things are being discussed, everyone can express their views. But it's not like a corporation where finally the church makes a decision.

"So the answer is always floating in the air," he laughs. "It's a very difficult process for architects because you don't know who to follow. Many times there is no conclusion. I don't know if other religions are like that. Perhaps this is something that is very Taiwanese or Chinese."

In the end, "Architects have to think whether it conflicts with our own values. In the end, if it does align with our values, then it's great. However, if there is a conflict of values, then you should say no and run away fast!"

Peitou Catholic Church

Mr. Yao's philosophical approach to architecture has resulted in some very creative projects. With Peitou Catholic Church, "It's a church to commemorate 100 saints. Because there had never been an official recognition of them or a place to recognize them, they decided that would be Peitou's theme, to commemorate all these saints from China. Since I didn't know too much about Catholics, I first asked my colleagues and they told me about it from a personal viewpoint. So they told me how you proceed into the church. You have to wash your hands and there are other rituals you observe. Then there's the concept of saints who support the divine."

To this, Mr. Yao's team performed additional in-depth research from books as well as conversations with the church hierarchy, and then they began designing: "Overall, the shape of the church itself is like two folding palms, it's like a cylinder shape that's narrower on top and wider on the bottom. It's also on a horizontal, linear site, with a longish frontage facing the tree-lined boulevard. So the depth is very shallow but the width is very long. We decided three-dimensionally to put the highlight of the church above the tree line. That way it will rise up above everything else, including the mortals on the street."

Mr. Yao explains the progression, "When one enters the courtyard, there's a small fountain in front. And then beyond the fountain, one goes up a ramp. That ramp is parallel to the street from the length. On this ramp, as you ascend, there are all these pictures of these saints lined up on both sides of the ramp. If there were only two, this whole thing wouldn't work. But with a whole procession, it is quite a sight. Once you arrive at the top of the ramp, there's another pair of grand stairs up to the main space itself. What we imagined was that when people go up the stairs, they would see a very impressive and stunning space with light coming from above. And that we felt was very Catholic. You're basically looking up to the light, and the idea is that you depend on it."

And the procession through the space to the main space is ritually significant: "The process coincides with their ritual procession. Bringing the church to the top of the tree line, once you are there you look down to the city. And the city in that area at that time was mostly lower-rise buildings. So you really have that feeling of rising above the city and normal, everyday life."

On Architects

"As a designer, we're limited by our skills and thinking" says Mr. Yao. "Overall, you can see there are underlying values, habits, or aesthetics—whatever you want to call them—that run through all the projects. That's very natural, that's nothing special. Sometimes people over-exaggerate that there is an underlying principle of a particular firm or person. But I think it's about the limitations; it's because of the limitations of our skills and the dominance of our habits that naturally happen that result in what other people see as a signature 'style.'

"The important thing," he says, "is how we architects use the tools we have. First there is space, trying to figure out the space. Second is the materiality. Those are the main tools we architects have." This understanding shapes Mr. Yao's own approach: "Even with this traditional style, I arranged the space with a lot of different layouts."

On Designing Sacred Architecture

Mr. Yao's own understanding of Buddhism informs his approach to architecture: "If we think that there is only one style or aesthetic that is correct, then we're caught in an extreme that Buddhists believe we should avoid. This is something that I started to realize after a few years of working." He continues, "Once there was a monk in China who came to me and this monk said he wanted to design a temple because he liked all my modern ones. But this one has to be in the Jiangxi style because that was just his requirement. I gladly accepted it because if that's the condition, then I don't really need to do something modern because as long as it inspires people, then it has served its purpose.

"Most of the religious projects I have done are Buddhist," admits Mr. Yao. "There have been a few other opportunities that I got involved with. There is the Catholic church and another Christian project where I was asked to enter a competition. But most of our projects are Buddhist temples and monasteries."

As in other religions, however, "Buddhism has many different sects or schools of Buddhism. So they're not actually entirely the same." That said, he admits, "For some reason Buddhist temple projects come to me. But they're each very different. Sometimes they're Mahayana or Zen, sometimes they are in the Tibetan tradition."

Notes

1 Kris Yao. Interview with Sherin Wing via Skype. Los Angeles, October 14, 2013.
2 "Peitao Catholic Church." Project description emailed to author, June 19, 2014.

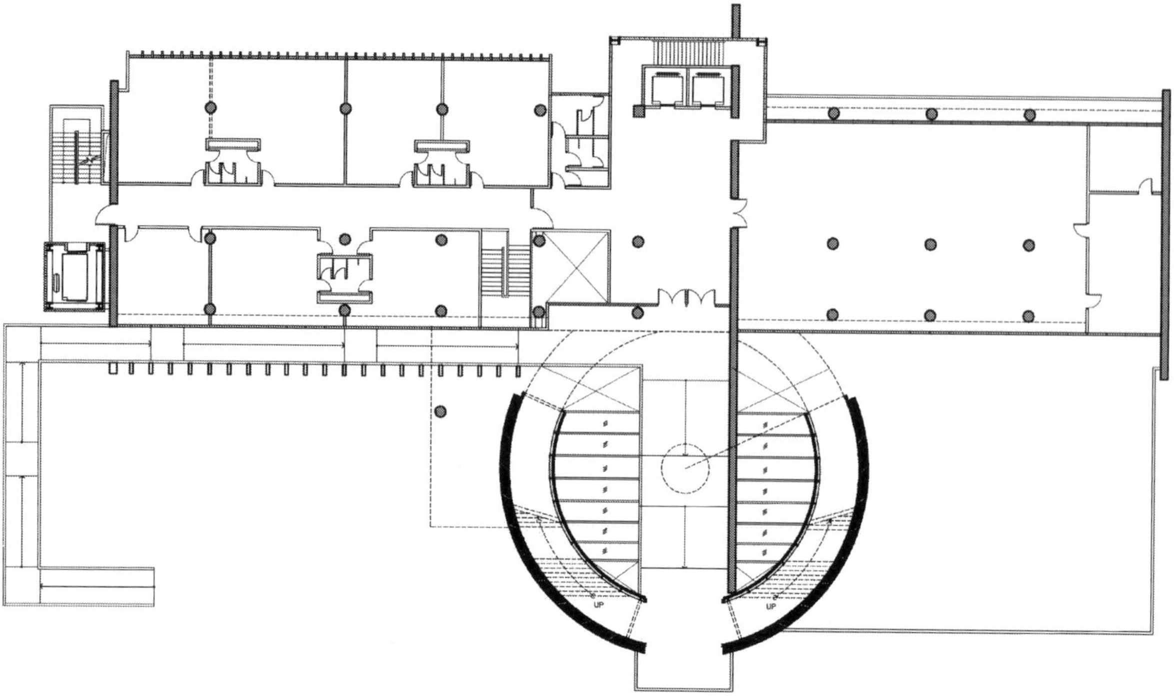
UP
UP

Peitou Catholic Church plan 1

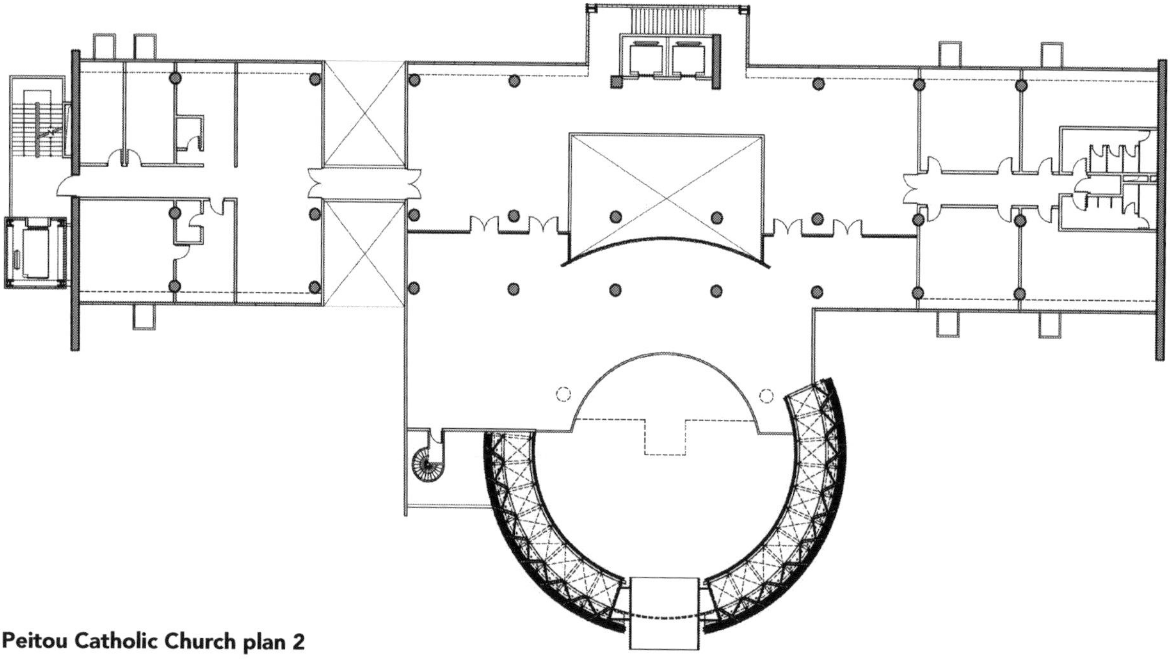

Peitou Catholic Church plan 2

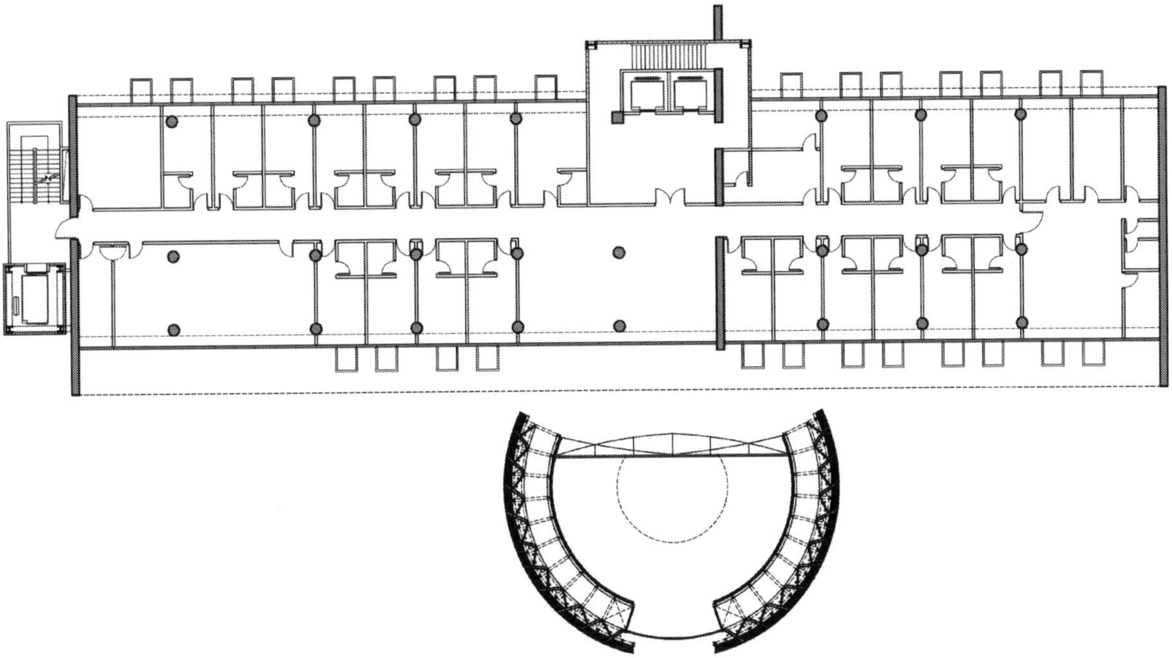

Peitou Catholic Church plan 3

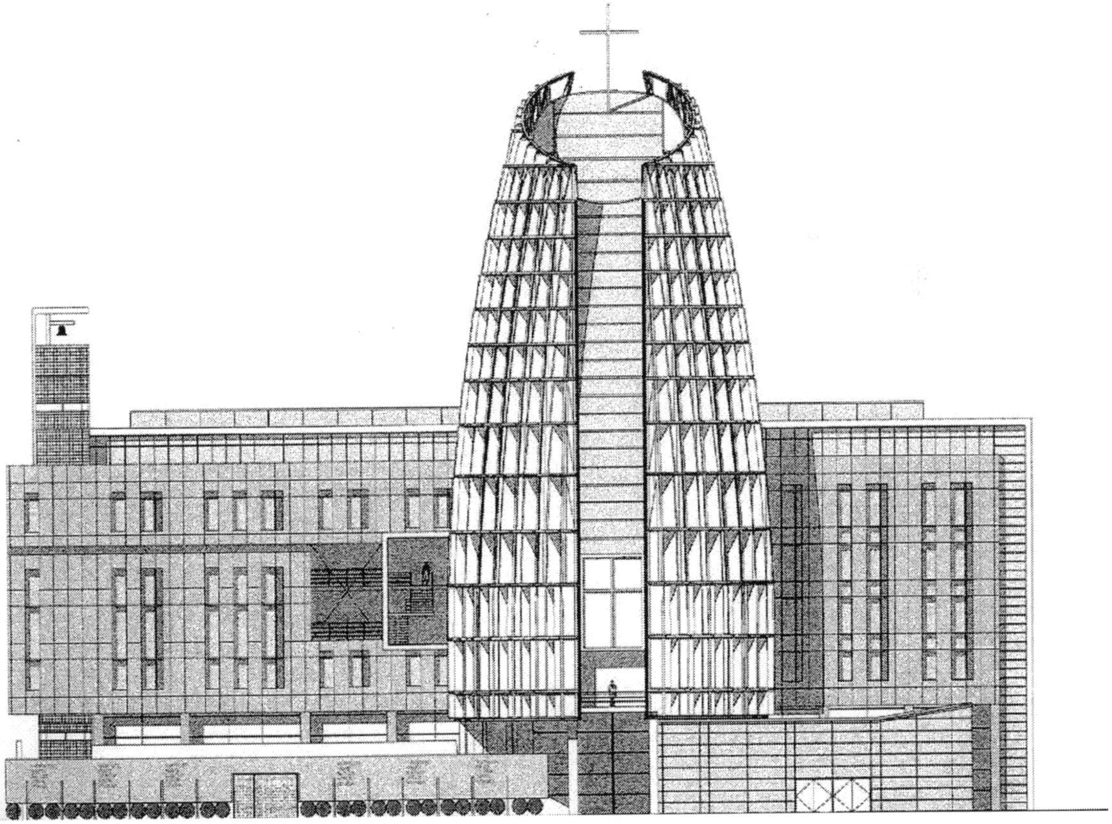

Peitou Catholic Church elevations

Peitou Catholic Church model

Peitou Catholic Church model

Peitou Catholic Church model

Chapter 8

Makespace Architects[1]

Mr. Shahed Saleem, Dip. Arch, RIBA, Founder and Director

PROJECTS

Mosque

Hackney, London

Mosque

Aberdeen, Scotland

On Adaptive Reuse

"One of the things that always fascinated me about the experience of mosques in London was the way you're always in ad hoc spaces. You're in buildings that have been used as something else. What's more, the alterations are quite rudimentary, quite piecemeal. And there's this direct connection between people using the building and the way in which the building's been adapted and made.

"This is quite fascinating, actually. I didn't mind the non-architectural-ness of these religious spaces, the fact that they are quite 'imperfect', because there's a kind of intimacy in them as a result. There is also a sense of real embeddedness of the community in that building because of its constant adaptation. This project is a kind of microcosm of all the issues that I'm interested in.

"For the first project which is in Hackney," Mr. Saleem says, "the long lead time of eight years was okay for me because it was also quite a formative period for me. It was a period of time in which I could just explore approaches to things. So I wasn't in a rush to get anything done quickly because I thought it was going to take some time anyway.

"It was an existing Georgian house that was a hundred and fifty years old sitting amongst a similar terrace of houses. The mosque is this converted building. Originally, it was a single-story mosque with a temporary building in the back. So we started by first demolishing the single story that was there and we built this new three-story addition. Through the main entrance door you can enter either the new building or the old building so it connects the two together."

Interestingly, the building combines the historical with adaptive reuse. He explains, "The front is still kind of traditional and is being actually completely restored as a historic building. In fact, the whole project is in a conservation area which is a historic area of East London."

Yet the interior had to be changed: "The inside is converted and used as the mosque."

On Culture and Design

Heritage and history exert important influences on the design process: "My designs employ remnants of the past and traces of history that don't replicate the past. For example, the patternwork in my first project, the Hackney mosque is partial where you only see a partial tile. Traditionally it's very complete, a wholeness, and this source is where every pattern is derived from, but mine is a reinterpretation. I employ it because that's what people understand and resonate with but in a way that the pattern is not intact. It's not being disruptive or disrespectful, but rather it is complex. It's meant to suggest that there are now a whole series of influences and ideas which constitute identity.

"I was trying to create an aesthetic which is simultaneously contemporary and of the historical conservation site it's in. The place in this context is the architectural environment, the aesthetic environment. It relates to a wider physical context. But," he says, "it should also be something which has a connection to systemic cultural heritage as well."

Mr. Saleem's solution was to use a design that referenced the Ottoman period. "This design is based on a tile, a 13th-century Ottoman palace tile. It's the top corner of the tile, with the rest of the tile down below. It's a way of taking an Islamic pattern out of its original context and out of its geometrical completeness and using a part of it that remakes it as a façade of a building. One can read the Islamic pattern, but it also doesn't read as a solely Islamic pattern; it has some ambiguity. People may not necessarily identify it as a mosque at first, but if they know it's an Islamic building, then they understand the reference."

In other words, the design references the cultural heritage of Islam that simultaneously accommodates new interpretations. "On the one hand it is an Islamic building but on the other hand it's also a design object within a certain part of the city. And it's a conservation area that also relates to Islamic history as well on a contained site."

He emphasizes that respect is an important factor in his designs, "The past is important, however it's understood, particularly for migrants in religious spaces. The past is quite significant. I'm not trying to tell people to forget it through my reinterpretations, but rather, that what I'm doing is using it in a different way." So, in fact, "There are a number of resonances between what was happening with mosques in the past and now."

Patience is another key element to the way Mr. Saleem works: "A lot of times it's a very long relationship with the mosque. The design process goes on for years in many cases because it starts out they've got some ideas and you start doing things, and then it takes a long time to coalesce. And then gradually you put something together."

Clients

Working with clients has one basic element: communication. "It's not just about the design in the type of work architects do, so it's very much about communicating. For example, sometimes people want something more traditional or more 'expected.' They want a mosque in the sort of image of what they think a mosque is. Which fulfills their stereotypes. So you have the dome or the minaret and so on."

In such cases, "I try different ways of trying to persuade them otherwise. It's not bad, but I don't think it adds anything to the conversation. It doesn't really take the conversation in another direction and in that sense it's not really using the opportunity that's available. But I guess every building doesn't have to do that."

For his first project, the clients found him, "I think because I'm so close by," he admits. "I think someone just gave them my name when they were looking to do something." He continues, "There's a localness about this whole endeavor that is also linked to my relationship with this project because it's been going on for so many years. It's a very personal relationship so it has this kind of foundational project sense; it's not something that I went to see where I don't quite know the area or don't quite know the context."

For the Hackney project, the client involvement in the design was initially minimal: "They didn't get really involved with the design and the aesthetics of it. They just went along with whatever I did. But I didn't really talk about the design until I presented the drawings. The discussion was more about the amount of floor space they'd be getting and how many people could be fitted in and how things were going to be arranged. The discussion was much more pragmatic. And as long as their practical needs were being met, they didn't have any issues with how it was going to look.

"With Aberdeen the client actually was an individual who wanted a contemporary proposal. So he found us because of our design in Hackney which was modern. So he was actually looking for that specific approach." The reason stems from the adaptive reuse conditions Mr. Saleem sees throughout the UK. "They were frustrated because they were using a converted series of houses as the mosque and a converted bank building. That was all they had."

For another project that is currently in the development stage, Mr. Saleem has been working with an immigrant Nigerian community. "In Camberwell the clients have been almost sanguine about the design. And I guess they kind of liked what I had done. They didn't want anything overly traditional. It may also be that these kinds of traditional mosque stereotypes are more for South Asian communities because they refer to the images of mosques you have in South Asia, like India and Pakistan. It's not so relevant to a Nigerian community because their register of forms is different. Maybe there's a little bit of that when they see the other stuff that's done, they think they can also go for something like that. They can see the direction the design can take.

"I'd like that to be the case, that people can see that this is what can be achieved through design. There have been cases where the projects were a lot more traditional than I would have wanted them to be just because the clients were very forthright about saying they wanted to have a mosque which looks like a 'mosque.'"

Community

For all Mr. Saleem's religious projects, connection to the community has been a central factor, "When I started designing mosques, I wanted to retain that connection. It's a connection between the users and the place, because it's very much about the place that you're in and taking what you have around you and shaping it into a religious space. You're taking a building that's already there and kind of shaping it which makes this a very space-based kind of way of making a religious building."

In the Aberdeen mosque, "The community is rather wealthy and has been established for about 30 years. But the only mosque provision was the sort of ramshackle series of buildings I mentioned. And the reason there haven't been any new mosque initiatives was because unlike in most mosques that were located in towns and cities, they were located in the country. In cities, there is a continuous process of change and improvement in the mosque facility. But Aberdeen hasn't had any tradition like that. No one was doing anything and so the client thought, 'I need to do something to get this mosque built.'

"It was a personal quest for the client. Which is unusual since here in the UK mosques are community endeavors, and they already have a presence and they have connections in that area. But that wasn't the case here. The client actually had to create a community."

He began with the site: "The client bought the site as a business. Then he created a mosque. Next he gathered together a small committee, who then reached out to other individuals to join the committee. And that committee became a decision-making consultancy body. But he didn't dictate things to them—it was a much more collaborative procedure."

The next order of business was to reach out to the larger community. "Essentially," he explains, "they had a number of ambassadors for the project, around fourteen people who supported the project and who got the message out to others about it. They held fund-raising dinners and events and over the two years they've built this project from the ground. It's been a very sensible, measured way of going from a personal idea to a community project, which is not an easy thing to do, especially with immigrants where you have a lot of different cultural issues."

Developing Design

For different projects and architects, the role of the architect changes. Mr. Saleem explains, "In a sense once an architect comes along and designs a mosque, it starts to professionalize that process because the architect has aesthetics and training and so on and so on. That creates a bit of a distance between the users and the final building.

"The geometry, the fact that your geometry is often skewed toward the sides can often be a positive contribution to the overall organization of the building. So you can use that to generate the form, the layout, how the plan works."

Program

"The mosques are actually quite simple in their program as well. There's really only the prayer hall and the place for washing. That's really the two main functions that need to be accommodated. And the circulation is how you get from one to the other and how you get to the street. Where you put your shoes. And there aren't many liturgical requirements in the mosque itself so you don't need altars in specific locations and you don't need icons in certain places."

Specifically, he says, "You just actually need a hall. So in that sense it's quite simplified, the process is simplified. Interiors aren't that important, except for the prayer niche called the Mihrab where the Imam stands."

Materials

The issue of materials actually comprises several factors. Mr. Saleem says, "I like the materials to be embedded in the traditional practice of making buildings. There isn't an unnecessary hi-tech-ness to them. I keep the materials understandable for myself and the clients before introducing other materials and types which may have other meanings for them."

Then there is the issue of using local materials to ensure that a project is contextual. For example, "One of the things the clients did insist on is that the project used granite because Aberdeen is known as the granite city. It's in Scotland and a lot of buildings there are in granite. So if the granite is not used as blocks, then it can be used as cladding. I used it as cladding. It locates it quite firmly within the surrounding environment."

Continues Mr. Saleem, "We're also using a ceramic artist to design some bespoke Muslim ceramic Islamic tiles. This is the first time she's done Islamic tiles. The idea was to bring something more contemporary to the tradition rather than a strictly historical reference to the design. So she's using a design that resonates with traditional Muslim art, including a series of ceramic stars in the pattern work. These will be auctioned off so people in the wider community can have a sense of ownership in the mosque and engage them while also being more creative with the mosque itself.

"Cost is an issue because materiality is going to be dependent on things that can be afforded. I'm working with a fairly limited palette at the moment. I'm working with stone cladding or ceramic cladding. And I'm also using brick in a slightly more contemporary way, but again it's a very traditional British material. I also use metal in a metal mesh façade. I'm also using a lot of stone. Both are traditional materials but are treated in a contemporary way."

Sites

"One of the interesting things about mosques in London or UK towns is that you're often dealing with existing sites," Mr. Saleem explains. "They already have a formal use within the fabric of the town. And the fabric of the town has been composed through various historical processes, generally industrialization, house-building or in industrial areas, commercial buildings. But they fit into this kind of industrial town-scape."

These conditions directly impact mosques in the UK. "Often what you find is that Muslim communities are concentrated in city areas because when they came to Britain and settled, it was to work in certain industries. They're often settled in working-class factory towns. So the mosques that are built within these communities are located in areas where there may be very few civic buildings. There are not big libraries or town halls. In other words, it's not where those buildings are historically built. There may be a church or other religious buildings, but the mosque can be one of the largest civic projects in a particular area in a particular part of town within these Muslim communities."

Situating a mosque in established towns or cities can be challenging: "The mosques are oriented toward Mecca, which may not necessarily fit with the site that the mosque is on. That means that you then have to reconfigure buildings to make the prayer room and prayer hall oriented toward Mecca. Therefore you might end up with a prayer hall that is at an angle in relation to the lines of prayer." In other words, "The direction of prayer doesn't really sit comfortably with the room. It's often at an angle or it's not quite aligned within the walls of the room."

There are different responses to this issue. "I think there have been various responses in the mosques in Britain," he says. "One of them has been the hexagonal prayer hall seen in a couple of mosques. It's the easiest way of getting the prayer lines posed within the geometry of the room. Or you might have a room that is at an angle to the rest of the building otherwise the prayer lines are not oriented right.

"It's odd situation," Mr. Saleem admits. "It does compromise the quality of the space. But that's just one of the realities you have to deal with in building mosques in existing contexts. You don't have the leeway to arrange things exactly the way you'd like and you don't have the towns arranged around the mosques, you have the mosques very much inserted into an existing urban context."

For example, the Hackney mosque's development was very much tied to the site. "The site is a long rectangular site. Within it there is a hall with various functions and the main prayer hall. But the direction of the prayer was such that you ended up with a nice square prayer hall. But the prayer hall was then placed obliquely on the site. I used that to generate the rest of the plan. The necessity for orientation towards Mecca affected the way the rest of the plan works."

Mr. Saleem observes, "If you've got a bit of space, and you've got potential, it can determine how the rest of the building works in a positive way." For the Aberdeen project, "We were initially at a different site and did some scheme developments. It's been a process. The final design is actually the second or third scheme, but it's very much what I envisioned. It's the same in treating visual language, symbolic language, and we've really just been discussing minor details. Finally we found this system after four years."

On Culture and Society

Mr. Saleem views architecture as an expression of society, culture, and identity: "I think there's potential for a new architectural language. There's a social context now which is generating these mosque buildings. It is a new phenomenon."

It begins with emigration: "The process of emigration and settlement of former colonial subjects encapsulates the whole history of imperialism, colonization, and globalization. It's all these global currents which started in the 16th century and continued into 19th-century empires." He continues, "These then ended up, morphed into WWI/WWII, decolonization, post-colonialism, the creation of commonwealths, the movement of people, and the migration of labor."

In fact, Mr. Saleem sees much of the current emigration as resulting from the world wars: "Diasporas include post-war economic environment as well, which precipitated these emigrations around the world. Immigrants from South Asia were coming to provide labor for the industrial base of Britain. And people from the West Indies were coming to provide services in health care, transport, and so on."

Migration has changed the shape of cities. "People are coming to provide a large number of services, which reforms the imperial powers, as it were. The economy changed, so industry declined some. Services grew. So the shape of the city changes because of that."

The mosque was an outgrowth of these economic changes from colonialism and imperialism to a trend of emigration to the UK: "Now you have this new building type, the mosque, that really has an impact on the urban landscape of the country because every town has a mosque of some sort. They've become part of the indigenous urban language, they've become part of the vernacular.

"What I'd like to see," he confesses, "is a real engagement. I'd like the buildings to engage that history because buildings speak of all of that complexity. On the one hand, buildings are just buildings and I think architects have quite grand ideas of what buildings can do. They're not novels. They're not great pieces of academic research. They're not great philosophical treatises. They are just buildings. They're only buildings. I think they can encapsulate things, but obviously they can't completely explain things."

On the other hand, he says, "In doing buildings, I'd like them to be able to reference this kind of social complexity which is an aesthetic. It's also an aesthetic history of Islamic art, as well. All these factors are amalgamated into a complex milieu which has a form with its own hope, beauty, and voice." In this way, "buildings can speak very much of where they are and what they are now, where they are now, and who's using them. And also where the surroundings are." In particular, he says, "These kinds of religious buildings have the potential to speak to things that other buildings can't necessarily. That's why I find it very interesting."

On Secular and Sacred

"Secular projects are mostly residential individual or apartment blocks, commercial, or public buildings," says Mr. Saleem. "So in a sense they're quite different types of building. Maybe my approach wouldn't be that different because you're still talking about different strands of society and how to represent that and symbolize that. I don't necessarily see the mosques as religious buildings. It's not the religious side of things that's driving these designs.

"Some people might talk about the relationship of the divine and sacredness and the kind of existential experience, but I'm not really talking about that in these buildings. Partly because they are of limited means and partly because the needs of the communities are very practical in that they need as much floor space as possible."

He elaborates, "We need to get this many people in, we need to have the space for washing dead bodies, having classrooms. So the way in which the users deal with the mosques is very pragmatic. Nobody's ever said to me we want to create a very spiritual space, a very sacred space. It's never been part of the brief. It's always about practicality. And I think that's partly to do with the nature of the religion. It's very embedded in everyday practices.

"When I hear people talk about sacred space, I think, mosques in a sense are not sacred. They're not formally sanctified. There also isn't this kind of separation within the secular lives and sacred lives. You don't stop being secular and then spend, you know, some time being sacred, because the way the religion is described, your condition of being an individual in a state of worship is continuous. So that when you're doing your secular activities, you're still in a sacred state.

"So that kind of separation you hear about in Western architectural narratives of sacred space doesn't really translate to Islamic buildings because the sacred vs. secular doesn't really exist. So you don't necessarily say, this space is going to be a sacred experience because there isn't really such a bifurcation. I mean, one can say that one has a spatial experience, because mosques are great experiential places and medieval spaces, but I think that they're experiential because they're built by rulers or they're built for political power as great public buildings. I don't think they're necessarily great spiritual spaces because the religion requires them to be spiritual spaces. That's just learned behavior.

"That's why I concentrate more on the symbols of the building. And why a lot of that is mainly about a kind of surface and materiality. Because the spatial side of things is really functional, how do we get it to work, how do we get as many people in because there's a great demand on the building's capacity, practically speaking."

Architecture's Role

"In doing my book on mosques in the UK," says Mr. Saleem, "I've realized that architecture really has a much more important role to play other than just creating tasteful, aesthetic objects, which is actually the objection that people have about the religious projects. They are a bit pastiche and vulgar, gaudy and so on. You get this criticism of the mosques that have been built in this country over the last 20 or 30 years that these buildings are all of no aesthetic or design value: they're just pastiche. And they're denigrated in a patronizing way.

"That might be true from a high architecture point of view, but I'm glad they're there. There's obviously something there that I value. I think they show a very direct, a self-built, direct relationship between the people who use them, their aesthetic aspiration, and the aspiration of the buildings that they've created. I've realized the importance of these very direct, readable symbols."

He explains further, "I think it's important not to lose that completely. Because then you risk alienating the people who use it because they have nothing to latch on to. Without a visual symbol people can easily latch on to, you run the risk of losing them.

"The trick," he says, "is to present something which is different enough that people think that, 'I never really thought that we could have a mosque that looked like that.' But it's also familiar enough for people to attach to it, as well. So there's that kind of fine line that one needs to tread." Toward that end, he states, "I don't believe in this complete avant-garde for mosque design because you need to take people with you. You need to be guided by how people respond as well.

"I believe that ideas, ideology, and cultures are fluid and historical," he says. "There is a continuous exchange and there has been a continuous exchange and interaction between beliefs, religions, ideas, and cultures. I don't have a dogmatic belief in a particular religious practice, but one religious practice or any other practice exists because of the interactions it's had along the way in a cultural context. I would like the buildings to have meaning on a number of levels and to a wide group of people."

Note

1 Shahed Saleem. Interviews with Sherin Wing via Skype. Los Angeles, October 22, 2013 and November 16, 2014.

Hackney exterior 1

JOHN TANN'S
RELIANCE
LOCKS,
FIRE&BURGLAR-PROOF
SAFES,
IRON DOORS, ROOMS &
WORKS

Hackney exterior 2

JOHN TANN'S
RELIANCE
LOCKS,
FIRE & BURGLAR-PROOF
SAFES,
IRON DOORS, ROOMS &c
WAREHOUSE 11, NEWGATE ST. &
WORKS
TREADWAY STREET

Hackney exterior 3

PORAN MASJID
IC CENTRE TRUST

Hackney exterior 4

RELIANCE
LOCKS
FIRE & BURGLAR PROOF
SAFES

Hackney panorama

Hackney interior

Aberdeen exterior 1

Aberdeen exterior 2

Aberdeen cutaway

Chapter 9

OOPEAA (Office for Peripheral Architecture)[1]

Mr. Anssi Lassila, M.Arch, Founder and Director

PROJECTS

Kärsämäki Shingle Church, Parish of Kärsämäki, Finland

The project was a student competition to rebuild the original parish church which was built in 1765 and demolished in 1841.

The structure consists of a log-built core. Cladding is a black-tarred shingle. The interior is hand-crafted wood.

Natural lighting from skylights is accented at night with candle-lit glass lanterns and tinplate lanterns.

Project is 200 square meters.

Completed in 2004.

Klaukkala Church, Parish of Nurmijärvi in Klaukkala, Finland

The project was an open competition to redesign an existing community center to provide an identifiable landmark for the Klaukkala suburb.

Exterior materials include existing brick façades on the original building plastered red. The new building uses copper cladding. The interior comprises white concrete walls. The wooden ceiling provides natural light through a combination of lighting fixtures and strip-like windows.

As a community center, the project serves multiple public functions that include a daycare center, a Scouts meeting place, office spaces for priests and social workers to meet with the community, in addition to the columbarium and church nave. There is also a new inner courtyard that in the summer serves as an outdoor church or event area.

Project is 3,500 square meters; 1,300 was a redesign of existing structure and 2,200 was a new addition.

Completed in 2004.

Kuokkala Church, Jyväskylä, Finland

Kuokkala Church was an invited competition for a church in a suburb that would serve as a focal point and as a clear identifier for the neighborhood.

The proposal accommodates the church hall as well as both a parish and a community center within a single large structure. The church and parish meeting halls can be combined into one large sacral space with adjoining youth facilities. A gallery between the halls houses the organ and the cantors' offices. Sacral spaces are flanked by service spaces including the sacristy, storage, kitchen, and lobby.

Materials for the exterior roof and walls include Spanish slate tiles and a wood- and copper-covered entryway. Finnish granite is also used for cladding. Interior materials include Finnish spruce wood walls with laminated timber for the ceiling.

Project is 1,250 square meters.

Completed in 2010.

Developing Design

Mr. Lassila, principal and founder of the Office for Peripheral Architecture (OOPEAA), began working while he was still a student. That first project was a religious commission, a competition to be specific. "It was," he says, "The first project I did and it was a competition which I entered as a student. I was just interested in making a very interesting, new public building. I was 24 or 25 years old. I made really interesting solutions and interesting details on the site and made the one-to-one scale prototypes before the final project. It was really an amazing experience to be part of this process."

Friend and translator, Ms. Juulia Kauste, Director of the Museum of Finnish Architecture, translates further, "Particularly at that age and because it was a competition, the first designs were much more guided by the project's needs outlined in the competition's program." From there, she says, Mr. Lassila, "Developed his design through more abstract ways of trying to get into a mode of designing. He listened to the music of Bach and thought about ideas of sacred spaces in general. So it was much less specific to that particular community or that particular location and place."

As Mr. Lassila notes, practical requirements provide, "Just a starting point. I am also very interested in exploring an ecumenical shape, a very universal space that could be a church." That involves not just practical skills, but also an initial interaction with the site. "I also always try to find what is spiritually interesting in the space, whether it is religious or not. So I ask, 'What makes it more than just a space?' What aspects are interesting changes for each project. So when you enter a space, you can feel what is spiritual, though it's difficult to pinpoint exactly." Adds Ms. Kauste, "The emphasis is on a spiritual experience, which is a fairly abstract starting point, rather than a specific quality."

Mr. Lassila continues, "After the initial ideas had been developed abstractly, then came the more specific considerations of the surrounding physical environment, cultural environment, and the religious context of that particular community." What's more, because Mr. Lasilla's design was guided by the competition's set guidelines, "The function of building as a church was interesting but it was not the most important thing in my view." In fact, says Ms. Kauste, "That's why he was able tackle this project as a graduate student, because it was guided by the guidelines."

Mr. Lassila then uses "renderings, sketches, and pictures." However, the kinds of images "depends on the specific project." As Ms. Kauste points out, however, this is not simply a matter of using photographs of the site or even drawing multiple schemes. Instead, "Mr. Lassila uses other kinds of images that might be associations rather than actual drawings."

Site

"One of the most important elements for the design of a building is how it fits in the landscape, the town, or wherever it is. It's important to examine the context and the construction of the place where the project is." Ms. Kauste reiterates, "The actual location and physical surroundings are very important aspects that define the entire building and the way in which it is designed to communicate."

Explains Mr. Lassila, "For example, in the first project, Kärsämäki, the site is in the middle of the field of nowhere and it's quite a small building. But within the landscape it's a big building, relatively speaking. I was very inspired by the ponds and agricultural buildings in the area. So I really wanted to fit the church into the landscape.

Adds Ms. Kauste, "For the church in Kärsämäki, the relationship between the surroundings is such that it's in the middle of an open field. It's the sole structure there and is very much defined by its existence in the open."

"I also wanted it to seem like it had always been there, like it belonged, but on a bigger scale," he says. "That was all important as I was trying to find the final shape of the building. What's more, Mr. Lassila explains further, "They were also very flexible in using the space. There wasn't any fixed furniture, so it's total. They can use the space in any way and there were no limits. There was no religious altar or anything on the inside. The building is very ecumenical."

That differs from the site for the other projects. For example, Mr. Lassila says, "For the Kuokkala church it was very inspiring to try to fit this church into a new suburb. It was a very rough context because there was a restaurant quite near and very cozy housing nearby."

Competitions

A central element that dictates the successful development of a project is client interaction. That is further inflected by the type of commission. Mr. Lassila says,

"If it's competition or commission it makes a difference. When it's a competition, you are much more free to try to find a solution that will satisfy the clients. If it's a commission, it involves more talking and dialogue and many other people so it's a different way to shape the project."

He explains further, "The first project is located in a really small village that has about three thousand people. They were a little concerned about the future of their religious community. That is when the priest got the idea of re-making the old church. It was first built in the 8th century and then it was demolished in 1861 or 1869. But they didn't have any documents of the old building."

It was at this point that the goals of the priest, the religious community, and the project itself, changed. "The priest and his committee called the university where I was studying. They asked a professor of restoration for help to rebuild the old church. But the professor got an idea to make a new modern building using old techniques. After that, they thought, let's make it a student competition.

"I didn't have any experience in designing churches at that age," he admits, "So I was lucky that I won. I was also lucky that I had a very good client because we had very good communication with the client and with the carpenters who built the building."

All these components were reflected in the project itself: "The building reflects part of their open-minded thinking. And it also reflects the very good communications we had with the clients and all the people who were involved in the project. What I learned with this case is that you can make interesting architecture anywhere."

Ms. Kauste translates further, "For this competition, there was a strong emphasis on trying to find a modern expression for this traditional, religious need. They wanted to create a space of contemplation and spiritual experience. So as a starting point, there was a very strong emphasis on that, which guided the ways in which he approached the project and the ways he tried to express those ideas."

Ms. Kauste continues, "Mr. Lassila says that in a competition, they have already created a program. So there has been a dialogue between the client and the organizers of the competition already. The requirements have already been clearly expressed in the competition, whereas when you don't have a competition, the process of figuring out what the client wants is more flexible and unpredictable. More is left to chance. But instead of feeling that it's more rigid as it might sound, it's actually just a less-defined starting point. And because it's a less-defined starting point, it's also very different to work in that way."

Mr. Lassila adds, "It's not a bad or a good thing, it's just a different kind of process." He elaborates, noting that, "Each case is different because of the background. Everybody has a really different kind of view about how it should be or could be, as well as how it functions."

A later project, Kärsämäki, provides a good example. Ms. Kauste translates, "In that project, the priest was very open-minded and had very liberal and flexible ideas in terms of how the space ought to be organized. In fact, he was actually very willing to leave it as open and flexible as possible. Which made it possible to create the space we designed. So the dialogue was mainly between the architect and that priest."

The Klaukkala project was also a competition: "It is a very multifunctional building because it is a small chapel. It's not all church or not all chapel but rather it's a multifunctional building. It's a lot more pragmatic. There is a space for the seating, there is a kindergarten, and there is office space. There are many different kinds of functions in that building."

The Kuokkala church was yet another competition. Here Mr. Lassila admits, "It was an interesting thing because they wanted it to look like a church. And it was a really funny thing because it was an invited competition and everyone had a totally different interpretation of what a church looks like. So we thought okay, let's make something very primal in a way."

Ms. Kauste interjects, "In that case, there was a much larger committee of people with whom Mr. Lassila dealt with at different phases of the project. They had much stricter thoughts and ideas about the placement of the altar and all different kinds of details. Of course, that attitude is also reflected in the end result."

For all these projects, a key component of working successfully with clients is communication. For Mr. Lassila, that is not just verbal, but also visual: "A lot of the communication is aided, and actually important means of communication is through images and drawings. It's not only verbal communication but its reactions to those presented drawings and images. In fact, along with talking, it's the drawings and images that communicate best."

On Designing for Religious Institutions

"There is a big difference between the US and Finland," says Mr. Lassila. "It's because we have a one large religion in Finland." In fact, he says, "All the churches we've designed are in the same religion. So it's a foundation in our culture. It's very different from many other countries."

Ms. Kauste continues translating for Mr. Lassila, "Mr. Lasilla says that there is the idea that because the Lutheran religion is basically so much part of the culture, it's almost internalized as a secular culture. People don't acknowledge it as a religious culture. It just permeates everything. Even for people who don't belong to church and who don't practice religion in any way and who don't even go to church will still share the same values. It's very much that you grow into it. In some ways you aren't even really aware of it and don't question it much."

This difference, she says, "Means that the whole cultural context is very different. That makes it difficult to draw the line between a religious cultural context and the secular cultural context in these projects." What's more, she says, "We have a state church. So the state and the church are together, which is relatively unusual nowadays in most places."

Note

1 Anssi Lassila. Interview with Sherin Wing via Skype. Los Angeles, October 10, 2013.

Kärsämäki floor plan

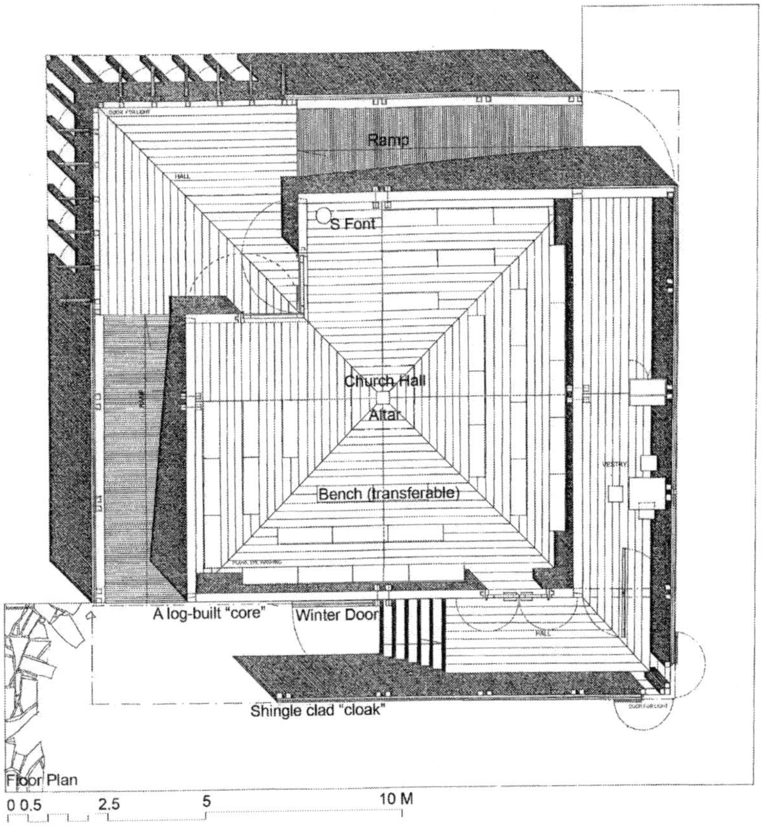
Ramp
S Font
Church Hall
Altar
Bench (transferable)
VESTRY
A log-built "core"
Winter Door
Shingle clad "cloak"
Floor Plan
0 0.5 2.5 5 10 M

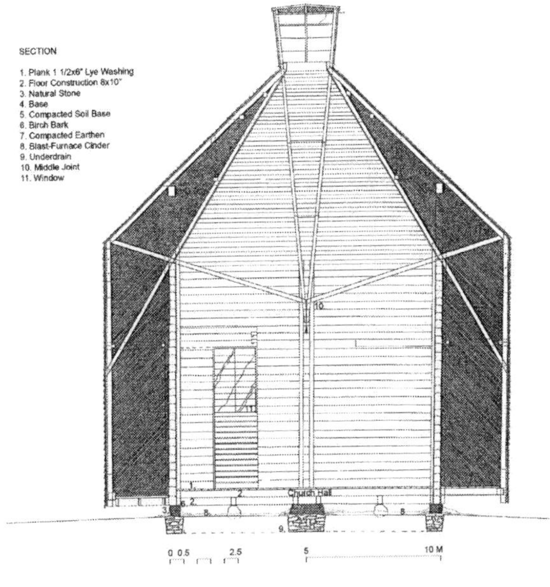
SECTION
1. Plank 1 1/2x6" Lye Washing
2. Floor Construction 8x10"
3. Natural Stone
4. Base
5. Compacted Soil Base
6. Birch Bark
7. Compacted Earthen
8. Blast-Furnace Cinder
9. Underdrain
10. Middle Joint
11. Window
Church Hall
0 0.5 2.5 5 10 M

Kärsämäki section 1

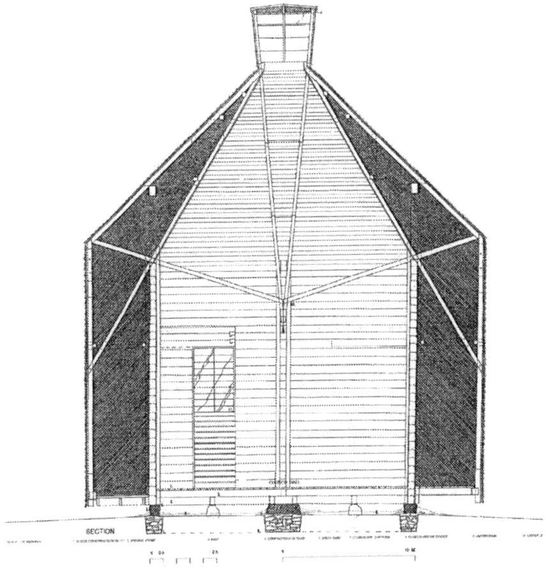
SECTION

Kärsämäki section 2

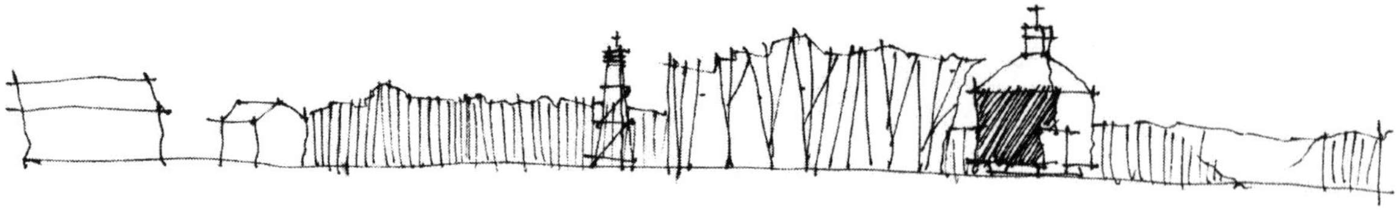

Kärsämäki sketch 1

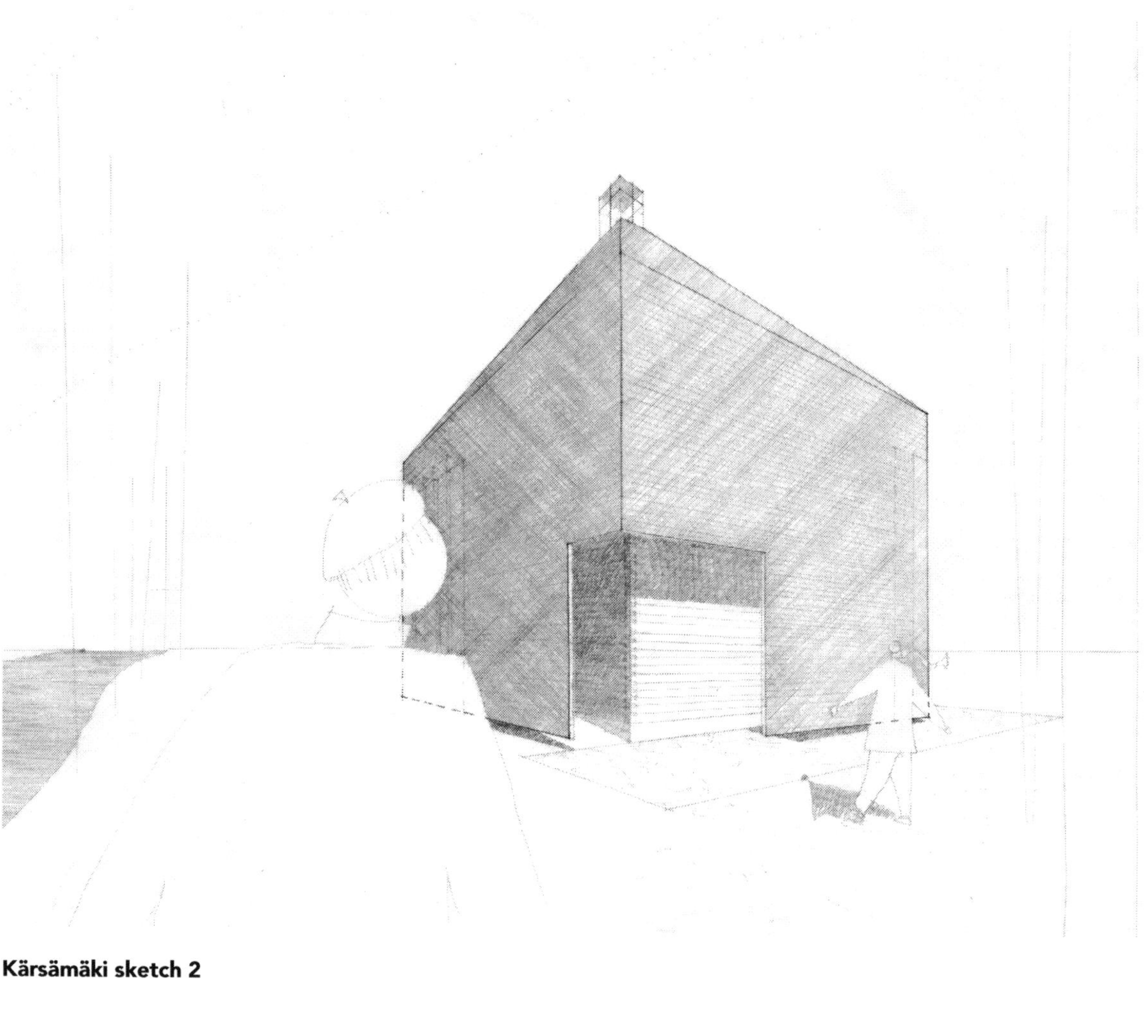

Kärsämäki sketch 2

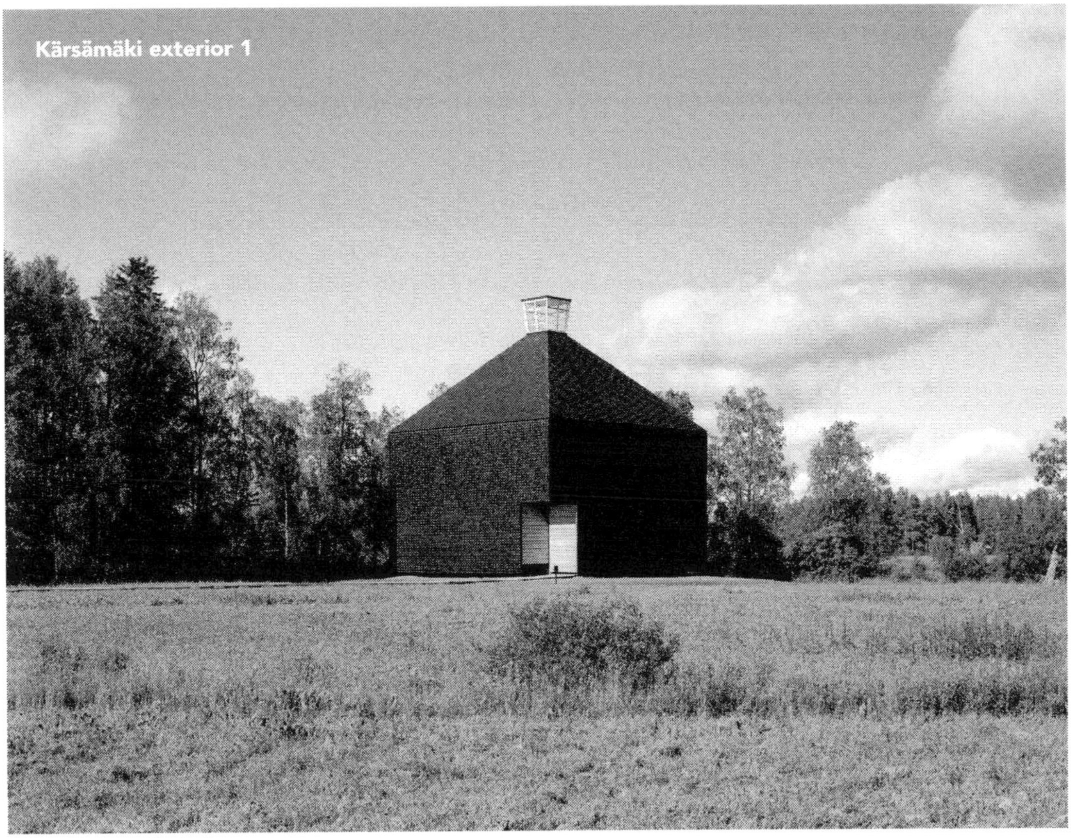
Kärsämäki exterior 1

Kärsämäki exterior 2

Kärsämäki exterior 3

Kärsämäki exterior 4

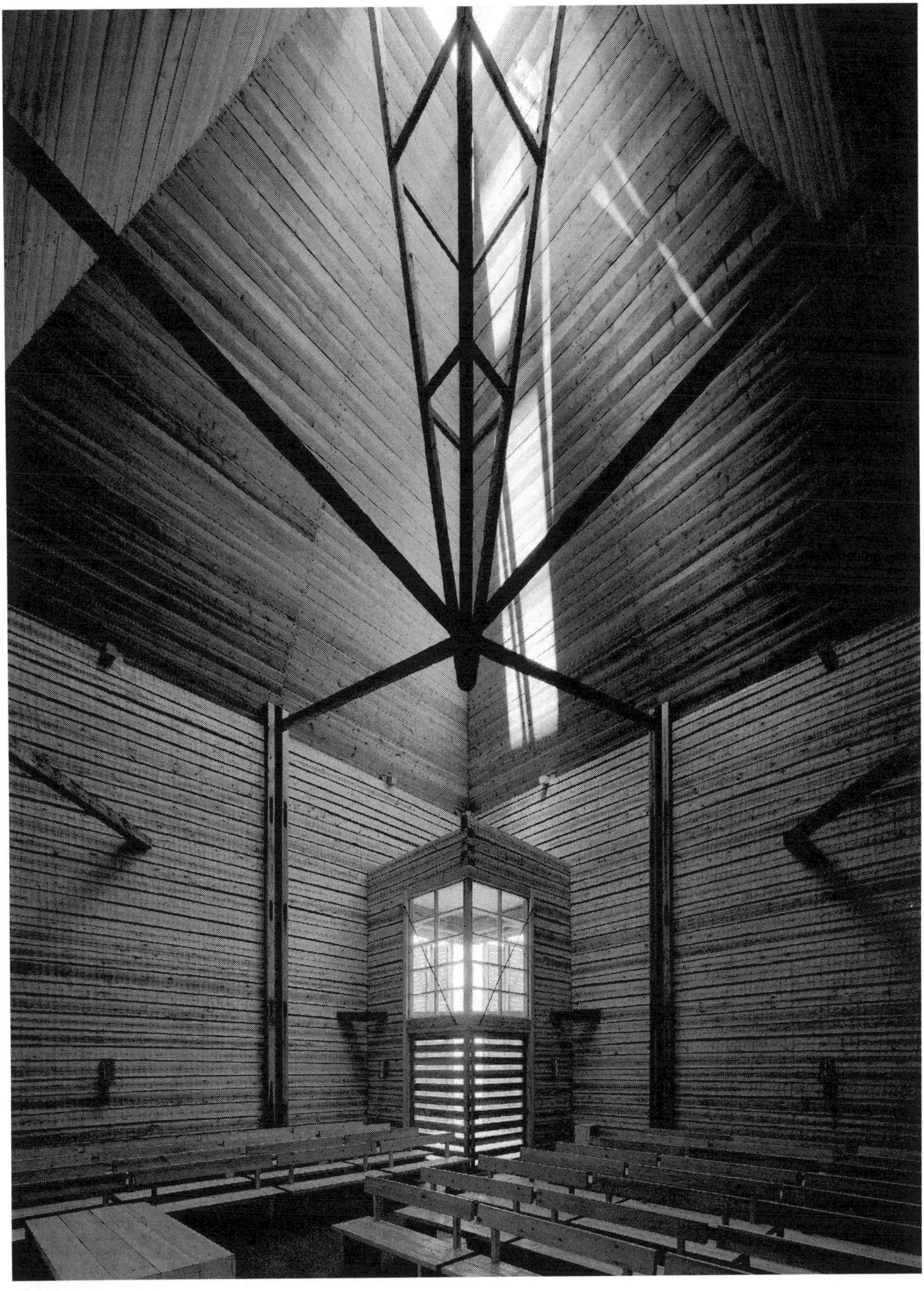

Kärsämäki interior 1

Kärsämäki interior 2

Kärsämäki, interior

Kuokkala plan

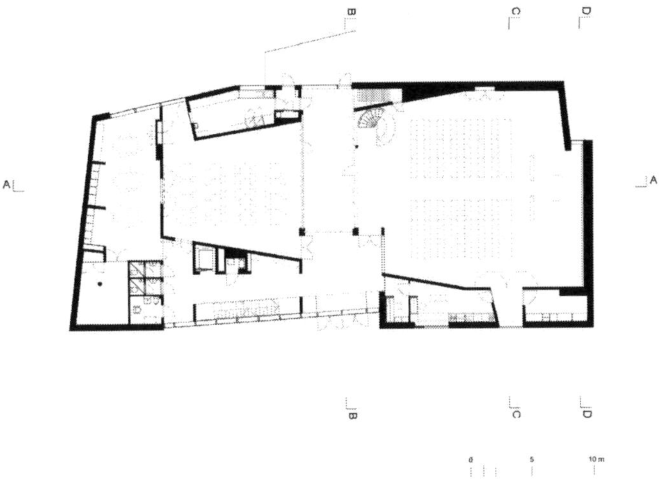

A
B
C
D
0
5
10 m

Kuokkala interior sketch

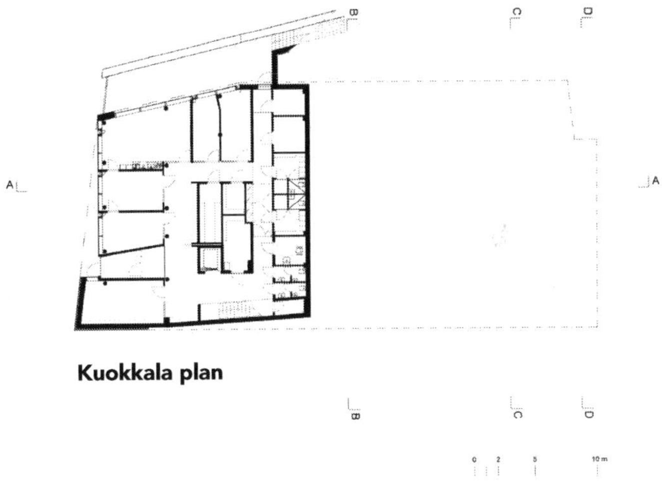

A
B
C
D

Kuokkala plan

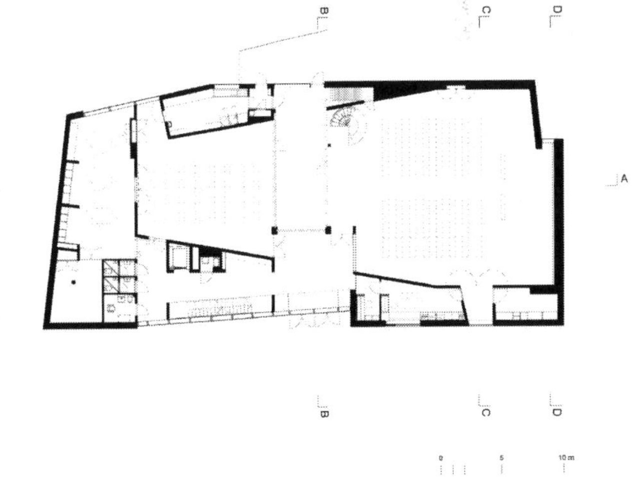

A
B
C
D
0
5
10 m

Kuokkala plan

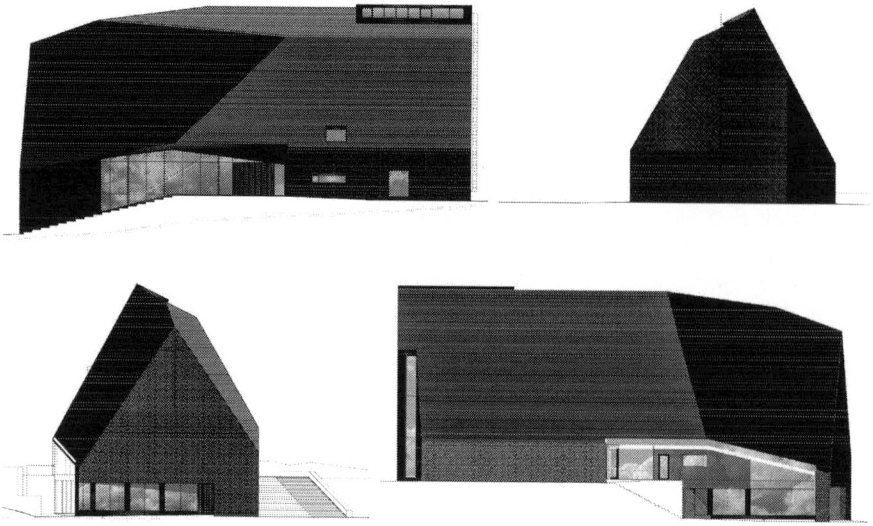

Kuokkala façade rendering

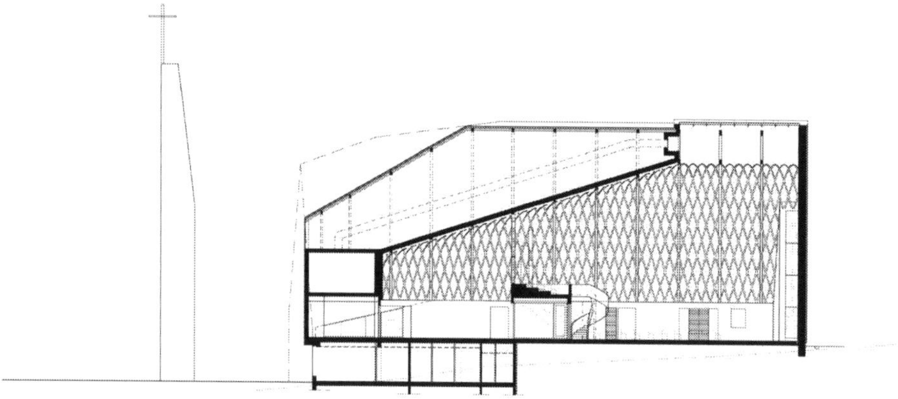

Kuokkala section 1

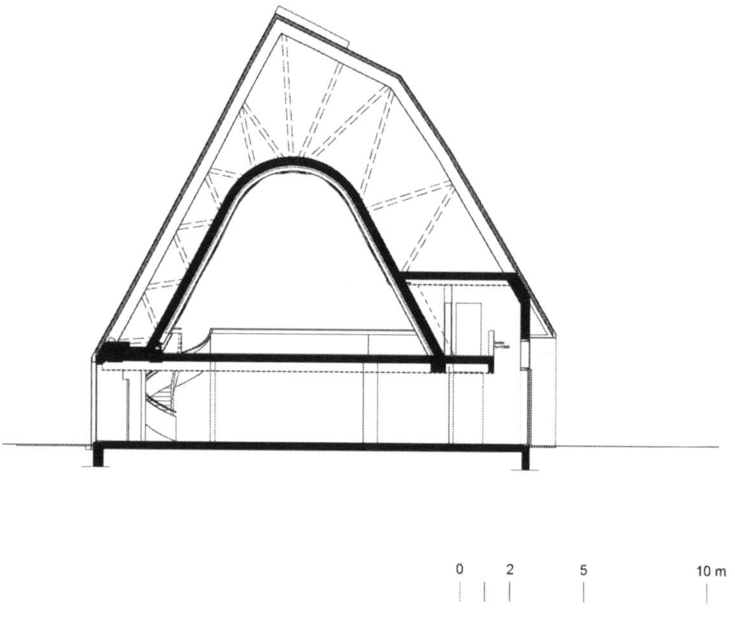
0
2
5
10 m

Kuokkala section 2

Kuokkala exterior 1

Kuokkala exterior 2

Kuokkala exterior 3

Kuokkala exterior 4

Kuokkala exterior 5

Kuokkala interior 1

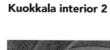

Kuokkala interior 2

Kuokkala interior 3

Kuokkala interior 4

Kuokkala interior 5

Kuokkala interior 6

Kuokkala interior 7

Klaukkala plan cellar

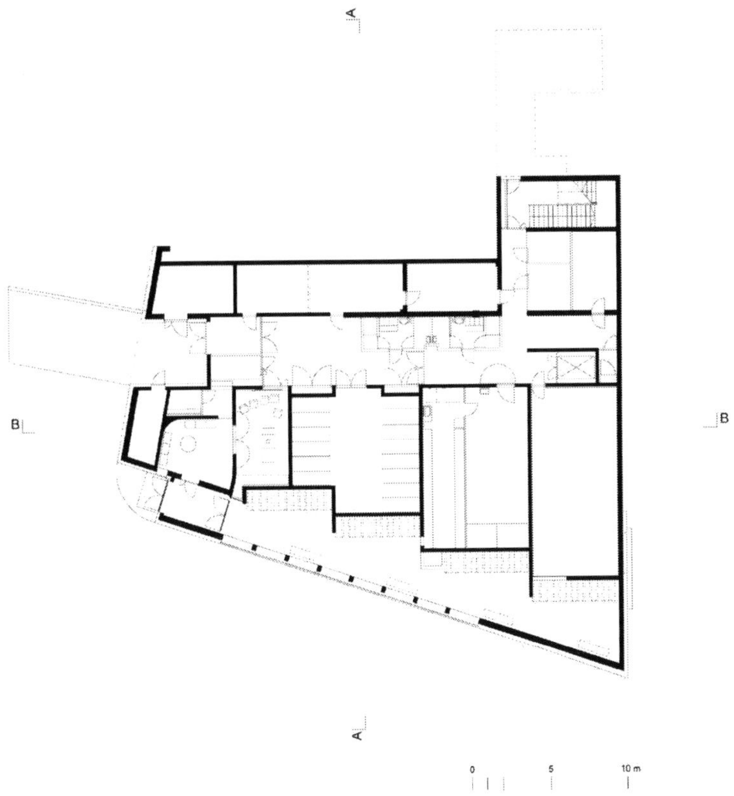
A
B
B
A
0
5
10 m

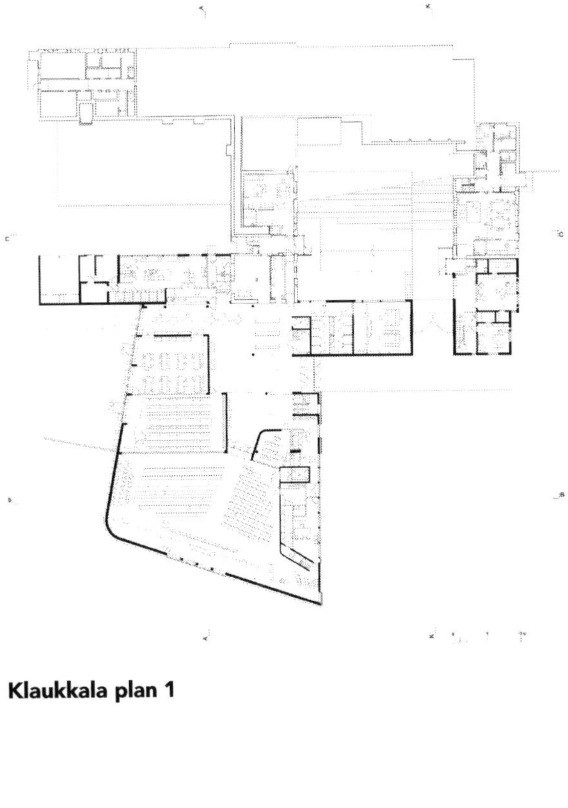

Klaukkala plan 1

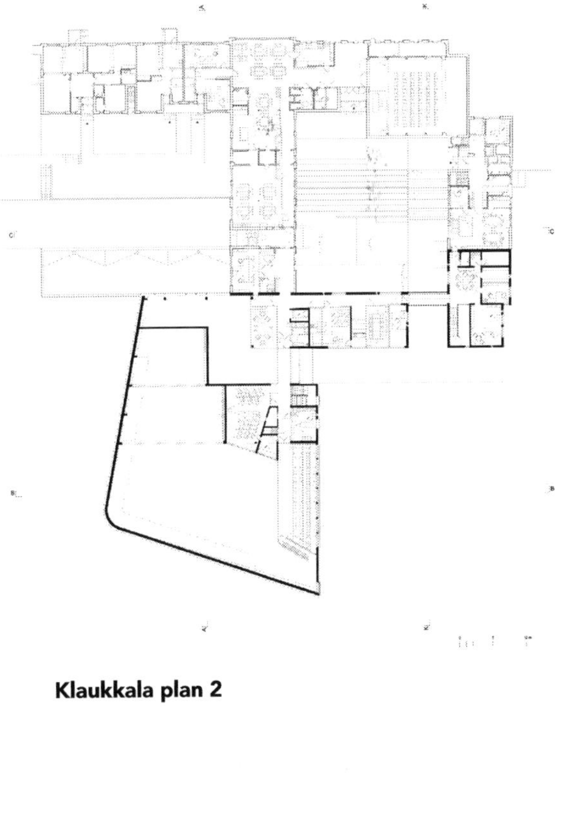

Klaukkala plan 2

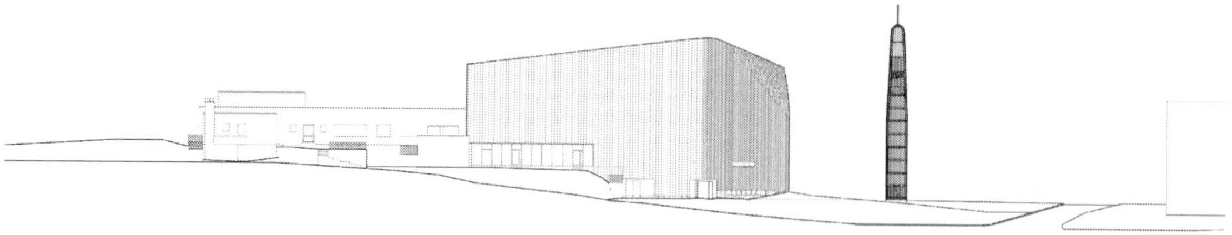

Klaukkala southwest elevation

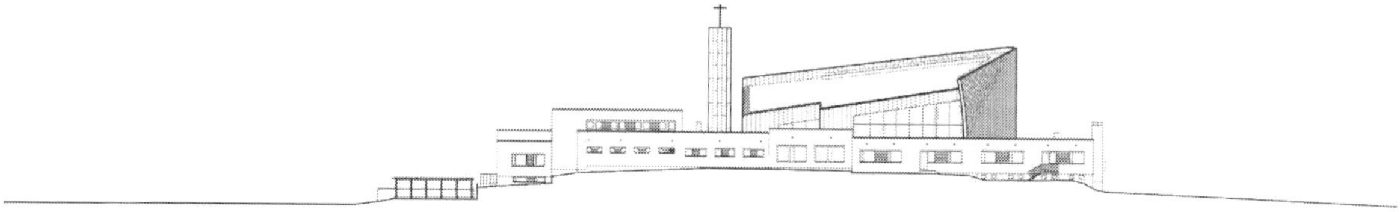

Klaukkala northwest elevation

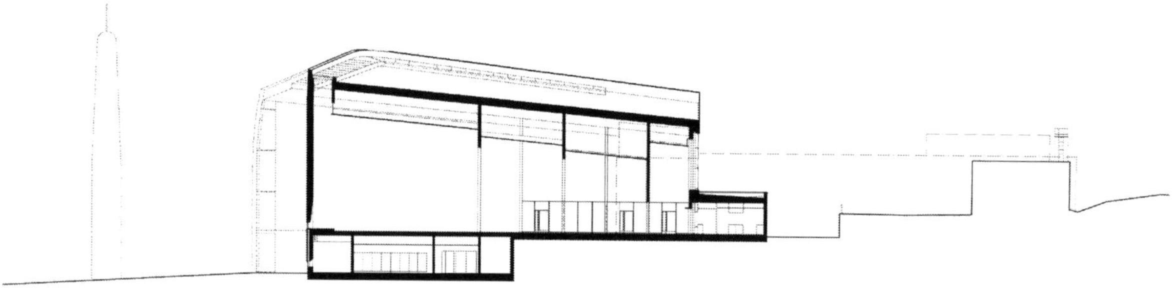

Klaukkala section 1

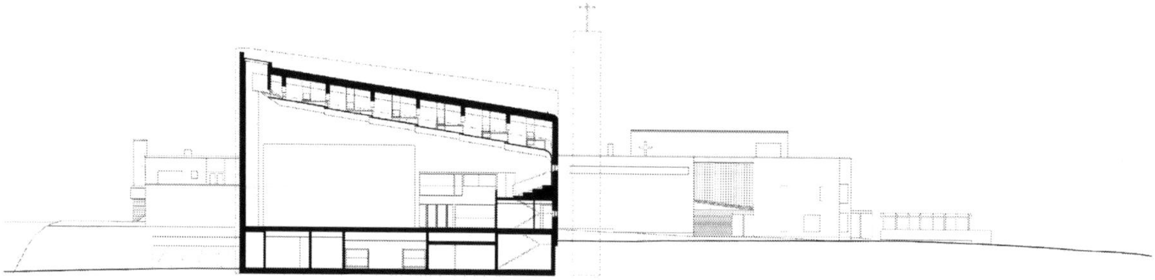

Klaukkala section 2

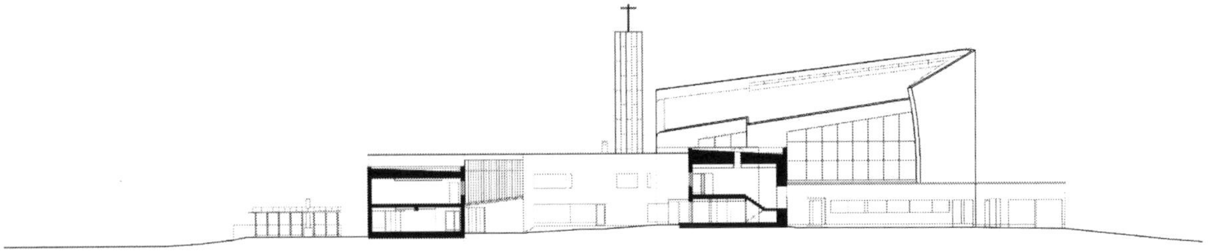

Klaukkala section 3

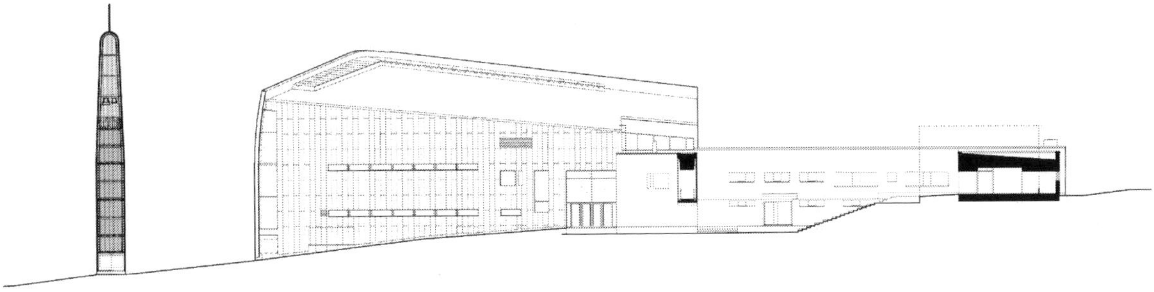

Klaukkala section 4

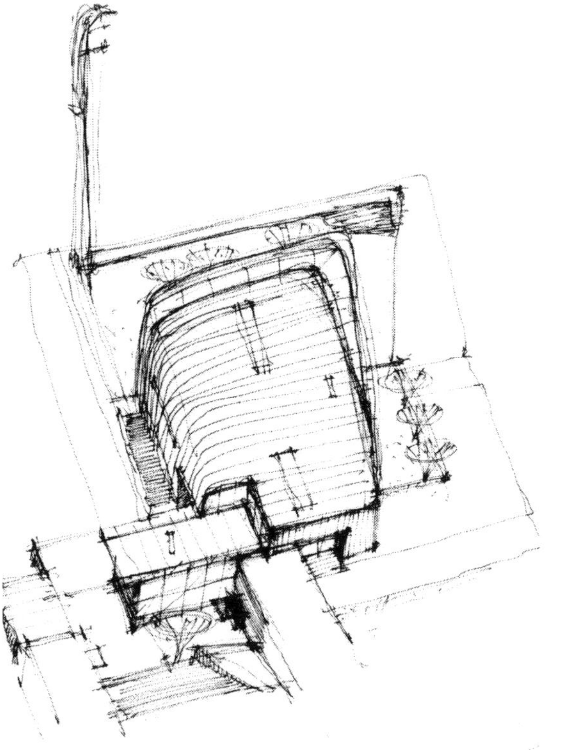

Klaukkala sketch, exterior axonometric view

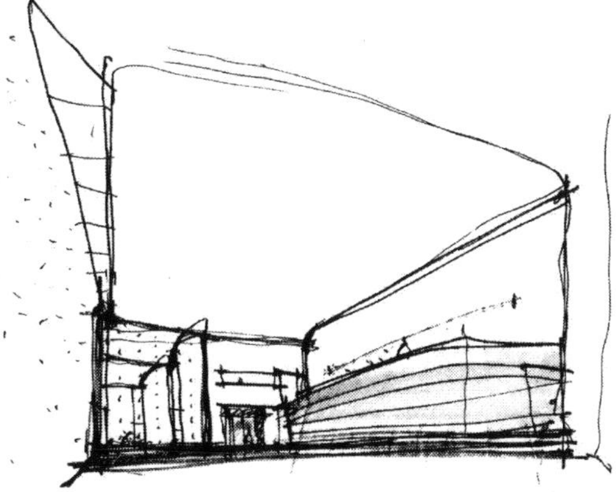

Klaukkala sketch, interior

Klaukkala exterior 1

Klaukkala exterior 2

Klaukkala exterior 3

Klaukkala exterior 4

Klaukkala exterior 5

Klaukkala exterior 6

Klaukkala exterior 7

Klaukkala exterior 8

Klaukkala exterior 9

Klaukkala exterior 10

Klaukkala exterior 11

Klaukkala interior 1

Klaukkala interior 2

Klaukkala interior 3

Klaukkala interior 4

Klaukkala interior 5

Klaukkala interior 6

PART 3

RECONCEPTUALIZING SPACE

Chapter 10

Conceptualizing Space: Scholarly Discourses

Space has multiple meanings in popular interpretations as well as scholarly ones. Each is dependent on context and privileges a specific set of analytical elements to define space, its function, and its importance.

For example, archaeology, architecture, and geography view space as a strategy of self-definition. That self is expressed materially and spatially, which means investigating material evidence is paramount to understanding how the self is defined.

Conversely, philosophy, theology, and cultural and social histories begin by examining intellectual and symbolic constructs of space. Because intellectual theories shape material manifestations such as those found in architecture, texts are favored over material evidence.

Yet for each of these disciplines, examining space ultimately provides a way to investigate self-definition and self-expression. In other words, all of these disciplines and their substrates examine and interpret economic, political, and social issues as they signify self-definition through space and its construction.[1] Depending upon the discipline's interpretation, people therefore have varying amounts of agency that manifests in space to "either reproduce or change social systems and structures."[2]

What's interesting is that until now, scholars have either focused on textual interpretations or material ones—rarely have they combined the two in studying built spaces. I propose to combine textual and material interpretations in a stroke that entails not just archiving but synthesis.

Let's examine this proposition more deeply. To construct a better, more comprehensive narrative, we must first use archiving methodologies.[3] These must be synthesized, however, using additional insights.[4] Explained differently, compiling and collating textual material—archiving—is merely the first step in creating a narrative. Archivists include theologists and historians who study idealized texts (i.e. doctrine) and intellectual constructs to the almost complete neglect of these issues. To construct a better narrative, those materials must be synthesized utilizing additional scholarly disciplines. Those explore material aspects of society including archaeology and geography to provide additional information.

Foregrounding all these insights is the acknowledgment that vested interests and agendas are embedded in all discourses. In other words, there are no pre-originary facts, nor can our goal be to strive for analyses that are pre-political or prediscursive. Why not? Because all analyses are by definition political.[5] In fact, politics pervades and informs all written and physical practices because written and physical work reflect ideals and values.[6] It is therefore essential to acknowledge specific standpoints or agendas embedded within narratives and projects, situating them within the cultural, economic, and social values they represent.[7]

Western Spatial Epistemology

Western philosophers have profoundly influenced general and scholarly concepts of space. Their discourses mark a diachrony of historical changes in culture, politics, and economics in Euro/American societies. To understand current spatial configurations, we need to delve briefly into these past philosophies.

We will find that several of the earlier philosophical narratives emphasize either purely physical or conceptual aspects of space. More recent explanations, however, combine the inherent dynamism and interactive exchange between people and space as an integral element of space itself.[8]

We begin with the Enlightenment, defined by Kant as pure reason, applied toward releasing humanity's potential for unlimited achievement and betterment.[9] His theory inaugurated an unbroken intellectual and material legacy amongst Euro/American intellectuals. The faith that their intellectual prowess could explain and uplift all of humanity in a purely "rational" and "scientific" manner shaped all subsequent philosophies.

In terms of space, Kant theorized that the body was instrumental in imputing meaning to space.[10] Specifically, the body provides directionality and orientation, undergirding space's meaning.[11]

Newton, however, posited that space itself was a physical absolute. Because Newtonian absolutism viewed space as fixed, it did not affect human behavior. Rather, space functioned primarily as a container for human interaction. Interestingly, this concept was shared by early Christian theology, a belief that directly affected the design of churches in Europe.[12]

Descartes shifted away from a concrete explanation of space. Instead, he proposed space as an extension of corporeal bodies.[13] His concept incorporated fluidity, defined and contained within the body and its action, into the definition of space. Including the body in his interpretation meant that space was no longer an absolute void or a vacuum.[14]

Descartes' theory reverberated throughout Western Europe, ultimately extending far beyond its physical and intellectual borders. First, Cartesian theory fundamentally changed European conceptions of history. History now became a linear narrative that could be mapped geographically. As a linear, single narrative, history now began *geographically* in the "ancient East".[15] As history advanced towards "modernity," it moved westward to finally end in the "modern West" of Europe and later, the US.[16]

Because Cartesian theory transformed the way European nation-states conceived of themselves and others, it profoundly altered the way they *territorialized* themselves and others.[17] Descartes' rationalization of the geographic progress of history justified colonialism as merely a "benevolent" bestowal of modern progress upon the "backwards" peoples "back" in the "East" and "South."[18] In other words, the economic exploitation of other peoples, their labor, and their raw resources, was a direct outcome of Cartesian theory. In fact, Cartesian spaces-as-territory instituted the aggressive territorialization and colonization that continues today. These real effects demonstrate the importance of understanding how theoretical models directly shape our material experience of space. Equally noteworthy, Cartesian spatial theory is remarkably similar to current definitions of religious space.[19]

Locke marks the early vestiges of contemporary spatial conceptions. Here, space is mutually defining: it defines while being defined by other spaces.[20] Note, however, that this definitional reciprocation does not yet involve a relationship between people and space. Merleau-Ponty, whose philosophical focus was the body,[21] asserted that its orienting function is the origin of space.[22]

These concepts have given way to current definitions of space. Space is now reciprocal: space "comes into being as a function of other processes and phenomena."[23] In other words, space is determined by its relationship with other spaces, objects, and people.[24] Most importantly, people inscribe spaces with meaning through "culturally dependent beliefs" and actions,[25] actions which are either secular or religious. The notion of culturally universalized, Eurocentric space has given way to the concept that local specificities define space.[26]

More importantly, the exercise of social power comprises a central component in definitions of space.[27] One version, the panopticon, views objects and actors as subject to a single gaze intent on locating and fixing them in space.[28] Spaces therefore become an exercise of human power, so that the panopticon replaces specific places with position.[29] Colonialist architecture exemplifies another exercise of social and economic power. It maintains oppressive, economically exploitative boundaries along racial and gender lines,[30] while simultaneously using certain elements that "hark back to a nearly forgotten way of life."[31]

For Western philosophy, the discourse on secular space has moved toward quantifiable, replicable terms "from which analytical and empirical consequences can be drawn."[32] Space has become "the outcome of a sequence and set of operations and cannot be reduced to the rank of a simple object."[33]

Most importantly, space is a product of social interactions that, ultimately, address the process of self-definition.[34] Given this, the definitional terms of built spaces are economic, political, and social, whether in the near-abroad, overseas, or domestically. What's more, there exists a reciprocity of space with people.[35] It is an ongoing process that is fraught and contested.

Space is therefore "a lived experience,"[36] and what's more, social agency and power are key to its construction and re-identification. Ultimately, space provides an arena for people to define themselves, and during that process, space itself becomes [re]defined: "spaces are composed of intersecting mobile elements [that] can be actualized. . .[containing] discursive formations of material and immaterial components."[37]

Notes

1 According to one study, "Scholars. . .are in the business of representing and thereby transforming and/or reproducing aspects of people's lives. . .[that] draw on pre-existing frameworks of meaning, which are inherently political insofar as they position ourselves and 'others' and in so doing help to reproduce or undermine structures of power and inequality" (Karner, 2005: 37).

2 Arthur A. Joyce, "Sacred Space and Social Relations in the Valley of Oaxaca," in *Mesoamerican Archaeology*, edited by J. Hendon and R. Joyce (Oxford: Blackwell, 2004): 193.

3 Wing, 2011; Janet Abu-Lughod, "On the Remaking of History: How to Reinvent the Past," in *Remaking History: Discussions in Contemporary Culture*, edited by Barbara Kruger and Phil Mariani (Seattle: Dia Art Foundation, 1989): 116.

4 Wing, 2011; Abu-Lughod, 1989: 116.

5 Paul Heelas, "Postmodernism," in *The Routledge Companion to the Study of Religion*, edited by John R. Hinnells (London and New York: Routledge, 2005): 270–271.

6 Karner sums up the intersection between a Eurocentric and a Postcolonial Deconstructivist view in his observation that on the one hand there is Foucault's view that a Eurocentric analysis focuses on power reiterated through "normalizing discourses" which limit the number of subject positions available and that on the other hand there is Said's proposition that no description can be innocent but, rather, is prescriptive and hence "profoundly political" (2005: 34).

7 Knott, 2005: 245.

8 Edward W. Soja. "Taking Space Personally," in *The Spatial Turn: Interdisciplinary Perspectives*, edited by Barney Warf and Santa Arias (New York: Routledge, 2009): 19.

9 Jung, Hwa Yol. "Enlightenment and the Question of the Other: A Postmodern Audition," *Human Studies*, Vol. 25, No. 3 (2002): 297–298.

10 Casey, 1997: 204.
11 Casey, 1997: 204.
12 Casey, 1997: 152.
13 Casey, 1997: 154.
14 Casey, 1997:154.
15 Anne McClintock, *Imperial Leather: Race, Gender and Sexuality* (New York: Routledge, 1995): 40; Gyan Prakash, "Who's Afraid of Postcoloniality," *Social Text*, Vol. 14, No. 4 (1996): 194.
16 McClintock, 1995: 40; Prakash, 1996: 194.
17 Cosgrove, 2004: 2.
18 John Corrigan, "Spatiality and Religion," in *The Spatial Turn: Interdisciplinary Perspectives*, edited by Barney Warf and Santa Arias (New York: Routledge, 2009): 158.
19 Casey, 1997: 153.
20 Casey, 1997: 173.
21 Jung, 2002: 299.
22 Casey, 1997: 230.
23 Cosgrove, 2004: 2.
24 Casey, 1997: 182
25 In a review of Louis P. Nelson, Ivey says that the "sacred *cannot* be manifest in the material. . .without human agents. . .with culturally dependent beliefs and rituals," and that "places become inscribed as sacred through belief and practice" (Ivey, 2008: 456).
26 Harkin, 2000: 52.
27 Casey, 1997: 184, 190.
28 Jung, 2002: 298.
29 Casey, 1997: 184, 190.
30 Say Lawrence and Low, "Class, gender, race, and culture relations are reproduced in the built environment" (1990: 486). They cite numerous studies that demonstrate how "political and racial domination are spatially expressed" (ibid.).
31 Harkin, 2000: 56.
32 Howarth, 2006: 110.
33 Henri Lefebvre, *The Production of Space*, trans. Donald Nicholson-Smith (Oxford: Blackwell, 1991): 73.
34 Cosgrove, 2004: 2.
35 Harkin, 2000: 53.
36 Lefebvre, 1991: 94.
37 Michael Kobialka, "Staging Place/Space in the Eleventh-Century Monastic Practices," in *Medieval Practices of Space*, edited by Barbara A. Hanawalt and Michael Kobialka (Minneapolis: University of Minnesota Press, 2000): 129.

Chapter 11

Geography and Space

A little known fact amongst non-geographers is that geography began as an enquiry into religion: it investigated spatial relationships linking cosmology, religious beliefs, and people.[1] As it developed into an independent academic discipline, scholars began exploring secular aspects of geography, focusing on the relationship between human behavior and sites.[2] Over time, secular geographical inquiries replaced religious ones. Subfields like cultural geography developed, which examine human perceptions of geography.[3] Others dedicated themselves to describing the "cultural landscape."[4] Such studies are furthered by anthropologists and psychologists delving into "reactions to density and crowding, privacy and territoriality,"[5] that result in clashes over community and national boundaries. During this time, studies on religion have languished.

Because secular inquiries have become the focus of geography, rigorous and refined analyses are reserved for it alone; all other investigations are portrayed in broad generalizations.[6] Religious spaces have become one of those broadly portrayed disciplines. Once their sacrality is identified, religious spaces are seen as inherently and forever transcendent.[7] In other words, geographically designated sacred spaces remain permanently sacred.[8] In short, they are merely territories that require safeguarding.[9] Other geographers view religious spaces as endlessly relative, in which religious practitioners project multiple meanings onto spaces they consider inherently sacred.[10] Recent geographers only see dynamism in religious pilgrimages.[11]

Such studies are more concerned with religious practice primarily as it shapes the movements and migration of people rather than religious spaces as they interact with people.[12] What they all ignore about religious geography is that interpretations and meanings result from interactions between people and space. Topography alone cannot dictate the location of religious projects, nor are religious spaces evanescent.[13]

It should come as no surprise then that the most useful insights geographers provide regarding how human relationships are spatial come from secular research.[14] It is now accepted that geography extends beyond merely mapping a geographic location.[15] Geographical terms—cartography, territory, space—have been co-opted by different disciplines to indicate movement and interaction.[16] Some researchers have even proposed that geography is a study of social process.[17]

In geographical terms, all spaces are political. Defining that space or geography is a matter of who controls it and determines which elements will be emphasized.

The question is which "self" will ally with the space to define both the space and the self.[18] Space and social position are thus in constant [re]production:[19] "Space is an ontological category that characterizes all social structures and any system of social relations, and not an ontical category that refers to particular sorts of space."[20] These interpretations share an emphasis on the *production* of space, not the *result* of that production. In other words, for both secular and sacred spaces, geography discourses have progressed from "place" and "container" toward "space as a process." Others use geography to examine the symbolic meanings attached to particular locations.[21]

For the few who study religion, the focus has shifted away from religious phenomena and geography.[22] Instead, these geographers have argued that "religions are constructed and maintained through simultaneous emphases on the power of the bounded place and the importance. . .of transgressing boundaries."[23] In other words, sacred spaces depend upon dynamism rather than fixed qualities for their definition.[24] In fact, there is a remarkable similarity between secular nation-state and colonialism projects with space in the religious sphere in that all rely on de- and re-territorializing.[25]

Seen this way, geography highlights the exchange between "competing social forces seek[ing] to fix the spatial positioning," of institutions.[26] Dynamism imparts meaning, which reaffirms the identity of not just people, but of the space itself. The process of de- and re-territorializing is therefore a process of imparting meaning. Any given space is thus a process of identification and self-definition.[27]

Notes

1 Hinnells, 2004: 3.

2 Stoddard, Robert H., "Perceptions About the Geography of Religious Sites in the Kathmandu Valley," *Contributions to Nepalese Studies*, Vol. VII, No. 1–2 (December, 1979–June, 1980): 97.

3 Stoddard, 1979–1980: 98.

4 Wolniewicz, Richard, "Ethnic Church Architecture," *Polish American Studies*, Vol. 54, No. 1 (Spring, 1997): 53.

5 Lawrence and Low, 1990: 479.

6 For example, see Stoddard, 1979–1980: 100, in which he asserts that phenomena are imbued with sanctity by human beliefs.

7 Eric J. Sharpe, "The Study of Religion in Historical Perspective," in *Routledge Companion to the Study of Religion*, edited by J. Hinnells (London: Routledge, 2004): 20.

8 Stoddard, 1979–1980: 100.

9 Corrigan, 2009: 165.

10 Sharpe, 2004: 23.

11 Robert Stoddard and Alan Morinis, "Introduction: The Geographic Contribution to Studies of Pilgrimage," in *Sacred Places, Sacred Spaces: The Geography of Pilgrimages*, edited by Robert H. Stoddard and Alan Morinis (Baton Rouge: Louisiana State University Department of Geography and Anthropology, 1997): x.

12 Chris Park, "Religion and Geography," in *Routledge Companion to the Study of Religion*, edited by J. Hinnells (London: Routledge, 2004): 439.

13 See, for example, the conclusions drawn by Park, 2004: 451.

14 Stoddard, 1979–1980: 98.

15 Soja, 2009: 23.

16 Soja, 2009: 19.

17 Soja, 2009: 19.

18 Howarth, 2006: 107.

19 Howarth, 2006: 108.

20 Howarth, 2006: 111.

21 Blake, 1999: 502.

22 Corrigan, 2009: 159.

23 Corrigan, 2009: 160.

24 Robert H. Stoddard, "Pilgrimage Places and Sacred Geometries," in *Pilgrimate: Sacred Landscapes and Self-Organized Complexity*, edited by John McKim Malville and Baidyanath Saraswati (New Delhi: Indira Gandhi National Centre for the Arts, 2009): 175–176.

25 Corrigan, 2009: 163.

26 Howarth, 2006: 106.

27 Howarth, 2006: 111.

Chapter 12

Archaeology and Space

Archaeologists investigate social organization as evidenced through materials and objects.[1] Their inquiries operate on different levels just like social organization itself, ranging from the individual to the collective scale.[2] Because archaeology examines society on micro and macro levels, it can offer useful insights into the religious realm.[3]

One of archaeology's most basic terms is "material culture." It primarily refers to both secular and religious ritual implements and handheld objects. Older discourses identify material culture as discrete objects that reflect both cultural and religious values.[4] In religious terms, material culture "symbolizes, represents. . . and informs the archaeologist attempting to explore the subtleties of ritual practice and religions."[5]

Unfortunately, archaeology is too often foregrounded by Eurocentric methodologies—both documentarian and material—resulting in narratives that are variations on Eurocentric-privileging themes.[6] Even more interesting is that archaeology ignores material evidence that exceeds handheld or relatively small physical dimensions.

One crucial oversight to secular archaeology is that "material culture" does not include built spaces and buildings. Similarly, archaeological research on religious material culture neglects investigating religious spaces, again concentrating solely on handheld ritual implements.[7] Clearly architecture comprises one aspect of material culture: one that further elucidates on the primarily archaeological investigations into social organization. After all, architecture is a material "object" and it is certainly a representative of a culture.[8]

For architects, materials refer to those used during the building process. These can include anything from brick and steel to glass and concrete. "Material culture" in the architectural view has no place: it is neither a recognized term nor is it important to theorizing architectural narratives.

Archaeology and architecture are seldom spoken of in the same breath unless one refers to ancient architectural sites. This is an oversight that must be corrected, not the least reason of which is because archaeology uses concepts that are potentially central to understanding architecture, especially religious architecture.

We must extend material culture analysis beyond both physical practicalities and handheld objects. Incorporating architecture and space into the concept of material culture allows us to investigate the theoretical underpinnings of architecture's material character. Examining that will reveal the importance of physical spaces and the role buildings play in the human experience socially, economically, and politically.[9] Specifically, combining the cultural analysis of material culture with the realities of architecture as an example material culture provides insights into culture, economies, politics, and social structure. In other words, using the archaeological theoretical framework of material culture allows us to understand architecture in terms of social organization, while simultaneously expanding the archaeological discourse beyond merely handheld implements.

For example, some archaeologists have begun widening their discourses to combat the primarily secular focus, notwithstanding studies on ritual objects.[10] One tactic has been to examine religion's function as a "primary structuring agent"[11] for those who investigate religious spaces; the focus has shifted from religious implements to rituals that occur in space. Others use structuralism[12] to interpret symbol, ritual, and myth as organizing "structures" of society and space.[13] For them, sacred spaces provide frameworks for people to use these "structures" to enact their religious beliefs.[14] People therefore constantly reify space as sacred through their religious practice.[15] For still others the debate turns on the meaning of ritual and symbol:[16] whether and how it incorporates not only architecture, but also implements used during ceremonies, as well as iconography.[17]

More recent archaeological studies investigate sacred space's role in the formation of identity. They examine how spaces generate specific kinds of social engagement or individual behavior.[18] Space in this rendering provides a framework or an "orchestration of (performative) space."[19] Another study coined the term "material religion" to define the physical components of Protestant churches.[20] Specifically, it refers to those physical elements which allow practitioners to access the invisible and the sacred.[21] It is a useful concept that points to how material manifestations of religious like space doctrine inform religious practice.

Still others have studied the "agency" of material objects, including architecture.[22] Without becoming too mired in the academic debate about architecture's "agency,"[23] we can accept that religious architecture is defined by the religious activities it enables.[24] While some view historical religious architecture as a space that "magnified and elevated [events] and it could also interact with them and engender the construction of ceremonial,"[25] in fact the same can be said of contemporary sacred spaces.

Mosques provide an interesting exemplar of how activation and engagement are central to defining a space as sacred. Unlike other religious traditions, mosques do not house icons. Their primary function is to provide a space for prayer, oriented toward Mecca. It is not the only place Muslims pray, however, since they do so throughout the day. It is one venue.[26] Yet in the contemporary sense of being activated and defined by the activity it houses, mosques *are* sacred spaces, especially as prayer is the primary activity that occurs there.

The consensus for much new scholarship is that people's interaction with and within space is what imparts meaning. That meaning, depending on the activities and the space, can be both mundane or religious.[27] However, while this space becomes a particular "place" through these constant engagements with and by people, that specificity does not proscribe their actions.[28]

In fact, contemporary religious spaces often house both secular and religious activity. Many of the projects featured in this book were designed to allow for a multitude of activities and options, individually and collectively. In some views, these multiple uses are what makes them "contested," since people may disagree about the proper use of these spaces.[29] But from an archaeological–architectural standpoint, their use and identity reflects the fluidity inherent in making space. Each project is also part of the material culture that addresses the cultural, economic, political, social, and religious needs of their communities.

Deploying archaeological intellectual methodologies to architecture begins with investigating how architectural projects organize society. There are additional questions we must keep in mind. For example, as one aspect within the cultural landscape, does architecture represent a microcosm of social organization? To what extent do architecture projects enhance or obscure economic, political, and social status of individuals and institutions? These are only some of the questions that archaeologists ask that must now be extended to architectural projects as an expression of material culture.

Notes

1 Lawrence and Low, 1990: 462.

2 Whitcomb, Donald, "Introduction: the Spread of Islam and Islamic Archaeology," in *Changing Social Identity with the Spread of Islam: Archaeological Perspectives* (Chicago: University of Chicago, 2004): 2.

3 Whitcomb, 2004: 1.

4 Timothy Insoll, "Introduction," in *The Oxford Handbook of the Archaeology of Ritual and Religion,* edited by Timothy Insoll (New York: Oxford University Press, 2011): 2.

5 See, for example, Insoll, 2011: 2.

6 Elizabeth Graham, "Mission Archaeology," *Annual Review of Anthropology*, Vol. 27 (1998): 26.

7 See, for example, Insoll, 2011: 2–3.

8 Insoll, 2011: 2. He says specifically, "questioned the framing of material culture 'as a passive reflection of cultural values, thoughts and cosmological beliefs'" (ibid.).

9 Hayden, 1994: 33.

10 Timothy Insoll, "Syncretism, Time, and Identity: Islamic Archaeology in West Africa," in *Changing Social Identity with the Spread of Islam: Archaeological Perspectives*, edited by Donald Whitcomb (Chicago: Oriental Institute of the University of Chicago, 2004): 88.

11 Insoll, 2004: 89.

12 Gregory J. Levine, "On the Geography of Religion," *Transactions of the Institute of British Geographers*, Vol. 11, No. 4 (1986): 433.

13 Levine, 1986: 432.

14 Jaś Elsner, "Material Culture and Ritual: State of the Question," in *Architecture of the Sacred: Space, Ritual, and Experience from Classical Greece to Byzantium*, edited by Bonna D. Wescoat and Robert G. Ousterhout (Cambridge: Cambridge University Press, 2012): 2–3.

15 Elsner, 2012: 2.

16 Levine, 1986: 433.

17 Amy Gazin-Schwartz, "Archaeology and Folklore of Material Culture, Ritual, and Everyday Life," *International Journal of Historical Archaeology*, Vol. 5, No. 4 (2001): 265–267.

18 Lawrence and Low, 1990: 462.

19 Elsner, 2012: 2.

20 Louis P. Nelson, "Sensing the Sacred: Anglican Material Religion in Early South Carolina," *Winterthur Portfolio*, Vol. 41, No. 4 (Winter, 2007): 203.

21 For example, Nelson says, "when material religion does come up, scholars embrace a functionalist view, discussing religion in terms of social structure, elite hegemony, or. . .as evidence of cultural identity" (2007: 204).

22 Branham, Joan R., "Mapping Sacrifice on Bodies and Spaces in Late-antique Judaism and Early Christianity," in *Architecture of the Sacred: Space, Ritual, and Experience from Classical Greece to Byzantium*, edited by Bonna D. Wescoat and Robert G. Ousterhout (Cambridge: Cambridge University Press, 2012): 201.

23 Say Wescoat and Ousterhout, "Architecture. . .magnified and elevated [events] and it could also interact with them and engender the construction of [the] ceremonial," which made it an "active agent" (Wescoat and Ousterhout, 2012a: xxiii). This proposal, while interesting, overstates the role of the building because it assumes sentience necessary in the theoretical use of the word "agency."

24 Lawrence and Low, 1990: 462–463.

25 Wescoat and Ousterhout, 2012a: xxiii.

26 Conversation with Shahed Saleem, October 25, 2014.

27 Desplat, 2012: 10.

28 Here "place" is put in quotation marks to acknowledge the definition of the term by geographers who see it as a particular locale that contains specific social meanings, imparted by people.

29 Desplat, 2012: 10–11.

PART 4

MONASTERIES

Chapter 13

Roto Architects[1]

Mr. Michael Rotondi, FAIA, Founder and Principal

The Architect's Role

For Mr. Rotondi, religious architecture and secular architecture share a similar genesis from a deep and critical investigation into the human condition: "I've been thinking a lot about the role we all play," he begins, "But in particular the role the architect plays and what role I play. It has to do with trying to be a positive force in the evolutionary inheritance imperative, the sweep of our evolution, the overall process.

"There are two aspects of us," he explains, "altruism and individualism. That's a constant. There are certain human activities that we've developed, invented and constructed along the way that help us in that regard. Architecture has one sole purpose which is to tangibly express the poetic side of human enterprise."

This, Mr. Rotondi says, is all related to the architect's own condition: "The better I take care of myself, the easier it is to be around me. I project a better person," he explains, "And then it's easier to interact with others and bring out the best in them. It doesn't mean there is no conflict." He explains further, "For selfish reasons because we want a benefit, we figure out how do we be generous and bring out the best of everything around us. That's the paradox. So is it possible to make an architecture to bring out the best, make us feel at ease, but challenge us to make us feel more progressive and make us grow?"

Unfortunately, most of architecture does not aspire to such heights: "Most of what is done today is the practical side of the architectural enterprise. This is the downside of reason. The upside of reason is moving into the realm of the unknown and the only way you can move further into that realm and seek more answers."

Seeking better solutions that challenge and uplift is the goal. Says Mr. Rotondi, "When you see scientists who are looking at or debating the relationship between faith and reason or are becoming friends with the Dalai Lama, that's what's interesting. We must ask, 'What is the way to make the best contribution?' The contribution you make is in proportion to the invisibility you have to what you're doing. You let subjects speak for themselves. You try to go into a selfless mode. You're nurturing and you bring your consciousness to the table not your personality and let it unfold, rather than imprinting your personality obviously on the project. So you seek the *qi* (气) points of this project that is unfolding."

The Role of Faith

"We're here for the benefit of others," Mr. Rotondi says, "And I think the work we do should be for the benefit of others. You have to have faith that it's going to come back around again. And that's the hardest thing to retain, is faith. But that's really the endgame. How to keep your faith alive and the inherent goodness of everyone, of humans. Then it's possible to believe that it's the context, the context that we're in is what we respond to and adapt to. We construct the world and in return it constructs us. We become the hardware and the world that we've constructed is the software. And I think that's easily turned around.

"That's why science of mind as its discussed and debated in Eastern religions, Buddhism in particular, is so important. It's basically being on top of all the things the mind does, and get it to stay in balance with the body. Which is a very hard task. That is, everybody has their version of how to get to a state of equilibrium and the fun of it, working with different religions, is to see how they get there. And then what spaces are required to facilitate that and stay out of the way.

"The most difficult thing I was trying to solve for many years was 'Am I supposed to take care of myself or other people.'" But, he says, "You never have that discussion." He continues, "For Buddhism, it's about the philosophy. You keep yourself in good shape and whole, you project that in the world and other people have the opportunity to take that energy and they can then bring it out in them and pay it forward. It's not about the ritual or the practice, it's about the philosophy."

In fact, says Mr. Rotondi, "There are so many decisions made in the language people use to get what they want." In other words, many decisions architects make are driven by the language they use." For example, "In academia, we talk about everything we think is necessary about full potential, we talk about cerebral, intellectual, mental, but we don't talk about the spiritual, spirituality and religion.

"Yet people still have difficulty with the relationship between faith and reason, which is probably a fundamental issue we have with ourselves. I think when you're at ease, you have faith, people think it comes when you're in fear but that's not true. That's not faith. It's when you feel at ease and confident. That's when you have faith." He explains further, "Faith and ignorance are not connected. Faith comes out of extreme deep intelligence."

In fact, Mr. Rotondi says, "It could be that this period is one where faith and reason become a hybrid rather than confronting each other or coexisting or being a confluence of a few things. It could be a time of seeing how faith and reason come together."

On Religion

"Generally all religions are about love and service," says Mr. Rotondi. "You're constantly trying to make yourself healthy and whole so that's what the influence is you have on everything and everybody around you. It's about giveaway; it's not about acquisition."

These principles have given way to something else: "The theory of economy in most religions right now is do what's good for you and to hell with the rest. Let them take care of themselves. That's the theory of economy in finance; it's the theory of economy in society and in religion.

"Then there's a certain amount of gesturing that you do to make it seem like you're on the straight and narrow and doing good for everyone else. And if anybody crosses you, let them be damned. What poses as religion is really a bad example for our young ones."

In fact, he says , "Religion is a really a personal practice. And you do it collectively because it reminds you you're part of some bigger thing. It gets you out of your self-centeredness and self-absorption. It's a curious thing when religion begins to be self-absorbed and self-conscious and that's when it's not working very well."

Religious Projects

For Mr. Rotondi, religious projects offer an opportunity to learn more about important subjects and issues. They also provide a chance to improve oneself: "I spent a lot of time with American Indians," Mr. Rotondi says. "When I started working with the American Buddhists, it was trying to bring back into the world whatever I experienced when I was in that world and start to have a different impact on students and coworkers.

"And that led to Eastern philosophy and at the same time how to integrate it with the stuff I grew up with. So I started reading a lot of Thomas Merton. And then I started working with American Indians in South Dakota. I was going back and forth for six years working on projects and spending time sitting with the elders.

"When I was working with American Indians, the elders made it clear that I was there to listen to their stories and convert their stories into buildings. The objective wasn't even the buildings, it was to help them rebuild their nation. That was kind of shocking to hear at first because it seemed too big a task. I was up there to do some building and didn't think there was anything that I could. Anyway, it put it into the biggest context."

He continues, "When I started working with Buddhist American Buddhist group in Barre, Massachusetts, for a couple of years, I would also practice sitting meditation. I practiced all through that period in a more formal way. But vipaśyanā is somewhere in between formal and informal. It's a meditation practice so I took to that. I also began spending time with a Tibetan Buddhist and I had been working with him for six to seven years.

"Taking projects like that on is an opportunity to spend time with the lamas. I was practicing so I could know in a more intimate way what needed to be designed. There are things we can extrapolate from a number of other experiences and recombine them. Architects design things, houses, whatever, we're really good at recombining things. But there are certain things that we can't know anything about until we've had direct experience of them."

For Mr. Rotondi, this should extend beyond intellectual knowledge to physical understanding. "It's not just knowing. When you're designing for people who are trying to get their bodies to a very high level of concentration which is basically a state of tranquility and alertness at the same time, you have to eliminate as many architectural moves as possible, as much noise as possible. That's literal and figurative noise, which is usually the architecture. At the same time it can't be reductionist because the body begins to pick up everything that is going on around it and if you have a reductive building, you begin to have a reductive imagination. So I had to know in my body to get really slow.

"Everybody has their own ritual and their own liturgy. So you have to know that. You actually have to get involved in the practice, you have to embed yourself in the middle of the practice so you know what you're designing for. Because there's no way to really know things like that until you experience them directly."

He emphasizes, "It's not just a symbolic memory that you need. You need an embodied memory and the only way you get that is experiencing something directly with the body. It doesn't just come from reading. Especially prayer, which many have been taught is really a negotiation with the divine and you can do that without doing anything. Just talk your head off and make promises. That isn't what prayer is for. It begins to work its way through your body. You begin to see the world differently. Literally.

"That's what happens with sitting meditation," Mr. Rotondi says. "You begin to see the world very clearly because you're seeing things in a more intense way. So instead of scanning something you start to see things more deeply. It's like looking at a building section, you can see into the building. So you can see basically surface and volume. It's like seeing a roadcut. If you want to know about the history of the earth, you drive east and west because that's where the major roadcuts are, because the mountains are running north and south.

"So I spent some time doing two-week retreats and began to understand the nature of the problem. It's a cross-section of listening, interpreting, and translating into architecture. That includes American Indian stories, vipaśyanā eastern philosophy by way of Sri Lanka, that whole area, and then Tibetan stuff."

Materials

These relationships architects have with their own intellectual and spiritual lives directly impact on their understanding of how to design, "If you apply this to materiality," explains Mr. Rotondi, "you look at it as something that has weight if you look at it metaphorically. You can then talk about lightness of material, and making material appear lighter and hiding how it is part of a structure.

"The symmetry operation the way I understand it is the way things momentarily come to a state of rest before they commune and go on their way. It's a stillpoint. It's where things become weightless. If you think of a pendulum going to and fro, the point where it's completely at rest.

"One thing that often comes up when you talk about materiality is not what the actual material is but the technology in the broadest sense. Anything we construct, anything we use to construct the world we inhabit. There's earth technology which is physical. And the site technology can be physical, as can be language. Language limits the way you organize society, how people live, how they interact, based on language. So materials can fit in there.

"Years ago," he says, "we did a little house in Venice for UCLA Professor, Anne Bergren. She had so many books, and they were all period books. She had a library that went from Ancient Greece to the present in Europe and the US. When we saw the books laid out, we realized that there was not only the physical weight of the books, but also the weight of the knowledge. When you go from the weight of the books to the weight of the knowledge, it actually makes you free and very light. So in our design we floated the books off the ground.

"Materiality can work that way, in that certain materials have certain associations," Mr. Rotondi explains, "And then they help you recollect certain memories. All of your recollections, of definitions of the material, its behaviors, but also how it connects to your emotions. What you connect to materials is emotional, so warm wood, cold steel, heavy steel. Those are the most conventional associations.

"With these basic associations, you can juxtapose emotional with sensual with intellectual," he adds. Those qualities and characteristics can then be "Combined in a way that is coherent. First you look at the anatomy of the material. Then you look at all the different categories you have to define it. Then you put it together and you start to read those layers," of emotional, sensual, and intellectual characteristics.

"You have to figure out the relationship horizontally and vertically which is where the creativity comes in. It involves all the different ways you know how to think. So you can really know what the material feels like, its relationship to other materials, then you start to relate those different materials like a relationship between siblings." This occurs, he explains, "On a number of different levels."

Mr. Rotondi adds, "Materiality gets into how do you get all the spectrum of colors to become one blazing line. That stillpoint is where all those colors compress to white. That we can visualize. If you picture a prism and take a look at it, you're reminded of the stillpoint. And that's the point of stillness and that's where inhale and exhale come together. Gravity and expansion and life pops up. And creativity."

On Work

"When I start sketching, I keep several books on my desk and read a passage and see where it goes," Mr. Rotondi says. "Or I can decide I will sit still for five minutes and clear my mind and body intensely and then start working. I don't start designing any particular way. It's just whatever puts me in a state of mind and then my mind starts working.

"Focusing on creating spaces that bring your mind to rest, invigorate your body, and then trigger the deepest intelligence of all which allows you to make contact with everything that exists. And that can happen through meditation or prayer."

Teaching Clients, Teaching Architects

Mr. Rotondi's work all contributes to a single purpose: "Teaching is the way I tend to relate to people, friends or strangers. I just assume they are interested in what I know, it's not proprietary. I call it a teaching practice. A friend of mind calls it a finishing school. I'm also teaching here. So people understand they're in a professional environment, they must behave professionally.

"For example, when I'm working with clients, you solve the problem and give them the confidence that you can solve it and deliver the goods. But beyond that, how do you make it as interesting to them as it is to you. So I give them ten-minute lectures like I'd give to students.

"So if a client wants an iconic building, I give them a different presentation from what they expect. First I give them a lecture on 'iconic' to broaden their ideas about what it means so they can participate in the creative joy I have when I'm working and understand the ideas more deeply. It also makes them more deliberate in commenting on whether they do or do not like something. They are able to connect it to different ideas, the way they enter a building, or whatever."

Specifically, they are able to understand ideas that relate to architecture: "It's like the Economy of Means, which is trying to do the most with the least. So in a building, you can make it a higher performance building with cladding: instead of using thick materials, you can use new materials like Kevlar on motorcycle protective clothing. Also, the shape of something's surface on the outside creates volume on the outside, the least amount of surface area creating the maximum amount of volume and then I'll show them a sphere. So then clients understand that greater geometry means more building material and more labor and more cost."

For students and architects, the approach is, "Helping them get in touch with why they're practicing. They obviously have a burning desire. I have an unshakeable belief that if anyone is here, there's nowhere else they should be, whether it's a class or in my studio. It's how they are deciding what's most important."

He admits that, "There are times I'm impatient because of the level of work they're producing. The thing about being here, there is knowledge, there is skill, and there are values. You have to have the knowledge of the profession you work in. And also knowledge that things are connected. Then there are manual and mental skills." He jokes about the lack of research skills in young architects, "One click on Google is research, deeper research is two clicks." He then continues on a more serious note, "There is now strong scientific evidence that manual dexterity and visual imagination are connected. I use that in my teaching, so clay as well as paper models. And values, light or dark side. If you want to be a warrior on the light side, you can join in."

Note

1 Michael Rotondi. Interviews with Sherin Wing via phone. Los Angeles, October 18, 2012 and November 22, 2014.

Xijuan Monastery render

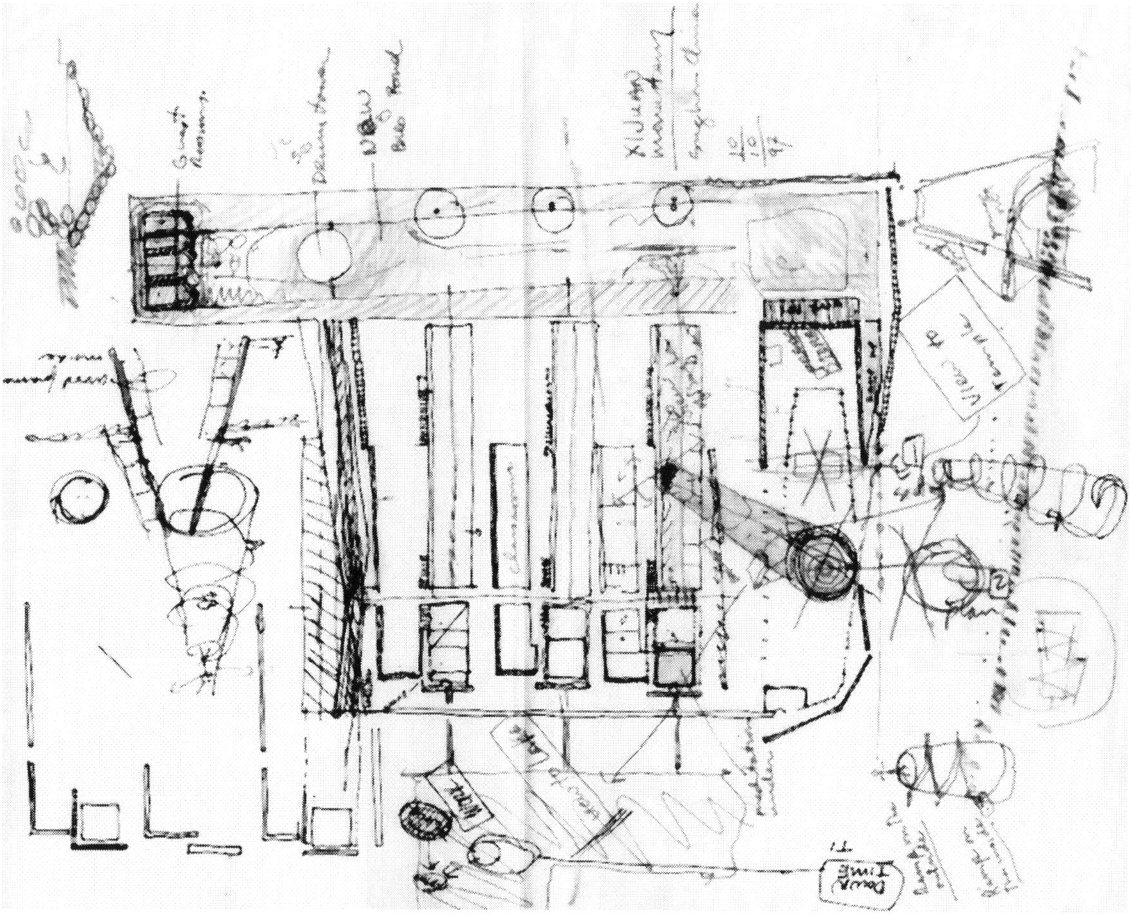

Xijuan Monastery sketch 1

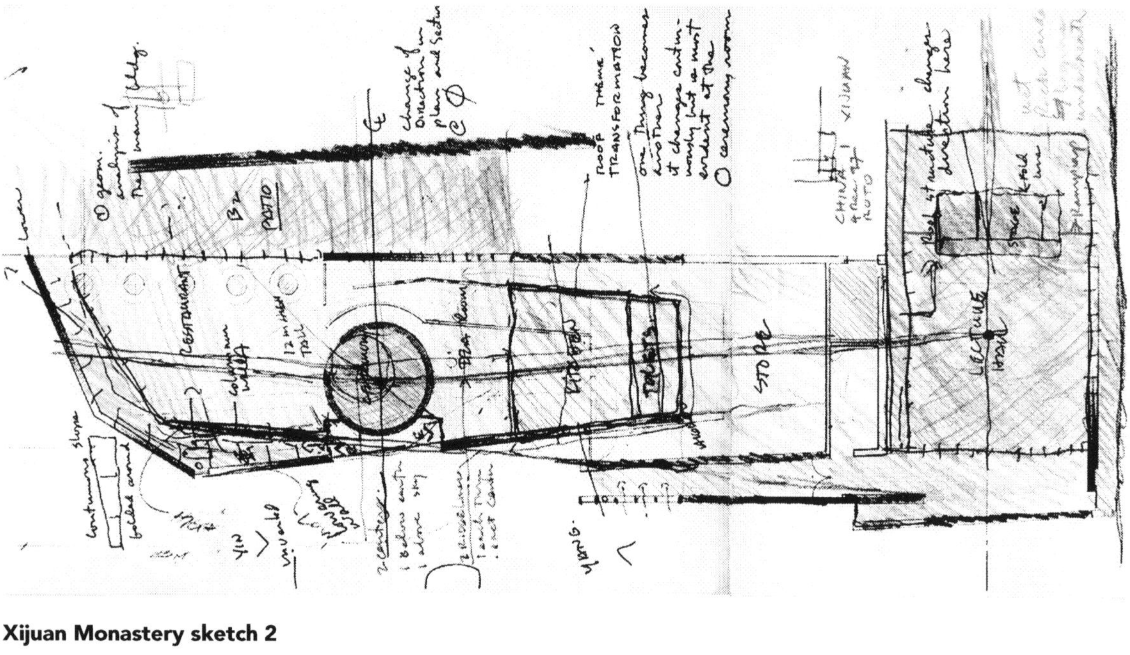
RESTAURANT
KITCHEN
TOILETS
STORE
LECTURE
PATIO
ROOF THEME TRANSFORMATION
YIN
YANG

Xijuan Monastery sketch 2

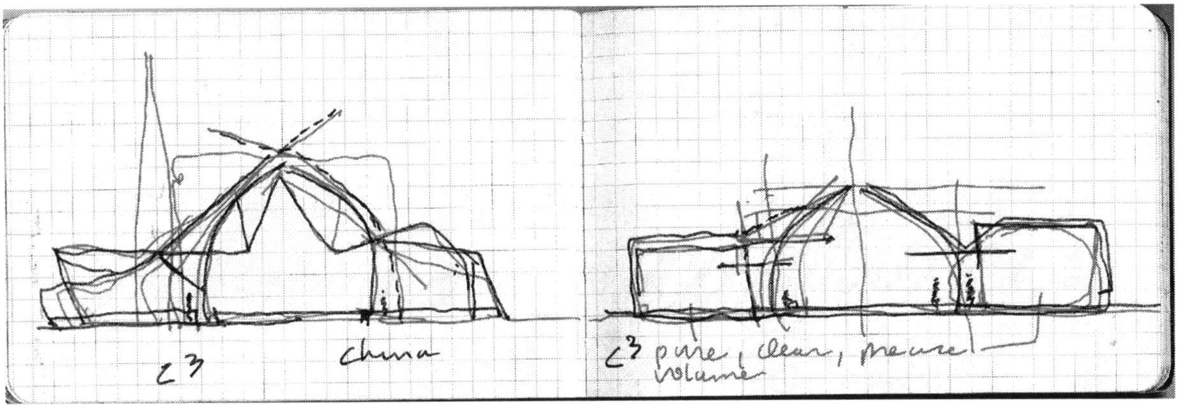
China
pure, clean, precise volume

China Catholic Church sketch

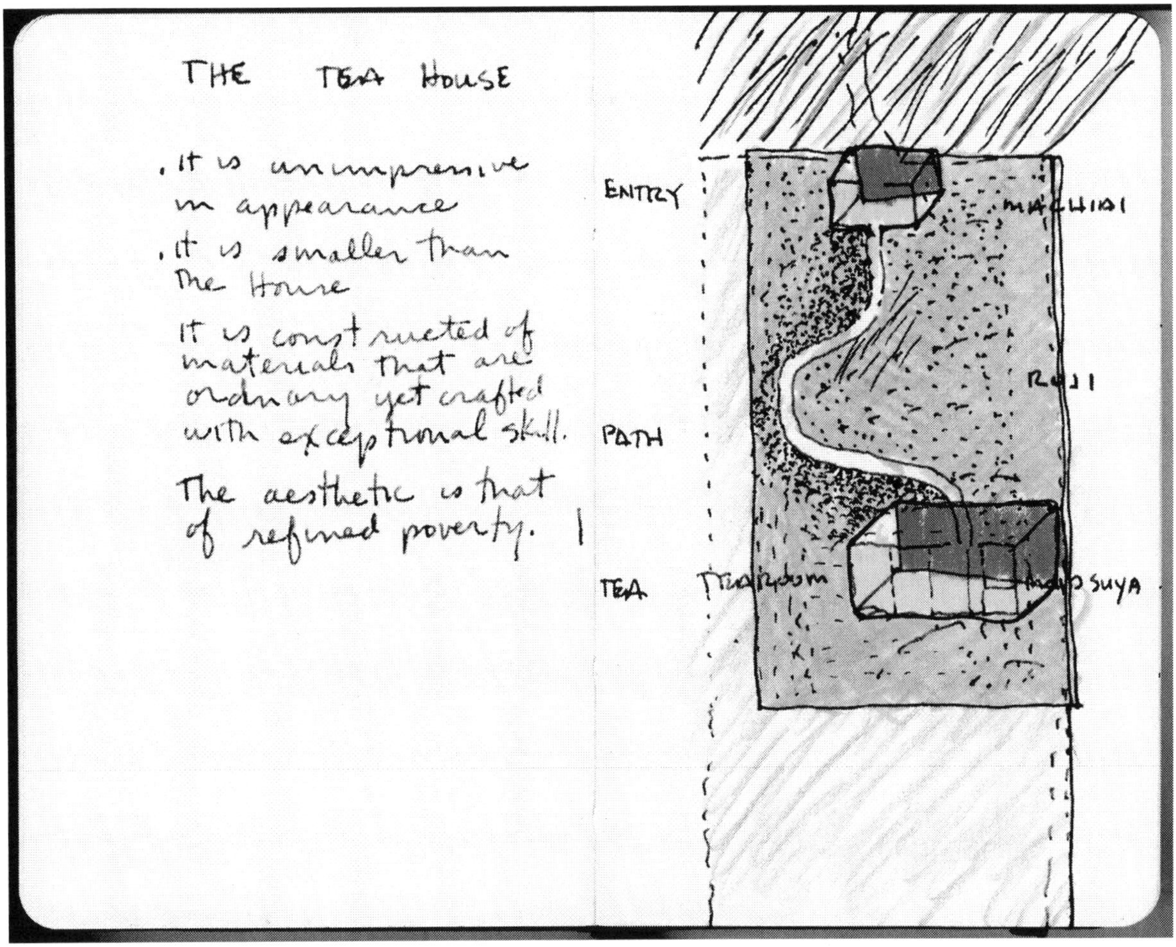
THE TEA HOUSE
. It is unimpressive in appearance
. It is smaller than the House
It is constructed of materials that are ordinary yet crafted with exceptional skill.
The aesthetic is that of refined poverty.
ENTRY
PATH
TEA
ROJI
SUYA

The Tea House sketch

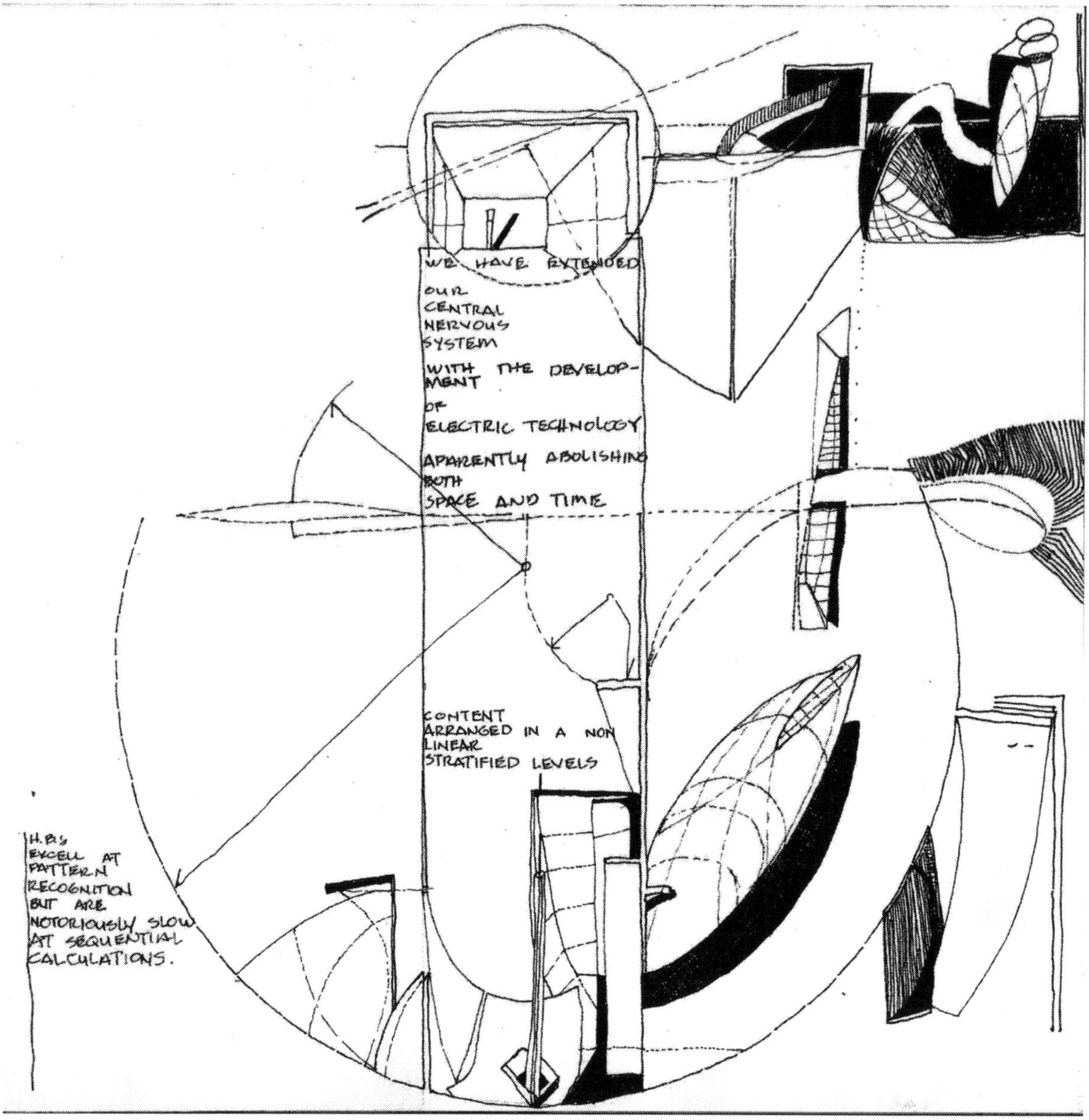
WE HAVE EXTENDED
OUR
CENTRAL
NERVOUS
SYSTEM
WITH THE DEVELOP-
MENT
OF
ELECTRIC TECHNOLOGY
APPARENTLY ABOLISHING
BOTH
SPACE AND TIME
CONTENT
ARRANGED IN A NON
LINEAR
STRATIFIED LEVELS
H.B.S
EXCELL AT
PATTERN
RECOGNITION
BUT ARE
NOTORIOUSLY SLOW
AT SEQUENTIAL
CALCULATIONS.

Conceptual thinking

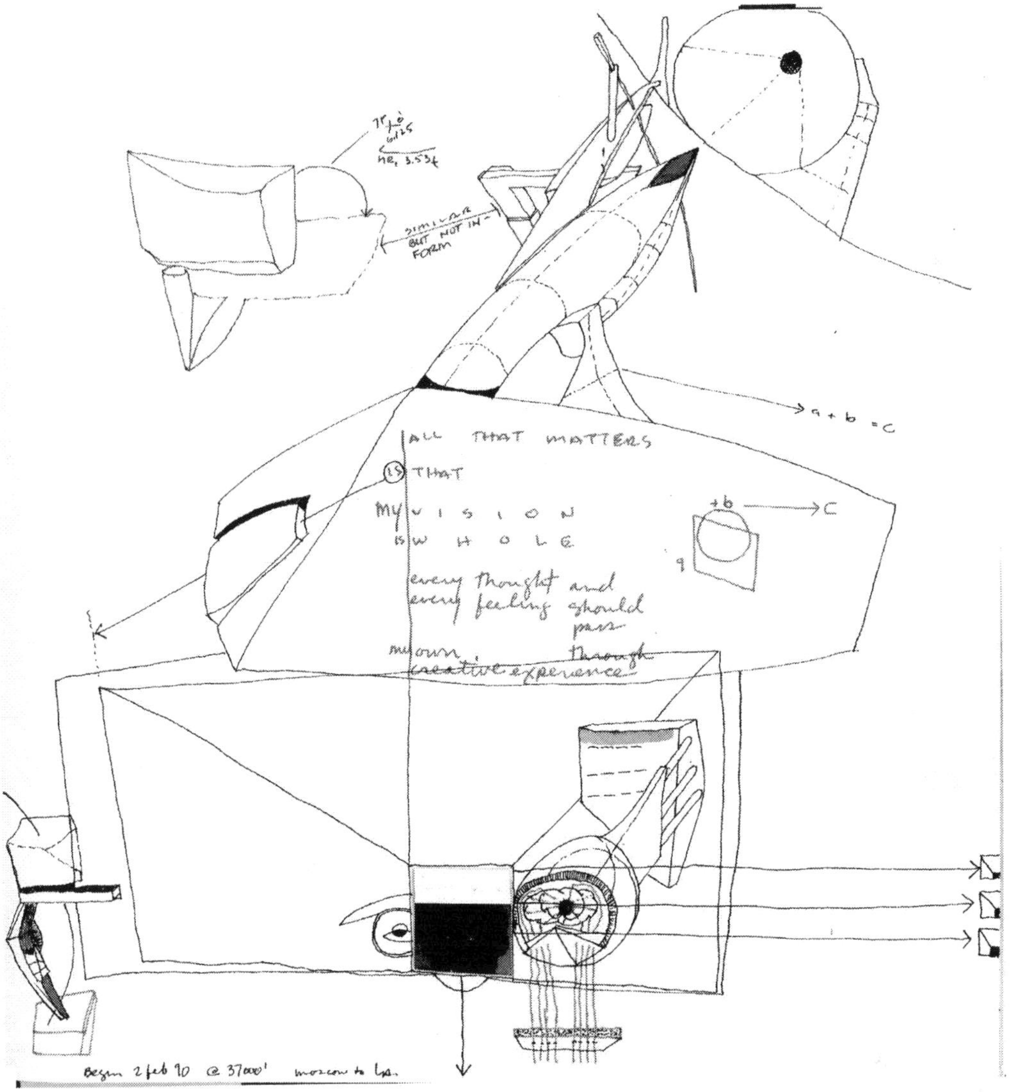
SIMILAR BUT NOT IN FORM
a + b = c
ALL THAT MATTERS
IS THAT
MY VISION
IS WHOLE
every thought and
every feeling should
pass
through
my own
creative experience
+b → c
Begun 2 feb 90 @ 37000' moscow to lps.

Conceptual thinking

@ ARI BHOD
ZANDOK PALRI

Ari Bhod Zandok Palri sketch 1

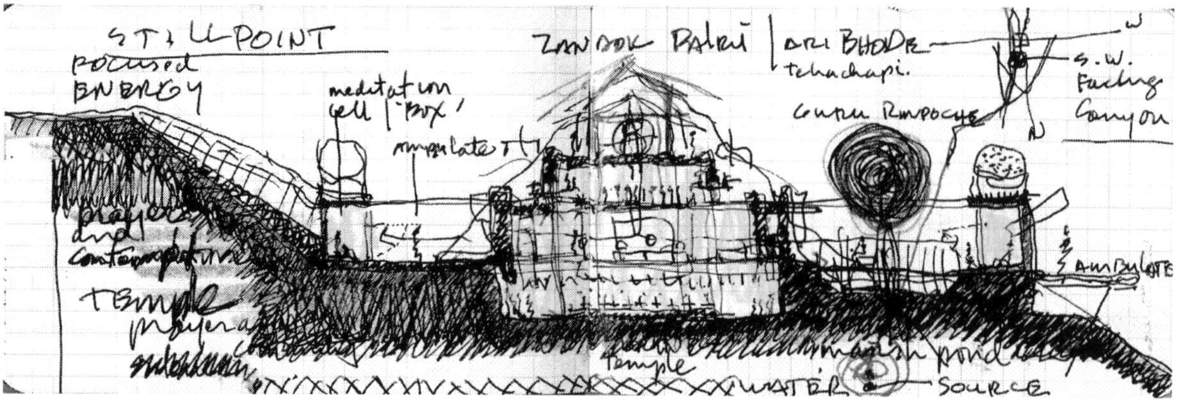
STILLPOINT
Focused
ENERGY
meditation
cell | 'BOX'
ZANDOK PALRI | ARI BHODE
Tehachapi.
GURU RINPOCHE
S.W.
Facing
Canyon
AMBULATE
temple
WATER
SOURCE

Ari Bhod Zandok Palri sketch 2

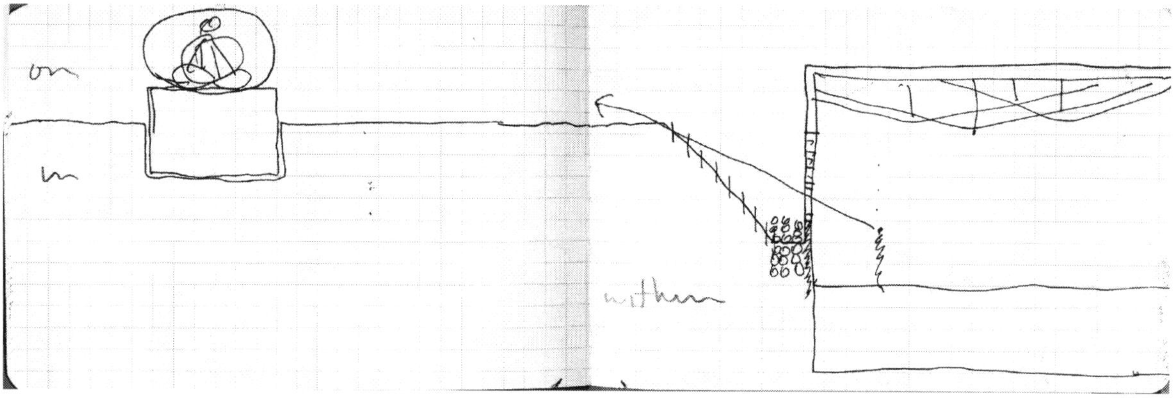
on
in
within

Ari Bhod Zandok Palri sketch 3

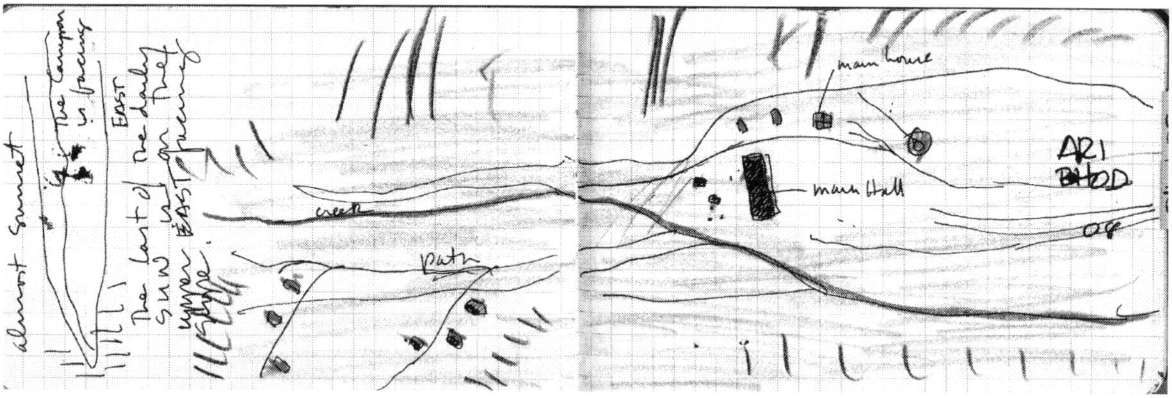
almost sunset
The canyon is facing
EAST
main house
ARI
BHOD
main Hall
creek
path

Ari Bhod Zandok Palri sketch 4

Chapter 14

Kris Yao Artech[1]

Mr. Kris Yao, FAIA, Founder and Principal

PROJECTS

Fo Guang Shan[2] Monastery, North Carolina[3]

Located in Raleigh, North Carolina, this project uses a gabled roof design to echo the style of the neighboring houses. The design is formed by interconnected, U-shaped corridors that also symbolize the open hands of the Buddha who offers refuge to all.[4]

The main building is of laminated timber wood framing which is anchored by reinforced concrete. It is clad in wood panels and asphalt tiles, while the corridors are colored cement.

The north end of the building houses the publicly accessible Grand Hall and meditation hall. The south end comprises monks' quarters, which includes living, worship, and study spaces.

Materials include laminated beams, T&G decking, cedar siding, and asphalt tile.

Project is 1,648 square meters.

Completed in 2008.

Fo Guang Shan Monastery, Bussy, France[5]

Located in a historical park in Bussy Saint George, this project contains three "walls" that run horizontally and house the main circulation corridors to all the functions. These provide for the three types of spaces which include a public zone, ceremonial spaces, and living quarters.

The public zone is in the outer section and includes classrooms, a café, an art gallery, and a bookstore. The second space houses a series of religious assembly halls. The innermost space accommodates the living quarters for monks and nuns.

The ceremonial Main Hall, the Mahakaruna Hall, the Zen Hall, and the Kṣitigarbha Hall are linked by outdoor courtyards or terraces on the east–west (horizontal) axis. The entrance lobby, the central courtyard, and the Zen garden connect on the north–south (vertical) axis.

"Visitors to the Main Hall ascend the ramp along the outer wall, enter the second floor lobby, then step down the grand stairs to the center courtyard in front of the Main Hall. The zigzag progression preserves the ancient ritual of approaching a temple."[6]

Materials include concrete and timber.

Project is 5,179 square meters.

Completed in 2012.

Water-Moon Monastery, Taipei, Taiwan[7]

The name comes from a realization about the monastery that the founder, Master Sheng Yen, had during sitting meditation: "It is a Flower in Space, Moon in Water," he said. "Let's name it the Water-Moon Monastery."

The monastery sits on the Guandu plain, facing the Keelung River, with the Datun Mountain as its backdrop.

The initial entry comprises two walls of different heights that serve as a buffer from the expressway outside. The Main Hall at the temple's entry sits at the far end of an 80-meter-long lotus pond. The pond reflects the large colonnades and golden drapes that line it.

The use of concrete is meant as a minimalist reference to the "the spirit of Zen Buddhism."[8] By making the lower section of the Grand Hall transparent, the upper wooden section is given the impression of being a suspended "box."

The Grand Hall's west wall is a massive wooden wall in which is carved the "Heart Sūtra" in Chinese characters. Outside the long corridor, the characters of the "Vajracchedikā Prajñāpāramitā Sūtra" are void-casted on prefabricated GRC panels. Both provide instruction, as well as lighting and shading effects.

Materials include concrete, teak wood, limestone, and glass

Project is 8,422 square meters

Completed in 2012.

Foguang Shan

The Foguang Shan temples that Mr. Yao's firm designed are for a Māhāyana school based in Taiwan. One of the projects is in Paris and another is located in North Carolina. For the North Carolina project, Mr. Yao says, "It's a very simple building. When things are simple, normally it's better.

"The site in North Carolina is a residential site," he says. "All around that area are all these East Coast pitched-roof suburban houses and we didn't want to create a big shock for the community. So what we did was interlock two pitched roofs with each other. It looks very much like a bigger house. But although it's a pitched roof, it goes all the way down to the ground so it's not a traditional house. It's a very modern architectural shape. The whole thing is built out of wood beams. It casts very interesting shadows. The wood goes beyond the building and hits the ground. That part is half inside, half outside."

This approach contrasts with that used in Bussy, France: "The Foguang Shan Paris project is for Taiwanese Māhāyanist Buddhist group and they have organizations everywhere. I think they serve Chinese communities all over the world. So that includes Chinese and Cambodians, Vietnamese, and other Asian countries, their diaspora and their descendants. And they all need somewhere to practice their religion."

The Foguang Shan project located in Paris presented some very interesting challenges. The site was a challenge because it was not suited to the normal plan of a Buddhist temple: "It's in a satellite city east of Paris in Bussy. It's kind of a new town and they have a huge green space. There's a lake and there's an ancient, half-ruined, 13th-century castle that still remains. The city designated a row of lots that were basically lined up alongside each other for different religions. Each lot has a different religious building. And they gave one to Foguang Shan.

Initially, Mr. Yao says, "Because it's in Europe, the clients hired two or three European architects to design it before they came to me. But the architects and the client just could not understand each other. Basically, these European architects didn't know what Buddhists do and didn't know anything about their culture." He pauses, "They probably Googled Buddhism or looked for books and then came up with all these lotus-shaped or imperial-roofed buildings, all things that I would probably do when I'm doing other religions. So the clients decided to come back to me."

"First, the site is located across the street from the castle. Second, the French government had very strict conservation regulations about the materials and the height of the building to protect the historic environment around the castle.

"Foguang Shan is also a very traditional Māhāyana Chinese group who have had a lot of temples built before this. There's a huge one in Los Angeles. And they always follow this particular Chinese Māhāyana style. You have this axis and then you have courtyards, one after another. So there is a sequence of spaces that you progress through. First you enter the gate with the Four Guardians (Ch. 風調雨順, Eng. Fengtiao Yushun). And then there is the first courtyard with the Dharma protectors on both sides. And then the first pavilion is for Avalokiteśvara (Ch. 觀音菩薩, Eng. Guanyin Pusa). And the second courtyard, and then there is the main shrine with Suryagama Buddha. And then the last courtyard is where you store all the dharma texts and sutras and also where you teach and there is a lot of symbolism, like body, speech, and mind. Buddha, dharma, sanga.

"I looked at the horizontal site. Because this site didn't fit the traditional axial spatial layout, I bent the axis horizontally. First one enters the temple on the lower right-hand corner. It slopes up to enter the building on the second level where the first pavilion is with Avalokiteśvara. Then after the Avalokiteśvara hall, one turns around to go down the grand stairs into the courtyard and then into the main shrine. So it's kind of a zigzag version of the old axial, but I tried to maintain the spatial sequence because the practitioners are familiar with the sequence. The living quarters for the monks and nuns are at the very back of the site."

Mr. Yao continues, "The other thing I did was add a three-dimensional element when you first go up, and then down into the main hall. If I hadn't done that, there would not have been the progression and drama that the old temples had, where you actually enter the first courtyard, then the second courtyard, and so on; my design would have been too indistinct. By adding the planar dimensions, using steps and stairways as well as varying heights, there is an obvious progression between spaces."

As to the limitations on the height of the building as well as cladding, he says, "For the exterior of the building, because the height and material is very restricted, basically diagrammatically, I did a few horizontal walls. If you saw the first sketch, it's just a few horizontal lines. But those walls basically connect the whole space.

And being in the park, all the roofs are done in green cover, so hopefully from the air, when you look down to this thing you only see those walls; the roof is all green to blend in with the central park."

Water-Moon Monastery Background

"Water-Moon is a modern Zen monastery," says Mr. Yao. "The Dharma Drum group is headed by a very revered master called Master Sheng Yen who is very respected worldwide. They are a practice-oriented group. And it's part of the Chan lineage or tradition. He asked me to rebuild this place because this was where he and his masters started it years ago. They moved from China to this location. But all the buildings were very rundown so they wanted to rebuild it.

"They bought a piece of land in front of which was designated farmland so they couldn't put an actual building on it. So the Master said to me that because the site was very limited, he wanted to build a monastery which was a landscape monastery. However, it's not the landscape in the way that architects think about it." In other words, "landscape" functions as a metaphor: "What he meant was using the setting of the temple to cultivate people's minds. The Master said there are many, many Buddhist temples in Taiwan but almost all of them are devoted to doing all kinds of pūjā or rituals. Taiwanese love rituals and get together and do things. There's not many temples in Taiwan where you feel tranquil and peaceful like temples in Kyoto. Temples here are more like a club."

The exchange that Mr. Yao engaged in with his client, Master Sheng Yen, became an essential starting point to producing a design. He continued, "I asked him, 'Master, you must have a vision of how the temple should be to fulfill that dream.' Surprisingly, he said, 'Yes, I have seen that temple in my dhyāna, in my meditation.' I was joking and telling him, 'That's kind of nice, Master, but the things you see in dhyāna cannot be expressed by words.' And he said, 'Kris, you are right.' So he gave me six words: Flower in Air, and Moon in Water.

"That was my architectural program, these six words. It's very profound. It gets to the core of Buddhism. Basically, Buddhism believes that all phenomena are not truly extant. It's all like moon and water. So I understood that part intellectually. But the challenge is, how do you create a solid, heavy, concrete building, into something that tries to express the illusory aspect of phenomena?"

From Philosophy to Design

Mr. Yao explains the process of translating a theoretical principle into massed material. "I used that piece of unbuilt land and made it into a huge pond in front of the shrine. So when there is no wind, the reflection is almost as if you are staring at the real thing itself. It's a mirror image of the thing. And when a little bit of wind starts to move the water, the images become blurry. In addition to that, I put some drapes outside of the temple so that when the wind comes, the drapes move. So the wind moves the drapes and the images in the water as well. That helped convey the illusory aspect of a solid building."

Embedding Doctrine in Design

Mr. Yao's personal experience and knowledge about Buddhism also aided him in the design. He says, "Chan is also a very uniquely Chinese lineage, and I have always found that Chinese sūtras are very powerful. You don't even need to read them. Looking at them, the aesthetics of the characters [words] is very strong for me. And from what I understand from many other people, they also think this way." That means that both the words themselves and the aesthetics of them written in Chinese characters are very powerful. "So in the sūtras, Buddha said if you write or read the sūtra to other people or teach them to other people or carve them in stone, you gather a lot of merit. So that's what Chinese or Māhāyana Buddhists do, copy the sūtras and read the sūtras every day."

Mr. Yao continues, "I told Master Sheng Yen, 'there has never been a instance where the Buddha's words actually came with a form of light. So why don't we do that, actually carve the building and have light coming into the building through these sutras. And he said, 'Okay, why don't you try it?' So that's what I did with these 5,000+ words sūtras, the Diamond sūtra and the Heart sūtra, the two sūtras that are beloved in Chinese Buddhist traditions. And also the two most important sutras for the Chan tradition. The sūtras were cast in concrete panels. I imagined all these lights would come in and form all kinds of interesting lights inside the shrine itself which would cast shadows outward."

Interestingly, these effects are all achieved through concrete: "The whole building is mostly done in concrete. So it's very plain. And the space has a very spacious, peaceful, and quiet atmosphere thanks to the big water pond."

General Observations

"Many people who come in just sit by the water. A few times I've even observed parents with small children come in and sit down. Even the children sit for a long time!

"Once in a while," he says, "they circumambulate while chanting Avalokiteśvara's name. It's very touching. They walk very slowly, around the shrine, in this serene atmosphere."

Says Mr. Yao, "The temple has become very popular after its completion. Suddenly lots of people started going there and I often go there myself. Sometimes I get recognized by these people. On a few occasions these Buddhists come to me and thank me for designing such a nice building. Some of them have tears in their eyes, and say they see things; they send me pictures of reflections of the Heart sūtra in the sky. The small Buddha statue on the wall of the shrine is actually reflected in the sky as well. With the overlapping clouds outside, I guess they feel they are in this wonderful pure land. They find it very inspiring, the space and light, all these unexpected effects of my coincidentally doing all these things."

Notes

1 Kris Yao. Interview with Sherin Wing via Skype. Los Angeles, October 24, 2013.
2 We use the Wade-Giles system of romanization for the actual name of the temple, "For Guang Shan", however, for all general Chinese names, the Pinyin romanization system is used.
3 "Fo Guang Shan Monastery-North Carolina." Project description email to author, June 19, 2014.
4 Ibid.
5 "Fo Guang Shan Monasteries Paris." Project description emailed to author, June 19, 2014.
6 Ibid.
7 "Water-Moon Monastery." Project description emailed to author, June 19, 2014.
8 Ibid.

Fo Guang Shan Monastery, second floor

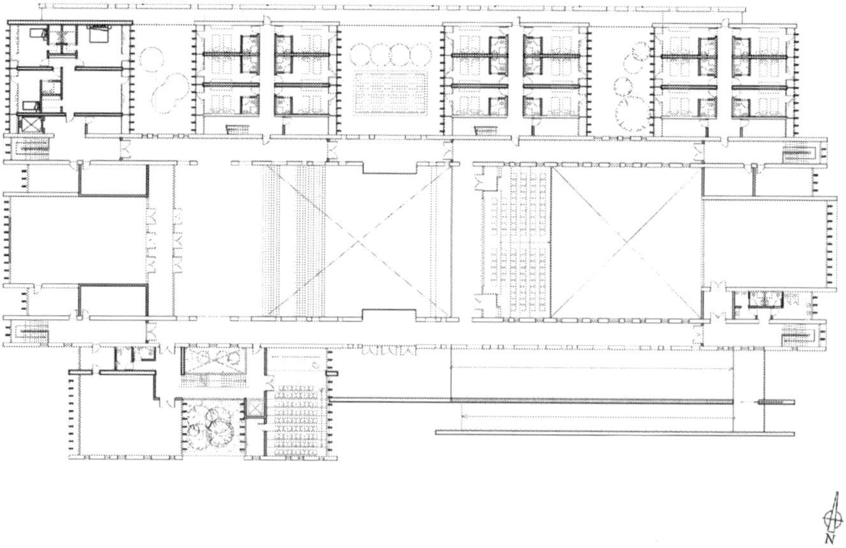

Fo Guang Shan, ground floor

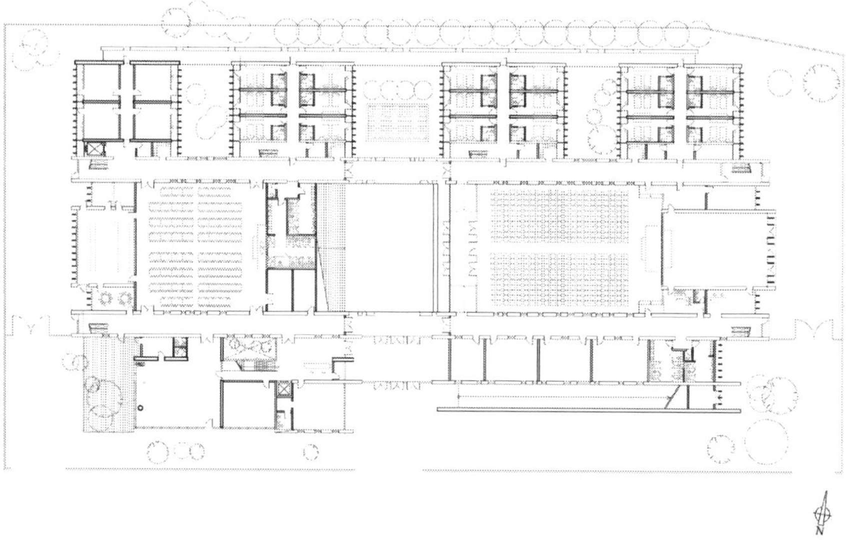

Fo Guang Shan rendering

Fo Guang Shan

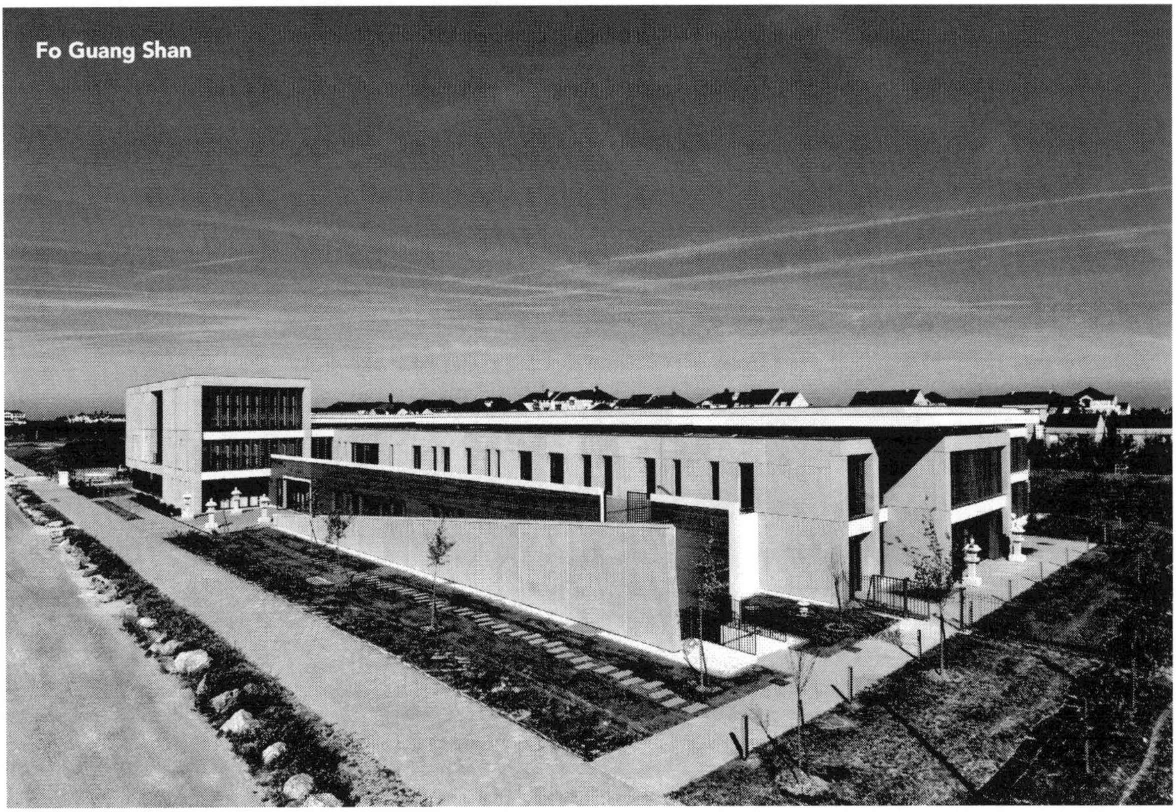
Fo Guang Shan

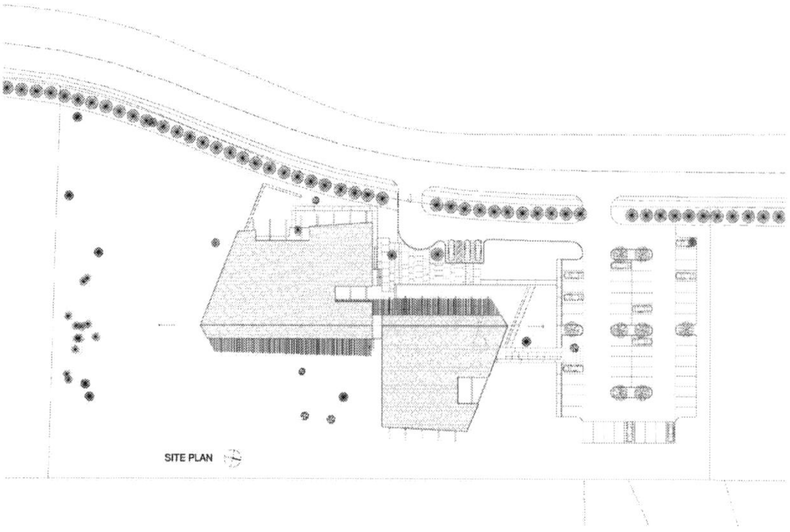
SITE PLAN

Fo Guang Shan,
North Carolina site

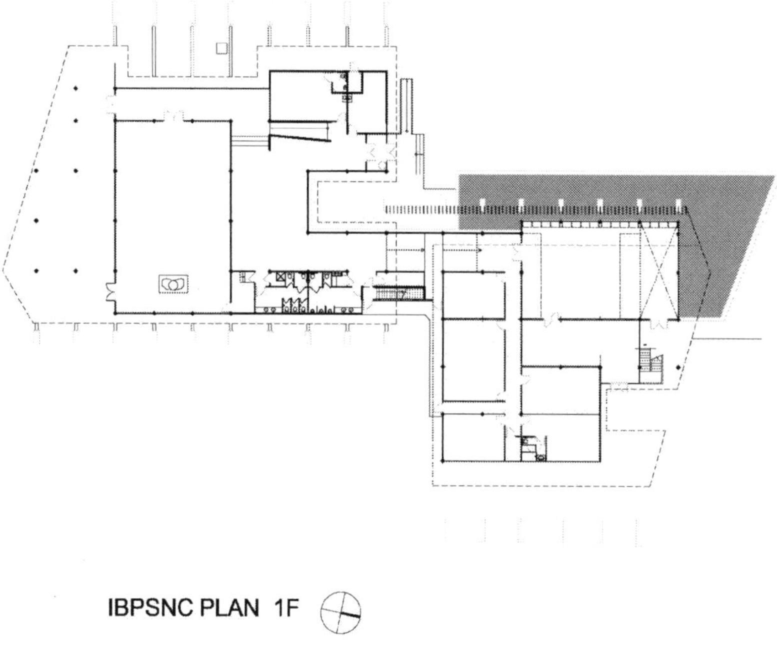
IBPSNC PLAN 1F

Fo Guang Shan,
North Carolina site,
first floor plan

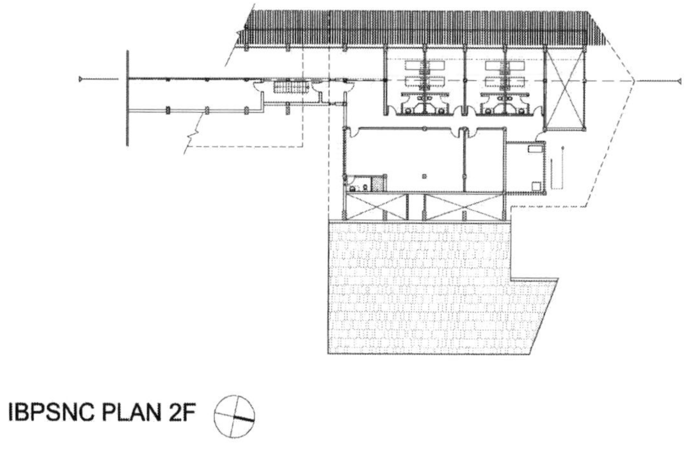
IBPSNC PLAN 2F

Fo Guang Shan,
North Carolina site,
second floor plan

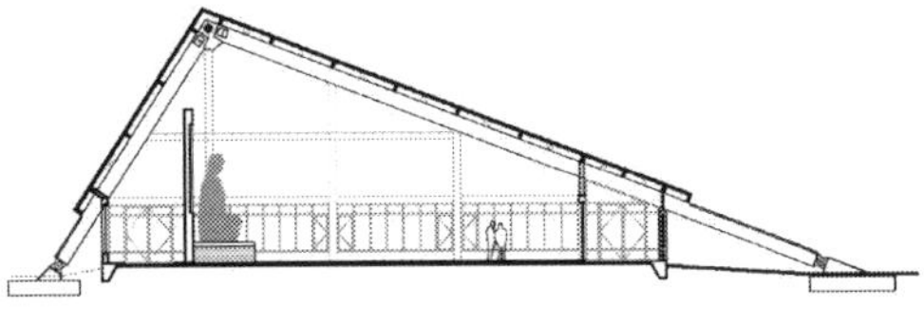

SHRINE SECTION

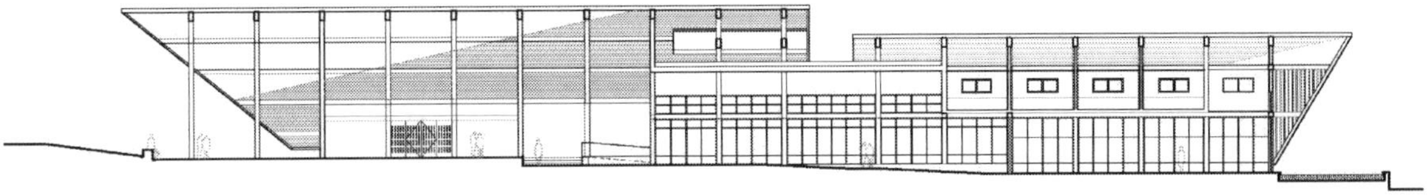

LONGITUDINAL SECTION

Fo Guang Shan, North Carolina, sections

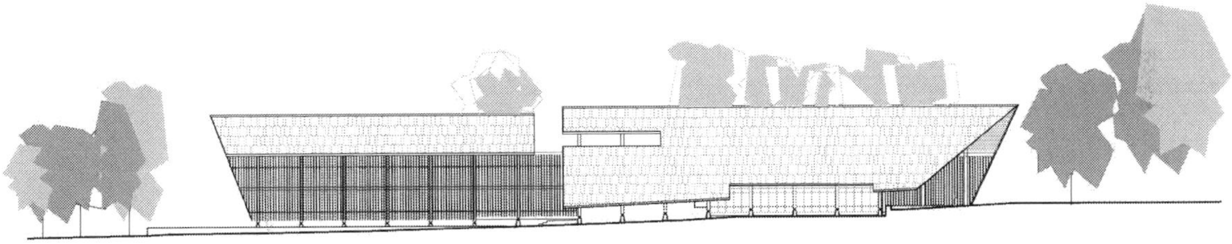

WEST ELEVATION

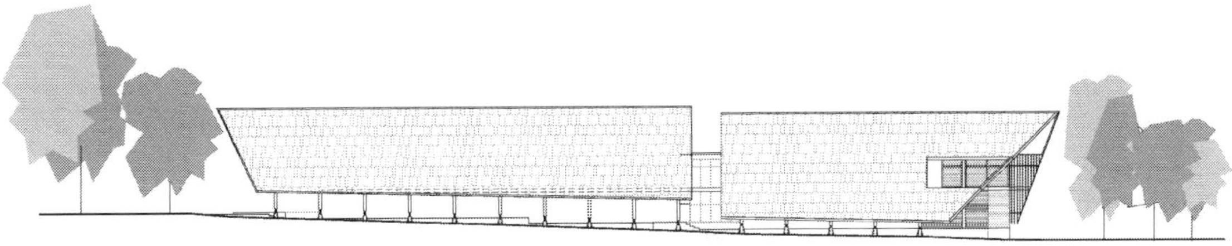

EAST ELEVATION

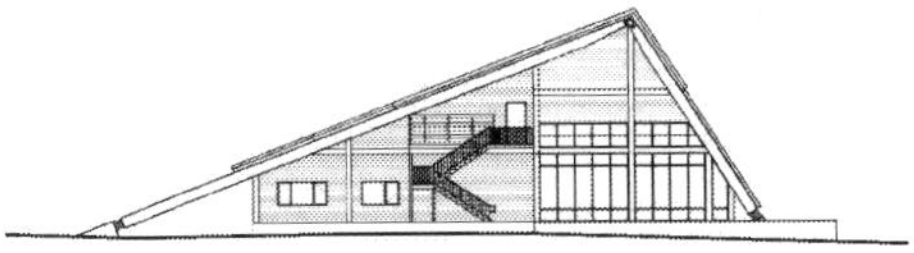

NORTH ELEVATION

Fo Guang Shan, North Carolina, elevation

Fo Guang Shan, North Carolina

Fo Guang Shan, North Carolina

Fo Guang Shan, North Carolina, interior

Water-Moon Monastery

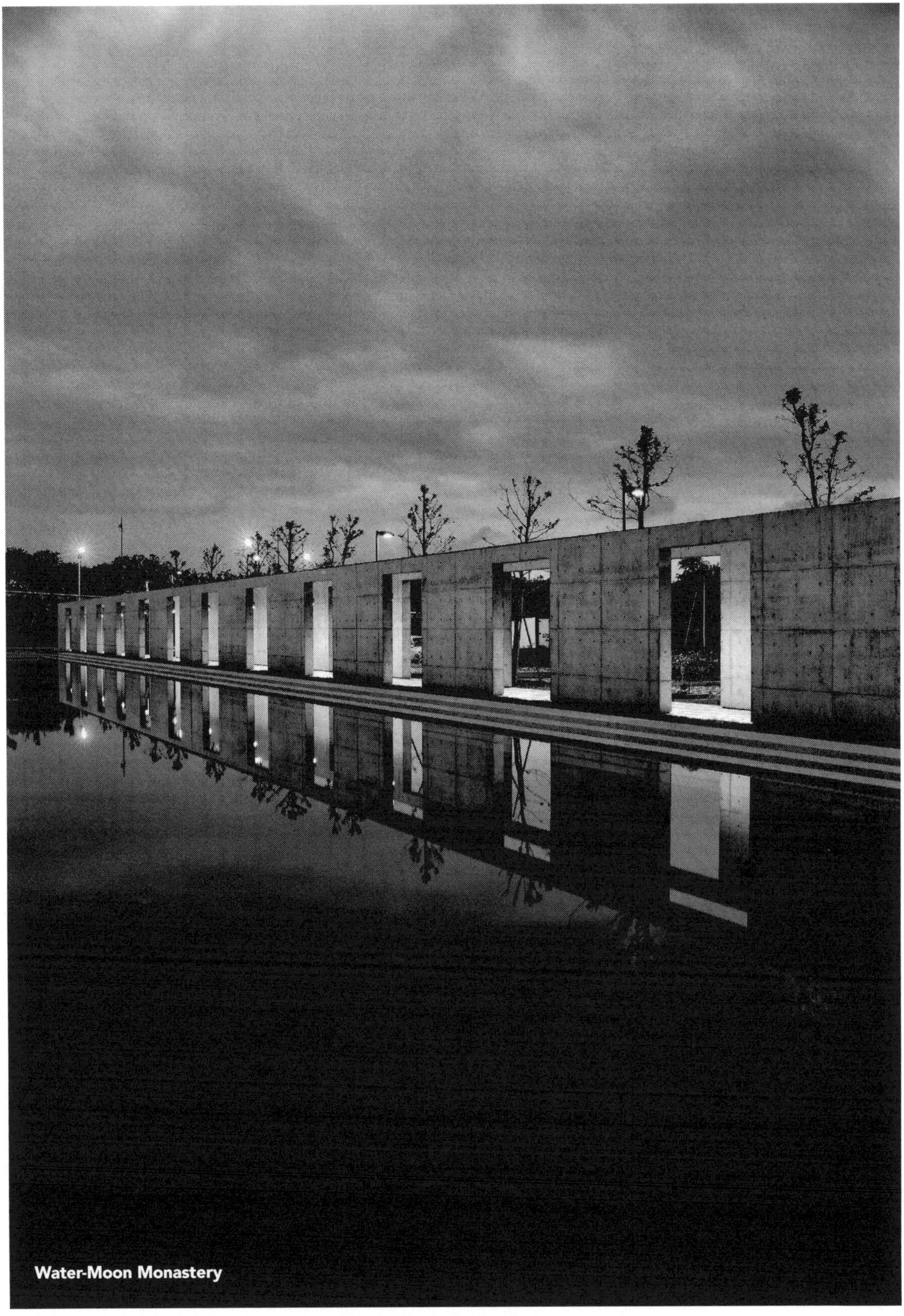

Water-Moon Monastery

Water-Moon site

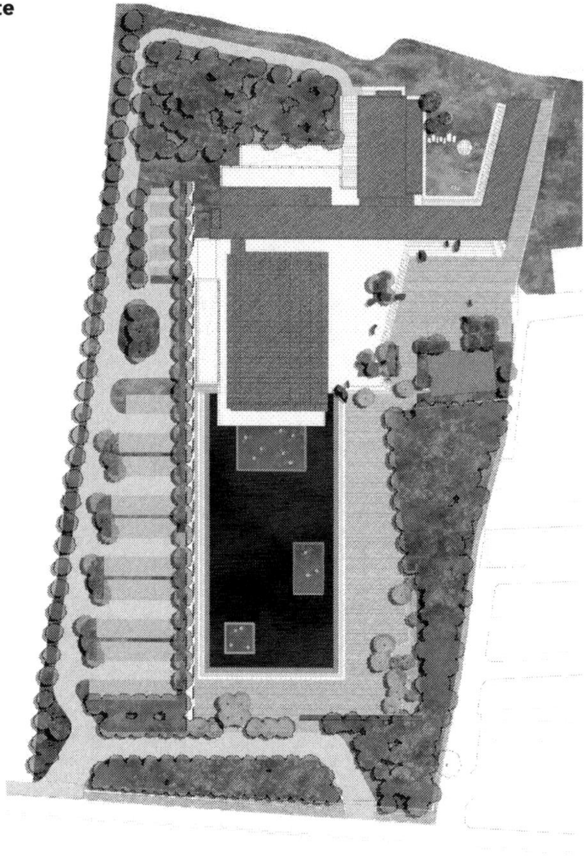

Water-Moon south elevation

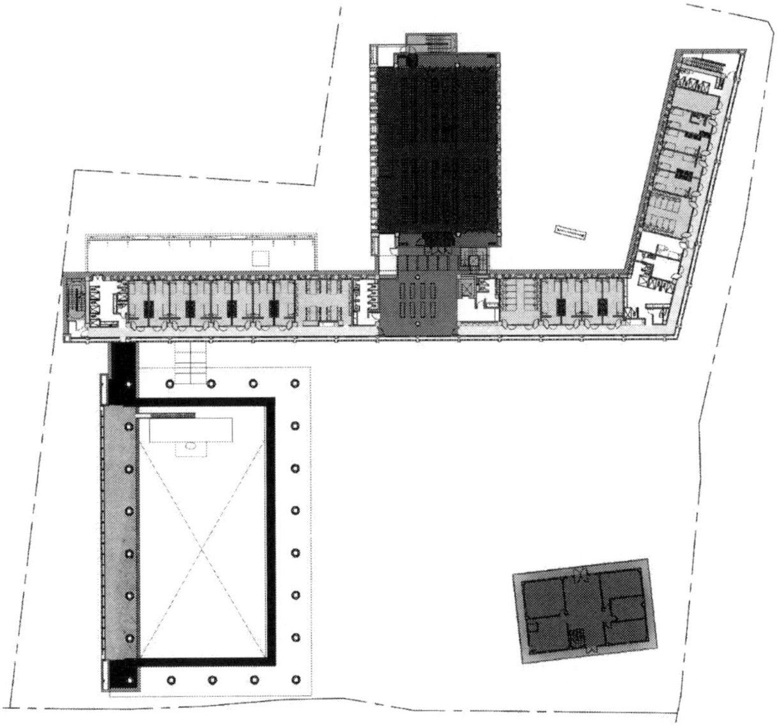

Water-Moon first floor plan

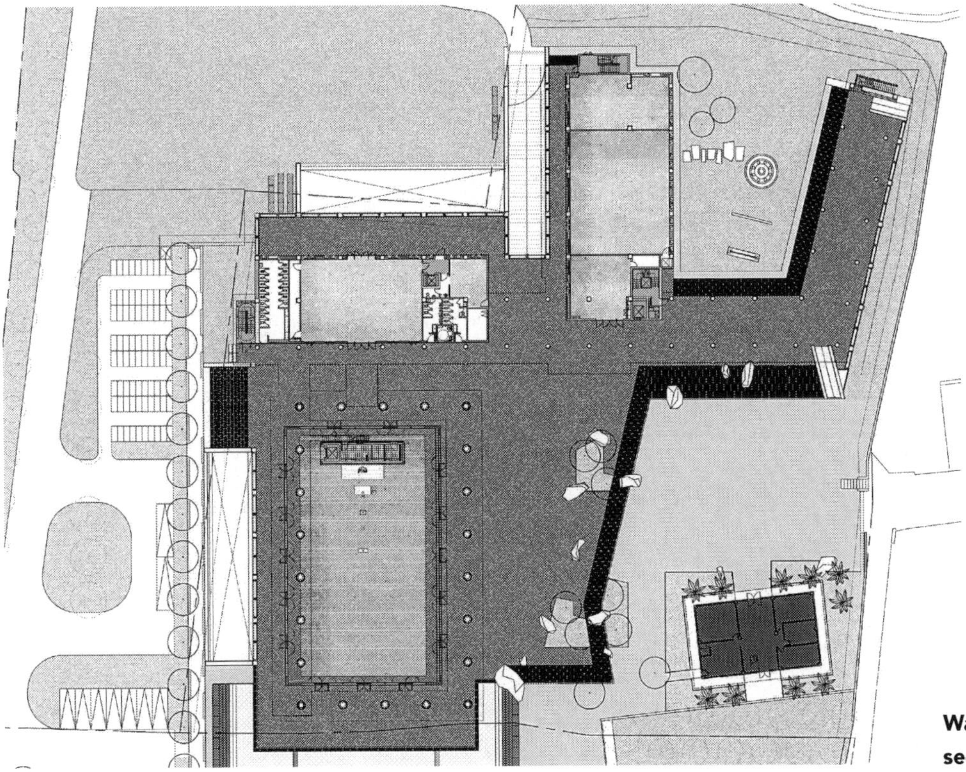

Water-Moon second floor plan

Water-Moon

Water-Moon

Water-Moon

Water-Moon

Water-Moon

薩為利益一切眾生故應如是布
施如來說一切諸相即是非相又
說一切眾生即非眾生須菩提如

Water-Moon

如來說三十二相即是非相是名
三十二相須菩提若有善男子善
女人以恆河沙等身命布施若復
有人於此經中乃至受持四句偈
等為他人說其福甚多爾時須菩
提聞說是經深解義趣涕淚悲泣
而白佛言希有世尊佛說如是甚
深經典我從昔來所得慧眼未曾
得聞如是之經世尊若復有人得
聞是經信心清淨即生實相當知

Water-Moon

PART 5

THE CONSTRUCTION OF RELIGIOUS SPACES

Chapter 15

Constructing Religious Space

Constructing sacred space—does it begin before breaking ground or when a space is ritually recognized? And what is the role of human behavior? Understanding these issues requires a complex approach that combines first-hand accounts with material and theoretical sources.[1] What's more, written sources should include not just official histories and documents, but also unofficial records and reports.[2]

Toward that end, scholars and architects must investigate sacred space using interdisciplinary frameworks.[3] Archaeologists, art historians, critical theoreticians, geographers, philosophers, religious scholars, and social historians have defined religious space through human interaction and "urban phenomena and institutional forces."[4] A comprehensive intellectual landscape now juxtaposes concepts of fluidity, liminality, and pilgrimage with practical considerations like circulation, lighting, materials, plans, and sound in the construction of religious spaces. In this way, environmental, physical, and social factors work together to identify a space as sacred.

Because religions have conceived and expressed sacred spaces differently, foregrounding all these methodologies requires cultural specificities.[5] In medieval Christian traditions, for example, sacred space meant "the way in which ancient and medieval patrons, architects, and masons physically shaped the environment in sacred cause."[6] The ideas and situations "generated by the built environment contributed to the cultural formation of the sacred [and] human engagement [in]. . .structurally organized, repeated, privileged, performed actions or rites."[7] In this view, there are clear thresholds that mark the end of a sacred space and the beginning of a secular space.

Contrast this with medieval Indian and Chinese Buddhist temples that were inhabited by study or practice monks and nuns with the wealthy donor laity as a third group. For practice monks and laity, procession through specific spaces was an exercise in indoctrination as well as devotional practice, and medieval temples and stūpas reflected this priority. So as one progressed from the outer spaces to the inner ones, the devotee was not only visually educated on doctrine, but also engaged in devotion.

Sacrality is also not limited to a particular space. For Islam, both historically and now, investing a space with sacrality involves engaging in prayer, which can be done anywhere. Therefore for Muslims, the mosque is but one locale of many throughout the day where individuals pray.[8] This brings an entirely different view to defining sacrality through human interaction.

Frequently the space as a whole conveys a religion's cosmology. It becomes a didactic metaphor for religious doctrine. For example, in Buddhist temples, the architectural plan of a religious space reinforces practitioners' understanding of basic ideology by directing them through edifying space in a specific, processional manner.[9] One can see the same intent behind the cruciform church plans in 1600 Europe.[10] The progress of practitioners through these cosmologically symbolic spaces not only emphasizes doctrine, it literally manipulates people's bodies to enact basic religious practice. Religious spaces can therefore educate and indoctrinate.

Certain religions also combine sacred and secular spaces into a single project.[11] That explains why recent scholarship defines religious and secular space in contrastive yet complementary terms. For example, secular activities like food celebrations or gatherings are not, strictly speaking, worshipful, but they occur as a complement to religious practice. Indeed, many projects in this book integrate secular spaces within their walls, including recreational, educational, ecological, aesthetic, political, and communal,[12] specifically sports, music concerts, and, of course, communal food events. Even sports activities occur within the walls of a religious project to facilitate the religious community's cohesion. Clearly, religious spaces can function in multiple ways, depending upon the interaction that takes place within them.[13]

People who partake in these activities are not just limited to members of the religious community. The general populace is also interested in engaging these sites as tourists or as patrons of secular events such as concerts.[14] In fact, religious sites can serve numerous secular purposes such as cultural and political events and discourses such as concerts, political rallies, and even tourism.[15]

Finally, some projects exemplify shifts in religious institutional identity: while the space was originally built for one religion, through a combination of necessity and human intervention, it was shifted to a different religion. The implications on constructing sacred spaces in contemporary times is profound, completely undermining the idea of fixed or intrinsic sacrality, toward a fluid, contrastive, and even contested definition.

Notes

1 Whyte, 2006: 159.

2 Nasser Rabbat, "Toward a Critical Historiography of Islamic Architecture," *Repenser les limites: l'architecture à travers l'espace, le temps et les disciplines*, Paris, INHA, 2005, http://inha.revues.org/642 (October 28, 2008): 4.

3 Branham, 2012: 201. Branham's own investigation involves the concept of mapping or the concept of providing a legend to "read" a particular terrain, including that of medieval churches and temples.

4 Lawrence and Low, 1990: 482.

5 Whyte, 2006: 153–155.

6 Wescoat and Ousterhout, 2012b: 365.

7 Wescoat and Ousterhout, 2012b: 365–367.

8 Conversation with Shahed Saleem, October 25, 2014.

9 Ronald L. Grimes, "Ritual, Performance, and the Sequestering of Sacred Space," Dunbarton Oaks Bynzantine Symposium (2003): 11; Desplat, 2012: 9.

10 Sergey R. Kravtsov, "Jewish Identities in Synagogue Architecture of Galicia and Bukovina," *Ars Judaica: The Bar-Ilan Journal of Jewish Art*, No. 6 (2010): 92.

11 Burgess, 2004: 312.

12 Blake, Kevin, "Sacred and Secular Landscape Symbolism at Mount Taylor, New Mexico," *Journal of the Southwest*, Vol. 41, No. 4 (Winter, 1999): 504; Hans Bakker, "Construction and Reconstruction of Sacred Space in Vārāṇasī," *Numen*, Vol. 43, Fasc. 1 (January, 1996): 38.

13 Burgess, 2004: 312.

14 Kang, Xiaofei, "Two Temples, Three Religions, and a Tourist Attraction: Contesting Sacred Space on China's Ethnic Frontier," *Modern China*, Vol. 35, No. 3 (May, 2009): 228.

15 Kang, 2009: 230.

Chapter 16

Symbols and Space

A religious tradition can be seen as a cultural system. One way of articulating that system is through religious symbols and iconography.[1] They comprise an important, theoretical dimension to constructing sacred spaces. Their characteristics have changed over time, however. What's more, they are religion-specific.

That said, in medieval religious architecture, symbols and iconography were more fixed than they are now. One reason is that religions were just developing their traditions, thus their ideology was less sophisticated. Physical representations, including symbols and iconography, were similarly less mature.

Early Indian Buddhist stūpas, for example, often consisted of simple earthen mounds that were circumambulated; later symbolic developments in China, which was the first East Asian country to receive Buddhism, included roofs that symbolized different levels of heaven. When Theravādin Buddhism spread to South East Asia, it also developed into different strands/classifications. This same process occurred in East Asia and Mahāyāna Buddhism. The symbolism and physical expressions for each of those schools/classifications therefore became more sophisticated. What's more, this all occurred very early in Buddhist history, specifically from the 700s through the 1100s CE.

Medieval European Christianity offers us another illustration on the earlier, fixed nature of religious symbolism. In medieval Christian churches, mimesis of the Old Testament "provided the inspiration for the tripartite interior," which, along with imitating other venerated sites, layered the symbolism invoked in these buildings.[2] Each spatial component worked together to represent an entire scriptural tradition. Sacred space was therefore "symbolically constituted" and pointed to a divine meaning.[3] That meaning had to be interpreted by specialists—the clergy—for the laity through doctrine, exposition, instruction, and ritual. Note, however, that it was not that a single symbolic or iconographic component stood in for the entire ideological narrative: every discrete constituent worked with other features to represent the entire system.

Another reason for the more fixed character of historical religious symbols is that there was also less competition. That includes within one religious system and with other religions. That meant there was less need for unique material representations to differentiate between schools or classifications within an overarching religion.

Iconography and material representations became more sophisticated as the religions began to splinter into different schools or strands. Today there are several different kinds of Islam and Judaism, Buddhism and Christianity. The proliferation of ideological differences manifest ritually and verbally, and also physically in architecture and iconography. To differentiate amongst themselves as well as from other religious institutions, they use unique symbolic and material expressions to identify themselves. In essence, each was marking itself off from a competitor.

Therefore as time progressed and religions proliferated, their architectures would convey religious ideology "by imitating a venerated prototype" within their religion.[4] In contemporary terms, if a very old and well-established building is venerated as a sacred space, the architectural and symbolic aesthetic elements it displays are by definition equally venerable or authoritative. In essence, reproducing older, established forms and elements references the religious lineage it purports to be part of, thereby invoking authority.

Similarly, when contemporary projects deploy historically established symbols and iconography, they are invoking their religious lineage, or so the thinking goes. The new space therefore establishes itself as part of a larger, unified religious tradition.[5] This is why many modern religious spaces will feature tropes such as tiered roofs, crosses on bell towers, or spired domes: to appropriate legitimacy through imitation. Using easily recognizable materials and architectural elements authorizes the new structure.

Yet while religious systems consist of symbols and iconography, they cannot be reduced to them.[6] And although today there are more fluid interpretations of what comprises sacred space, it remains especially true that a single or even series of decontextualized signifiers cannot properly evoke a complex series of beliefs, behaviors, and relationships. Especially when designing religious spaces, one should not simply choose a signifier discovered on the web and assume that it alone can evoke an entire religious tradition or culture.

Throughout this book, we will find that the projects do not decontextualize historical or medieval religious symbols and tropes. Instead, most of them use different architectural tactics to promote religious practice, as well as to foster the associated activities that accompany worship, including communal activities before and after ritual services.

Notes

1 Abdulluh Al-Jami and Michael H. Mitias, "Does an Islamic Architecture Exist?" *Revista Portuguesa de Filosofia*, T. 60, Fasc. 1 (January–March, 2004): 204–205.

2 Heldman, 1992: 231–234.

3 Steve Brie, Jenny Daggers, and David Torevell. "Introduction," in *Sacred Space: Interdisciplinary Perspectives within Contemporary Contexts*, edited by Steve Brie, Jenny Daggers, and David Torevell (Newcastle upon Tyne: Cambridge Scholars Publishing, 2010): 3.

4 Heldman, 1992: 224.

5 Alex Brenner, "'Some Imperial Institute': Architecture, Symbolism, and the Ideal of Empire in Late Victoria Britain," *Journal of the Society of Architectural Historians*, Vol. 62, No. 1 (March, 2003): 54. While Brenner is discussing the unifying effect of symbol in secular architecture in the imperial project of Victorian Britain, heuristically his insight is useful.

6 Say Al-Jami and Mitias, "An empirical, critical survey of the multitude of churches in the Catholic, Eastern Orthodox, and Protestant denominations would show that these churches do not exhibit a consistent system of visual symbols," an insight that can be applied equally to any religion (2004: 205).

Chapter 17

Project Sites

Throughout history, secular and religious power have been closely entwined. Quite simply, religious and secular authority, legitimacy, and patronage were reciprocal. This symbiosis occurred in medieval Western Europe, East Asia, and the Near East. It is much the same today in many parts of the world. Can anyone imagine a US president who does not subscribe to some type of Christianity, or a northern European royal who does not attend church as an affirmation of legitimacy and therefore worthiness of secular power?

The effect of these entwined relationships on secular and religious built spaces was profound. Medieval religious institutions frequently located their buildings near political seats of power.[1] Christian churches,[2] as well as Islamic mosques, Buddhist and Jewish temples, and convents and monasteries of all religions were often situated in the middle of towns near government buildings.[3] Positioning themselves near political institutions gave them access to secular power, whether it was a local municipality, regional, or even a national governmental body.[4]

The question is: why did religious institutions do this? Often it was necessary to gain the favor of local, regional, and national politicos and rulers to cement their own legitimacy and thus ensure their own continued existence. For example, when Buddhism was first establishing itself in China, competition with Daoist and local folk priests was fierce. Skeptical Confucian advisors balked at any religious influence over elites and rulers. In this environment, securing royal patronage meant that temples, monasteries, and convents would not be dismantled nor would monks and nuns be defrocked. But to do that, it was necessary to establish temples, monasteries, and convents near elites and rulers to curry and then maintain their favor.

The relationship between secular and religious authority was reciprocal because secular authority also gained legitimacy by invoking a religious mandate. Rulers and local officials could claim their regime had been sanctioned by a heavenly authority, through the mediation of a powerful religious leader. Oftentimes, national and regional officials would seek endorsements from different religions, depending on which was ascendant at any given time.

Other religious beliefs such as that in the inherent sacrality of sites also influenced location decisions. Religious sites reflected an institutional-level faith in intrinsic topographic sacrality.[5] Religious institutions chose building sites in the belief that only they could facilitate contact with the divine.[6] Essentially, a scriptural site was made manifest on earth at a specific location.[7] This is why several religions perceive mountains as earthly connections to the divine. Sites were considered inherently sacred because they marked significant doctrinal events. In fact, academics continue debating the issue of inherent sacrality even today.[8] Not only did sacred sites mark important doctrinal events, they also symbolized a divine/mundane connection.

These historically important forces starkly contrast with the considerations shaping site choices today. Many of the projects in this book reflect the shifting perceptions about site sacrality.[9] Choices today demonstrate how human perception of space and site shapes decisions.[10]

First, most contemporary religious spaces are not preoccupied with acquired secular legitimacy, so they don't necessarily site themselves next to governmental seats. Siting religious projects near buildings of secular authority such as in historical times is unnecessary because seeking secular legitimacy for a religious institution is no longer a predominant concern. One recent exception was the religious center project to be sited near the World Trade Center. The irony was that those who objected to it as somehow sacrilegious to Christianity or on the basis of racism failed to understand that the goal of the project was ecumenism and reconciliation.

Nor, as in medieval times, are they sited where the divine—however defined—has appeared. Rather, they reveal a different kind of religious and practical utility. Like ancient Indian Buddhist sites, many contemporary sites are neither pre-ordained nor "received" from a heavenly source. Of course, contemporary clients may still consider sites sacred, but institutional recognition of those sites as sacred is rare. In other words, on an institutional level sites are not considered inherently sacred,[11] despite the fact that individual clients may perceive them as such.[12]

What's more, although some sites are consecrated either before or after construction, that, too, does not point to inherent sacrality. Rather, consecrations express gratitude for using the site. Alternatively, ritual and formal consecrations accept a project within the religion. That is an important distinction. Therefore, while we cannot dismiss feelings regarding a site as an important factor, we likewise cannot use "pure subjectivity" as a measure for inherent sacrality precisely because it is unquantifiable.[13] Indeed, many contemporary projects, including those in this volume, exemplify the transformation from secular to sacred.[14]

Other projects epitomize the conversion from one religion to another.[15] By definition, these spaces of adaptive reuse reject the idea of inherent sacrality. Instead, they exemplify the process of producing and uncovering meaning.

Adaptive reuse also exemplifies how "architecture is not. . .simply a language, and buildings cannot. . .simply be read [using structuralism]."[16] Instead it is a "process of designing, building, and interpreting."[17]Architecture, after all, is not simply words on a page and projects are not texts: architecture is a part of the larger material (i.e. physical, not as in "materials used by architects to build") culture created by humans.[18] It orients space, and in so doing, architecture comprises meaning. That meaning, unlike in literature, must be understood not just as aesthetically, symbolically, or lexicographically—a literary structuralist influence;[19] architecture also functions on physical and practical levels.

Secular, practical considerations that governed medieval site choices have also changed significantly. Contemporary factors have shifted to: 1) accessibility for the religious community; 2) proximity to other desirable services such as schools, healthcare, transportation, and food; 3) site availability; and even 4) proximity to or distance from economic or political centers.[20]

Land availability exerts considerable influence today regardless of the religion, especially for projects located in urban areas. Many institutional projects, including those in this book, are either urban infill or are located in rural settings precisely because that is what is available. Wherever the location, the goal is to resolve the tension between establishing a unique identity while also blending into the surroundings. From a design perspective, that issue was dealt with according to designer aesthetics, client needs, budget, and the surrounding community.

Convenience for the religious community is another factor in site choice. Because seeking secular political legitimacy is not an issue, accessibility for the congregation takes precedence. Interestingly, in the case of the mosques presented here, the space itself is not technically sacred; rather, the space enables religious practice. What's more, almost all sites serve multiple functions. They facilitate religious interaction and identity along with secular activities and identities. That approach can, in fact, be applied to many other religious projects.

With these new considerations influencing site choices, we must ask, what is the interaction between project and the surrounding landscape? The key is to quantify the complementary interaction of religious projects and the landscape.[21]

Notes

1 Bakker, 1996: 37.
2 Wilbur Zelinsky, "The Uniqueness of the American Religious Landscape," *Geographical Review*, Vol. 91, No. 3 (July, 2001): 566.
3 Bakker, 1996: 37.
4 Bakker, 1996: 37.
5 Robert A. Segal, "Theories of Religion," in *The Routledge Companion to the Study of Religion*, edited by John R. Hinnells (London and New York: Routledge, 2005): 51.
6 Segal, 2005: 51.
7 Stoddard, 1979–1980: 101.
8 Park, 2005: 439.
9 Stoddard, 1979–1980: 101.
10 Stoddard, 1979–1980: 98–100.
11 Segal argues that "sacred. . .spaces are one venue for encountering god. Religious sites. . .are built on those spots where god is believed to have appeared" (2005: 51). Clearly, this is not the case here, as many of these projects are adaptive reuse or urban infill, while the projects built in rural areas were chosen because of their beauty, but not necessarily for their *intrinsic* sacred nature.
12 Bakker, 1996: 33.
13 Douglas Allen, "Phenomenology of Religion," in *The Routledge Companion to the Study of Religion*, edited by John R. Hinnells (London and New York: Routledge, 2005): 187.
14 Bakker, 1996: 33.
15 Bakker, 1996: 33.
16 Whyte, 2006: 154.
17 Whyte, 2006: 154.
18 Bell, 1992: 31–32.
19 Whyte, 2006: 165.
20 Bakker, 1996: 33.
21 Levine, 1986: 429, 431–432.

PART 6

RETREATS

Chapter 18

hMa (Hanrahan Meyers Architects)[1]

Ms. Victoria Meyers, M.Arch, Founder and Principal

Won Dharma Center, Claverack, New York 2

The Won Dharma Center is a recreational and spiritual retreat in Claverack, New York for a Korean Buddhist school. The 500-acre site is located on a hill that looks out to the Hudson River Valley and the Catskill Mountains.

The facility includes permanent and guest residences for 24 and 80 people respectively, an administration building, and a meditation hall.

The buildings are oriented south to maximize natural light. The symbol of the Buddhist organization is an open circle, symbolizing Buddhist concepts of void without absence and infinite return. These concepts were incorporated into the design of the buildings and the walking meditation paths, which link with the site's 350-acre nature reserve.

The use of wood was requested by the clients for framing the buildings, as well as porch screens to provide solar protection and filtered lighting. Rooms are furnished in especially designed furniture in plywood and oak.

The residential and administration buildings are based on traditional grass-roofed Korean farmhouses that are loosely clustered and internally organized around central courtyards. Each courtyard building supports silent walking meditation around the inner courtyards and adjacent outdoor porches and spaces.

Ecological strategies include passive cooling from the courtyards that allow cross-ventilation. All interior lights are low-voltage fluorescent or LED. All exterior lights are solar-powered fluorescent low lighting that also emit zero light pollution. The heating and cooling system includes geo-thermal wells, a photo-voltaic array, solar thermal roof panels, and a central bio-mass boiler. The Won Buddhists have committed to harvesting only fallen trees from their nature reserve as fuel for the boiler, resulting in a zero-carbon footprint for the heat system. The buildings employ state-of-the-art construction systems, including spray-foam insulation, low-E glass insulated windows, and a radiant in-floor heating system to minimize energy costs for year-round occupancy. The entire complex is designed as a net zero-carbon footprint project.

Project is 48,000 square feet.

Completed in 2012.

Design Narrative

The project's design narrative is very clear in Ms. Meyers' mind: "The Buddhist project has to do with the idea of dislocation and edges. All these buildings will turn a dark black-brown as they age because there's no finish on them. So they will disappear into the trees because the tree bark is the same color that they will turn into." In fact, says Ms. Meyers, "We were involved in developing the ideas they had to create a compound that had a strong relationship to nature because that's part of their sect's beliefs. We encouraged them to have everything framed with FSC wood.

"Silence," she says, "is also a huge aspect of the project. The notion of silence is a really, really strong element because that references John Cage's 4 minutes and 33 seconds, which was a complete redefinition of sound. That operated at the level of everything that Marcel Duchamp did. It was a severing of how we critique sound and music. So when I see that project, I call it Absolute Zero. Because it does have silence embedded within it. It's also Absolute Zero because it has a zero carbon footprint."

Another important element of the design was the circle: "Even though we had a series of squares which were the compounds, which were the residential compounds, we made them spirals. We also increased the sense of the spiral by cracking the roofs up into these fractal shapes. As you walk around this spiral under the entry and around the courtyard, you begin to trace it more and more as a circle in your mind. So the circle is present in those spaces, although they're different from the meditation space."

Clients, Community, and Developing Design

The Buddhist retreat is located in Upstate New York and working with the community was a key element in developing the design: "The Buddhists had initially worked with an architect who was not of a very great caliber before they made a more serious shortlist. It was a crisis for them because the community told them they had to build something that was architecturally acceptable to them or they wouldn't get permission to build."

The problem was an issue of approach which dovetailed with cost: "At first the clients thought they could cut corners with the design. The result was the community was furious because the design was really horrendous. The community where the project is located in upstate New York is very sophisticated and highly educated. They also had someone on their board who is a registered architect. Their response was very negative. The client recognized they had to put together a qualitative list of people who could make a qualitative design, or else the community was not going to approve of their building."

In fact, says Ms. Meyers, this is a common problem: "If you're trying to go with someone who is really cheap and easy to work with, your neighbors might get angry because the results are so unaesthetic and unappealing that it damages the real estate value of the area. So they are going to try to prevent you from going on with your project."

There were other considerations as well: "The Buddhist community also didn't like being cut off from the surrounding communities; they want to be connected to them; they wanted to provide a retreat for people in the urban area in the Northeast.

"So after the community reacted so negatively to the first proposal, they presented our plan. Our approach was to create this very natural set of buildings, make it low to the ground and make it out of wood that would weather and would become the same color as tree bark as it did, so that the built buildings would eventually disappear."

Communication was also central to the process: "In discussing the project with the community, I referenced Swedish architect Gunnar Asplund in regards to the screens we used in front of all the buildings, including for the meditation hall. Basically, the twigs, trees, and everything around the site, those trees will be the same color as the twigs. The surrounding community was thrilled that they had an architect who even knew who Gunnar Asplund was," admits Ms. Meyers. "I think they were also intrigued by the notion of a blurred edge between the buildings and the landscape, which made a reference to an infinite eternity of time in the way the project was devised."

Symbolism

Religious symbols are a difficult element to incorporate. Often symbols are either literally interpreted or hyper-abstracted, especially if the extent of "research" is a cursory review of websites and blogposts. But with proper contextualization, symbols can offer a powerful tool in developing a meaningful design. As Ms. Meyers says, "When you deal with symbolism, you have to look to the writings each particular religious group is looking at. Because they're going to want some interpretation of that in a very respectful way in the envelope you provide for them.

"In the case of the Won Buddhists," she says, "they wanted this round circle to set the room up. So that there is a wall which obviously is a very special wall with light washing outside. That would be washed with a glow light that could also become a really strong focal point. And that's what they are looking at when they meditate. They believe that in staring at that circle that their minds are released from the everyday and they can go into this spiritual sense of meditation and find a higher purpose and a better connection to nature."

Site

Practicalities extend beyond community and client needs. Site and zoning laws shape projects as well. Ms. Meyers explains, "The project was also about zoning the site. The site is very carefully zoned with the clients for sound." In other words, "People can talk and have normal conversations in the residential building and they can talk very softly when they're walking in the pathways on the site."

There is, however, an "Edge of silence that's maintained around the outer perimeter of the meditation hall. And within the meditation hall, it's a hundred percent silence. So the only thing you hear is the bell." This effect was embedded into the design: "We installed very careful soundproofing in the doors that open to the outdoors. All the windows are triple-paned with gaskets." The result, she says, is "everything is closed, and you're in a completely silent chamber. So they have the choice of being completely silent and separated or opening the doors and hearing nature. But they also have the zone of silence around them."

Notes

1 Victoria Meyers. Interview with Sherin Wing via Skype. Los Angeles, March 18, 2014.

2 "Won Dharma Center." Accessed November 14, 2014. www.hanrahanmeyers.com/sacred_won.html

Won Dharma exterior 1

Won Dharma exterior 2

Won Dharma exterior 3

Won Dharma exterior 4

Won Dharma exterior

Won Dharma exterior

Won Dharma exterior

Won Dharma exterior

Won Dharma exterior

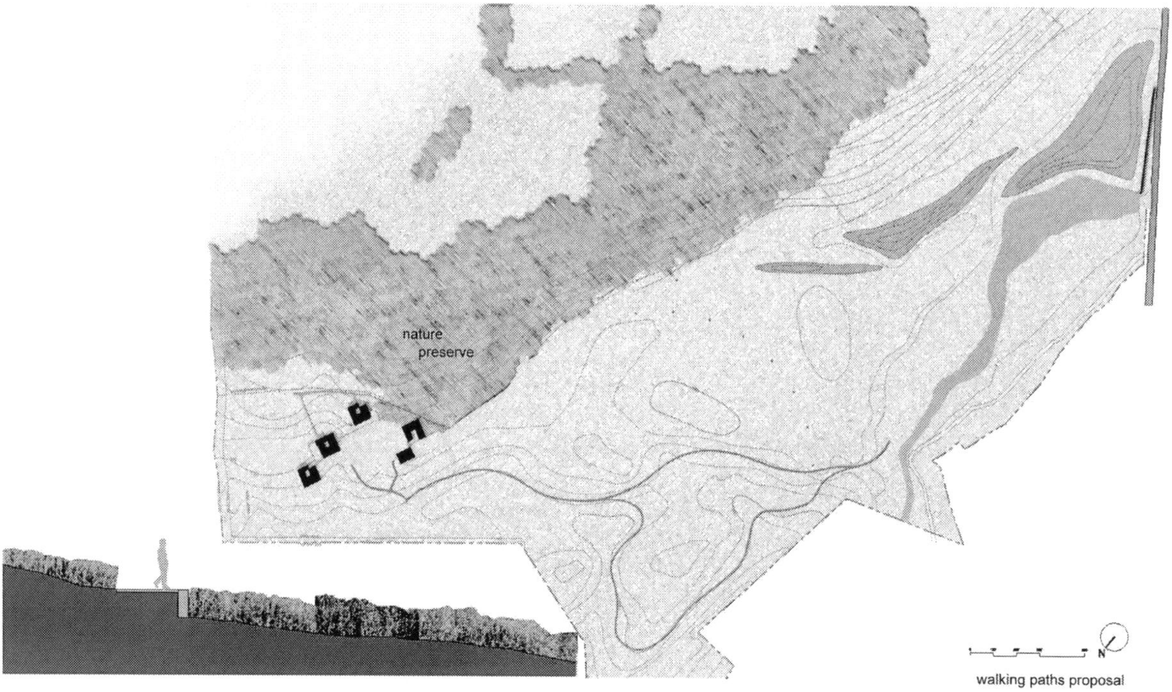
nature
preserve
N
walking paths proposal

Won Dharma landscape planting

Development Concept :

Skogskyrkogården :

trees + stones = 'infinite bleed of edge'

Buddhist retreat :

trees + screened buildings = 'infinite bleed of edge'

The natural state of the site recognized in the architecture itself.

DIAGRAM

Won Dharma infinite bleed edge diagram

prototype : 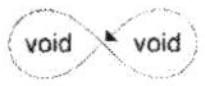

void
void

continuous loop; infinity - no edge, no end

1

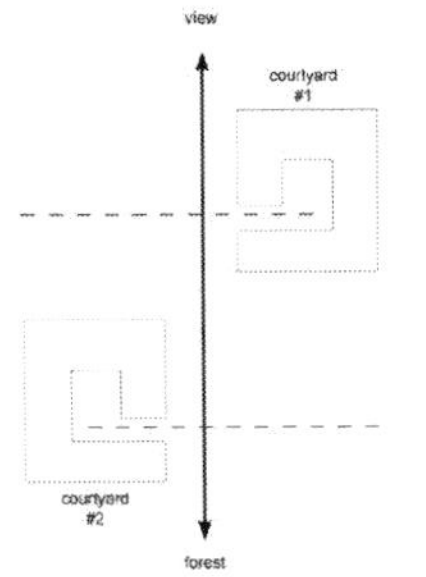

view
courtyard #1
courtyard #2
forest

broken loop = guest residence 1 + 2

2

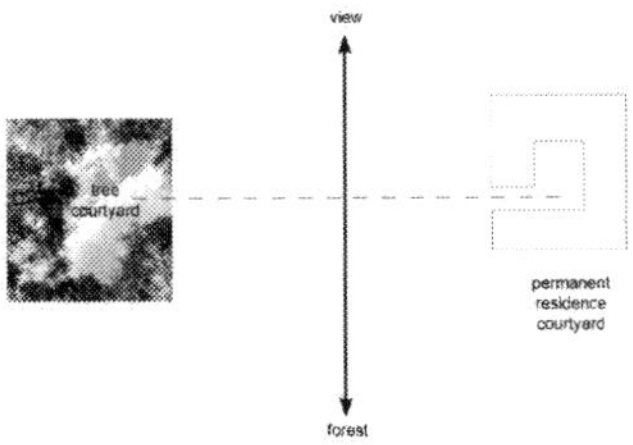

view
tree courtyard
permanent residence courtyard
forest

nature loop = permanent residence

3

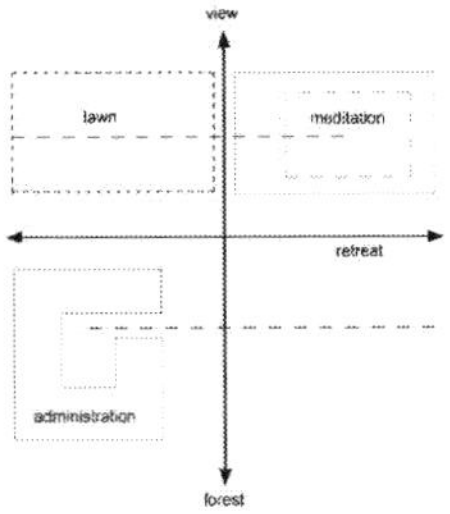

view
lawn
meditation
retreat
administration
forest

intimate void to public void = administration / meditation

Won Dharma void diagram

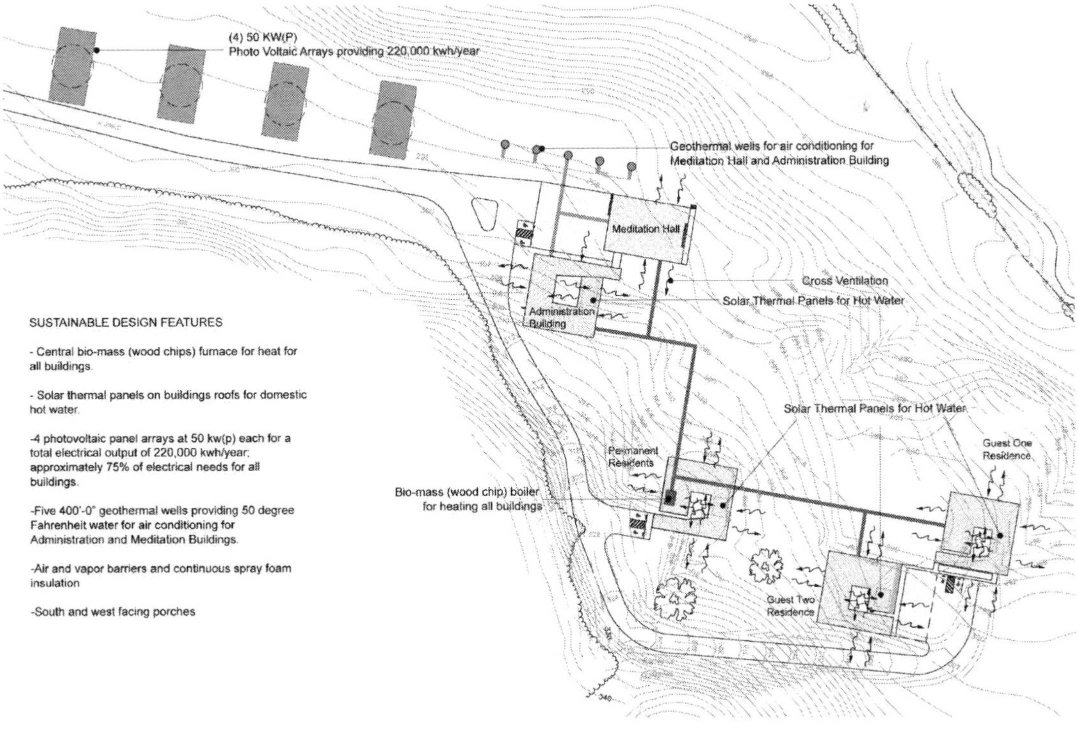

(4) 50 KW(P)
Photo Voltaic Arrays providing 220,000 kwh/year
Geothermal wells for air conditioning for Meditation Hall and Administration Building
Meditation Hall
Cross Ventilation
Solar Thermal Panels for Hot Water
Administration Building
SUSTAINABLE DESIGN FEATURES
- Central bio-mass (wood chips) furnace for heat for all buildings.
- Solar thermal panels on buildings roofs for domestic hot water.
-4 photovoltaic panel arrays at 50 kw(p) each for a total electrical output of 220,000 kwh/year; approximately 75% of electrical needs for all buildings.
-Five 400'-0" geothermal wells providing 50 degree Fahrenheit water for air conditioning for Administration and Meditation Buildings.
-Air and vapor barriers and continuous spray foam insulation
-South and west facing porches
Solar Thermal Panels for Hot Water
Guest One Residence
Permanent Residents
Bio-mass (wood chip) boiler for heating all buildings
Guest Two Residence
N

Won Dharma ecology diagram

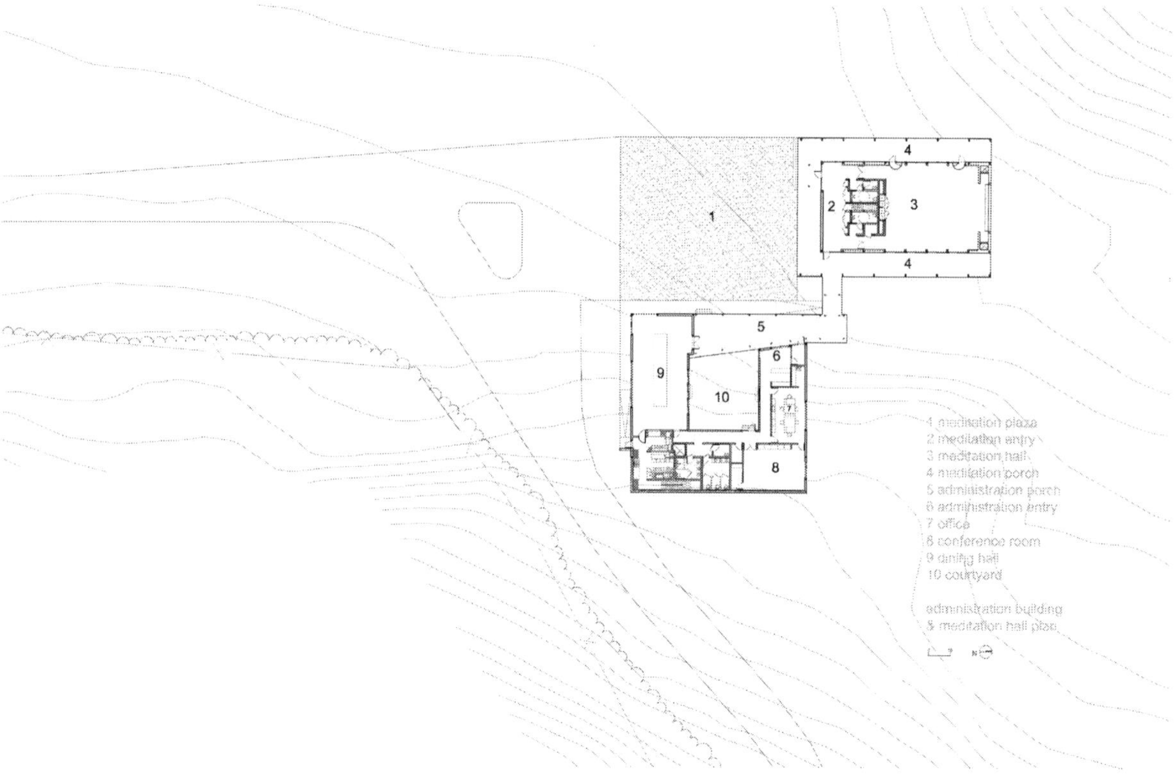
1 meditation plaza
2 meditation entry
3 meditation hall
4 meditation porch
5 administration porch
6 administration entry
7 office
8 conference room
9 dining hall
10 courtyard
administration building
& meditation hall plan

Won Dharma plan 1

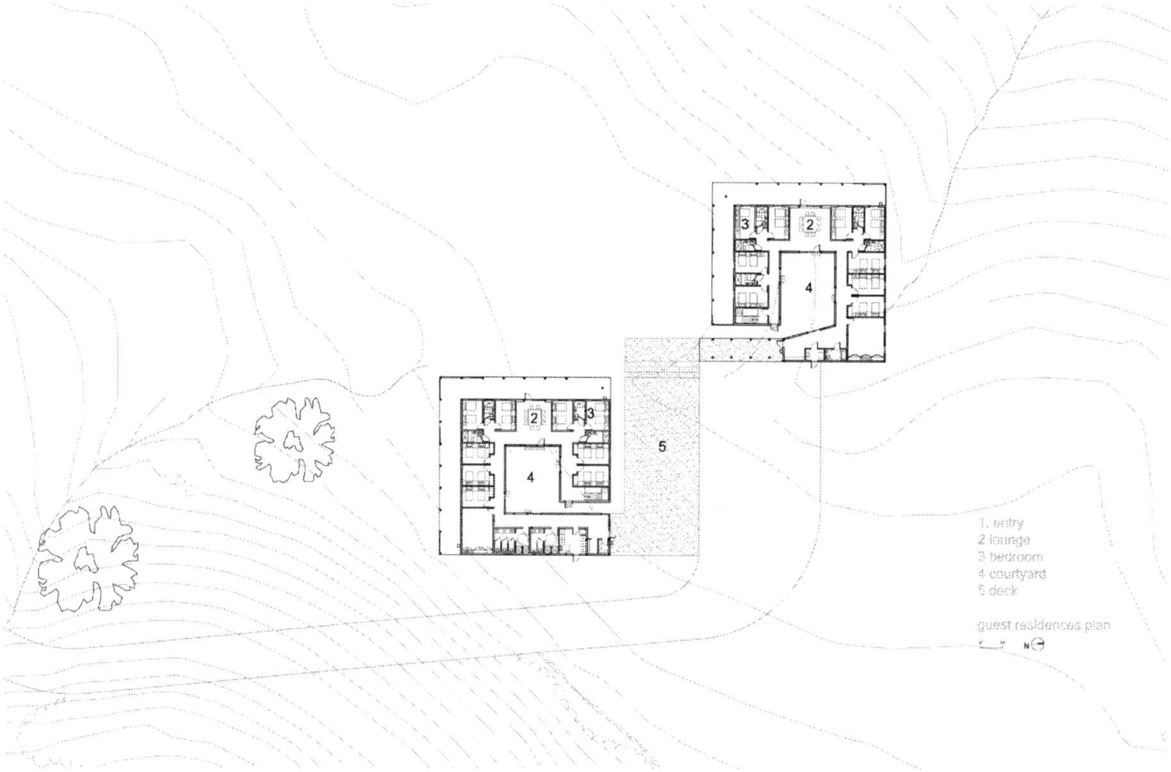
1. entry
2 lounge
3 bedroom
4 courtyard
5 deck
guest residences plan

Won Dharma plan 2

Chapter 19

Imbue Design[1]

Mr. Hunter Gunderson, Founder and Principal

Mr. Matthew Swindel, Founder and Principal

Mr. Christopher Talvy, Founder and Principal

PROJECTS

Buddhist Retreat, Torrey, Utah[2]

The project is located flush with the site. The entry deck projects horizontally over a large boulder and the sloping terrain below. The main living space functions as kitchen and living room with floor-to-ceiling, wall-to-wall views. There is also an operable glass wall.

The master bedroom angles off the main living space. There is also a guest bedroom with large views.

Exterior walls supporting the meditation deck are clad in gabion cages filled with volcanic rock found on the site and surrounding area, which helps dissipate heat in the summer. The deck is of Ipe wood. A steel standing seam rounds out the exterior materials.

Interior walls and floors are concrete, with Ipe wood cabinets and doors.

Project is 1,350 square feet.

Completed in 2012.

Olympus Cove, Salt Lake City, Utah[3]

The project is a five-bed, three-bath house with a deck and sunroom.

Materials for exterior façade is of steel standing seam panels with cedar insets. Roof is also of steel standing seam panels. Windows are wood-clad aluminum. Interior wood is walnut, with walls of painted gypsum board.

Ecological features include radiant heated floors and radiant cooled ceiling, combined additional passive heating and cooling strategies. Solar screens offset heat from floor-to-ceiling glazing.

Project is 3,570 square feet.

Completed in 2014.

Personal Retreats

Retreats can be on an institutional level or they can be more personal endeavors, designed for single users. The partners at Imbue Design embarked on two retreat projects that also served as residential homes for their clients. That said, their clients still viewed them as retreats and there were specific religious components that needed to be addressed and fulfilled.

Research

From the outset, what dictated the process was communication with the client. "It doesn't vary that much from our general practice," says Mr. Gunderson. "It begins with a very intimate conversation with the client. We ask the client for information, books, any materials they think are pertinent to the conversation. But ultimately the biggest deciding factor for a lot of the decisions came down to the client and their perceptions. That's really where a lot of our design decisions come from. Because the client perceives his/her religion in a very specific way and pinpoints the aspects of the religion that reflect him/her. For example, if you were to look at the Buddhist retreat, there are some people who are Buddhist and say, 'Well, this isn't Buddhist at all because of these certain elements.' Yet it is ultimately an interpretive process."

For the partners of Imbue, the process also included meeting a religious leader. Mr. Gunderson continues, "Our client introduced us to the Rimpoche who happens to be the US representative from Tibet. We talked to him and interviewed him to gain a better understanding. We also read a lot of books, some of which the client gave us."

The conditions and requirements of the Buddhist Retreat differ sharply from the Olympus Cove project. "We asked him about the religious elements and one thing the client wanted was, as you walk through the entry, a statue of Vishnu who is the guardian of the house standing at the entry. The client also wanted a special outdoor moment with running water that had religious significance."

Adds Mr. Talvy, "The running water in the backyard is one of the more spiritual places in the house which was very unique and driven by the client seeking that moment in architecture."

Site

Both of the projects by Imbue were located in relatively lightly populated areas. For the Buddhist retreat, "Capturing views leads to that spiritual experience," says Mr. Talvy. "We tried to offer our client a lot more from this landscape by framing views and adding to the intensity of the experience in a positive way."

Mr. Gunderson agrees, "The site down there is a very spiritual site and that isn't necessarily a religious thing. There's a spirituality to that site. We wanted to take advantage of it through not just views but by making these strong connections to the landscape."

This was achieved on several different levels—the site in its entirety as well as individual aspects of it: "In addition to the amazing juniper trees, there were great boulders which became part of the design. For the client especially, it really came down to these amazing views."

Continues Mr. Gunderson, "You just listen to the client and she would talk about how you'd have this view outward. And again this really came down to where she would place her prayer flags and things like that. Where she was most interested in and what she thought was the most sacred.

"For example, there's a window where you can't see anything except what's immediately outside the space. So some of windows were framed views. Some views had these old twisted juniper trees, others had sweeping views. Our goal was to make each action that occurs within the space its own special moment, its own sacred moment even though it's also an everyday moment."

The site is also relatively rural. "We were kind of lucky too," admits Mr. Swindel, "because these views were unobstructed. There isn't much development around and its very pastoral. This valley with grazing pasture below, but no development. Because it was fairly rural, we were able to maximize the views the client wanted to capture."

For the Olympus Cove project, the site was unique in that, "There's the dichotomy of the city from one perspective and nature from the other," explains Mr. Swindel. "You basically turn 180 degrees and you cancel out the city view and instead you have a mountain view. It's a pretty prominent mountain in Salt Lake called Mount Olympus and the neighborhood is called Olympus Cove." So, once more, "it came down to views. The client wanted just very particular, small, discrete, more poignant and direct moments rather than having the entire space be sacred. In that way, it made those sacred moments even more significant because not everything is."

Materials

Each partner in the firm has his own sensibility regarding materials. These are deployed independently as they develop their own proposals for each client. Mr. Talvy explains, "We approach materials independently as the project develops. We love natural materials and how they reflect the site or perhaps a client loves a particular material that we can incorporate."

Mr. Gunderson agrees, "Materials are interesting because they have so much intrinsic character to them. So if someone says, 'If I put wood in here, it will warm it up,' they're talking about the quality of the material itself. If you touch wood, it feels warm, and not because the wood itself is warm but it acts as an insulator and so it reflects your own heat, whereas you put your hand on steel and it will suck the heat right out of your hand. So it feels cold. Then there's concrete, which inherently is mass, and you can make really light concrete structures, but it always reads as mass because it's always a monolith that reads dense, thick and heavy."

Given this, he says, "As you go to project, you want to take the ideas of the qualities of the materials and then you want to see what the relationship of those materials are to your intent and the site. For example, we were able to use rock found on the site in various ways."

"It was an obvious choice," says Mr. Talvy, "because there is this very beautiful volcanic rock on the site, throughout the landscape."

Mr. Gunderson continues, "For one it ties directly to the site and adds a very strong component to the site. It also allows it to blend into the site. So using rock harmonizes with the site. It also creates a mass and heaviness while also making the solid base the deck rests on."

Using rock common to the site has a functional purpose: "It acts as a barrier: a rainscreen. It also acts like a radiator during the cold season; it absorbs the sun in the daytime and radiates that into the house and expels it back into the environment at night. In terms of design, the characteristics of the rock contrasted well with other design elements."

Adds Mr. Gunderson, "By its nature it's very raw, but we also used a standing seam which is not raw at all and it functions as a counterpoint that draws attention to its opposite. So that raw nature really stands out when you juxtapose it with something sleeker."

On Work

The partners at Imbue established their relationship during graduate school and that style of work has continued to this day. "We have three partners," says Mr. Gunderson, "and for each project, we create individual proposals for the clients by each taking our own direction. Specifically, and very deliberately, we vary those directions. So we see maybe that I'm going down the same path as Talvy, I'll diverge and I'll go a different direction. The reason we do that is because it gives a broader spectrum. Then we let the client see that entire spectrum we've created, we're better able to pinpoint where the clients land in that spectrum. So that way it becomes much more specific to them. If we just brought them one proposal and then they told us what they did or didn't like about it, that leaves a lot wide open. But if we give them three options, we can start to really triangulate between the three to figure out where they land in the universe."

Mr. Talvy elaborates, "As we're going through design development, certain ideas will surface and become better than others. And in design, we talk so formally about it and that might be a bit of a problem with it. Design should be a little more informal and it should be personal and not so serious all the time. Most architects are very strict and there's a reason for this and a reason for that and we do this and we do that and then when it comes down to it, you should have a more informal conversation with your clients and informal experiences with the site and work through the process and allow it to come to its own being."

This approach shifts their relationship with their clients: "We try to become involved in their lives as much as we can without being intrusive and balancing friendship with professionalism," he says. "We've camped with our clients, they've invited us to special moments in their lives, whether it's a house blessing or a baby shower."

Mr. Swindel jokes, "And to make sure we're involved, we have it in our contract that they have to hold a party after the house construction and the certificate of occupancy is a wine and cheese party."

"But in seriousness," says Mr. Gunderson, "it's a fun relationship we get to have and we're friends with our clients."

Rituals

Religious buildings, whether they are institutional or personal, often require rituals to sanctify both projects and the site. The partners at Imbue were fortunate enough to participate in their clients' rituals first hand. Says Mr. Gunderson, "The rituals for both projects occurred almost within two weeks of each other."

The rituals, however, occur at different times. They attended the Buddhist ceremony first. Explains Mr. Gunderson, "The Tibetan Buddhist ceremony occurred after everything was completed. There were a couple of rituals that happened along the way. There was a blessing of a capsule that was placed at the hearth of the home before the construction. But the blessing that happened after was the main ceremony."

Mr. Swindel elaborates, "They blessed each space. It occurred in each space and then you turned toward the four cardinal directions and said a blessing for each direction. And the Rimpoche did that in each room of the house. The client then circumambulated the perimeter of the walls while the priest was saying a prayer. That was one way we were involved. It was interesting that we were witnesses to both of these events as a way of being included in the ceremony."

The sequence of events was exactly opposite for the Olympic Cove project. "For Olympus Cove, the Hindi ceremony occurred prior to construction," he explains. "Given the intention of the building, that the clients had thought a lot about it, that they had given us so much information about what they wanted, and that we had thought about it, the building already spiritually existed. Blessing the land and the spiritual building was necessary so that when the actual construction began, it would happen in a way that was pleasing to the gods and that was appropriate and that would be safe for the family."

Specifically, "They had to appease all these gods," Mr. Gunderson says. "For example, if you're Hindi, you wouldn't use iron instruments to dig or pierce the earth. Because we were going to use metal to really pierce the earth, we had to ask for forgiveness and we had to ask for permission so that everything would be okay. We also had to make offerings to different gods, those who were benevolent as well as those who were opposed. You want to make sure they're all appeased so when you build this thing, everybody is satisfied."

Attending these ceremonies were a gesture of respect to the clients, one that reaffirmed their close working relationship. "I don't think it would have bothered them too much if we had wanted to bow out and not be there," says Mr. Gunderson. "But from our point of view, I think that it is important to the clients. I also think it's important for people who are fundamentally involved in the creation of the home to be involved in these ceremonies that are so sacred to clients and that make their home a sacred space."

Secular and Religious Projects

There is a clear difference between working on secular and religious projects. Programmatically, there is often a hierarchy that must remain intact, whereas with secular projects that program is not necessarily rigidly assigned using a value-based hierarchy. There are other differences, too, notably how designers approach designing religious spaces. Mr. Gunderson observes that, "the process can be a little more direct with a client in a religious project. There are a lot more specifics of what they need in that spiritual space, as opposed to someone who isn't working with a religious space.

"We had a professor who always asked us, 'Where do I cry?' In other words, where do clients feel and where can they have the emptiness to allow them to feel. We're always searching for that moment," says Mr. Gunderson. In other words, where do the clients feel safe enough to express themselves completely. To create such a space requires an understanding of what the client's needs are. Mr. Swindel explains, "To put it simply, it's about building a home that's specifically for them because the homes they have lived in before aren't working for them in the way they need.

"I think that's what a lot of traditional homes don't do very well, give you that moment where there is, in Buddhist terms, emptiness," says Mr. Gunderson. "Everything is often so packed with function that we forget there is a space between function and spirituality which is that emptiness. I think that's where we find these moments in every home though we probably wouldn't describe it that way to every client. There is a very particular moment or two or three that really sets it apart for the client whether it's a view or a space where something happens or a room, and it could be anything. A lot of times that just comes from the site or the client. But in architecture where you're dealing with someone who has a religious or very specific spiritual elements they're looking for, it is drawn from them personally. It's more direct."

"Yes," agrees Mr. Talvy, "it's a process of self-discovery." Toward that end, Mr. Swindel says, "We always ask them how do they live, how do they want to live. What are the spaces they need to facilitate their lives."

Adds Mr. Gunderson, "We also ask what are their hobbies, what are their fears. We're not trying to be deep or random, but the more information we can get from them, the easier it is for us to understand what it is that makes their minds tick and make the space work for them."

Notes

1 Hunter Gunderson, Matt Swindel, and Christopher Talvy. Interview with Sherin Wing via Skype. Los Angeles, December 13, 2013.

2 "Buddhist Retreat." Project description emailed to author December 15, 2014.

3 "Olympus Cove." Project description emailed to author December 15, 2014.

Buddhist Retreat breezeway

Buddhist Retreat north side, night

Buddhist Retreat entry stairs

Buddhist Retreat north volume

Buddhist Retreat pre-dawn deck

Buddhist Retreat site plan

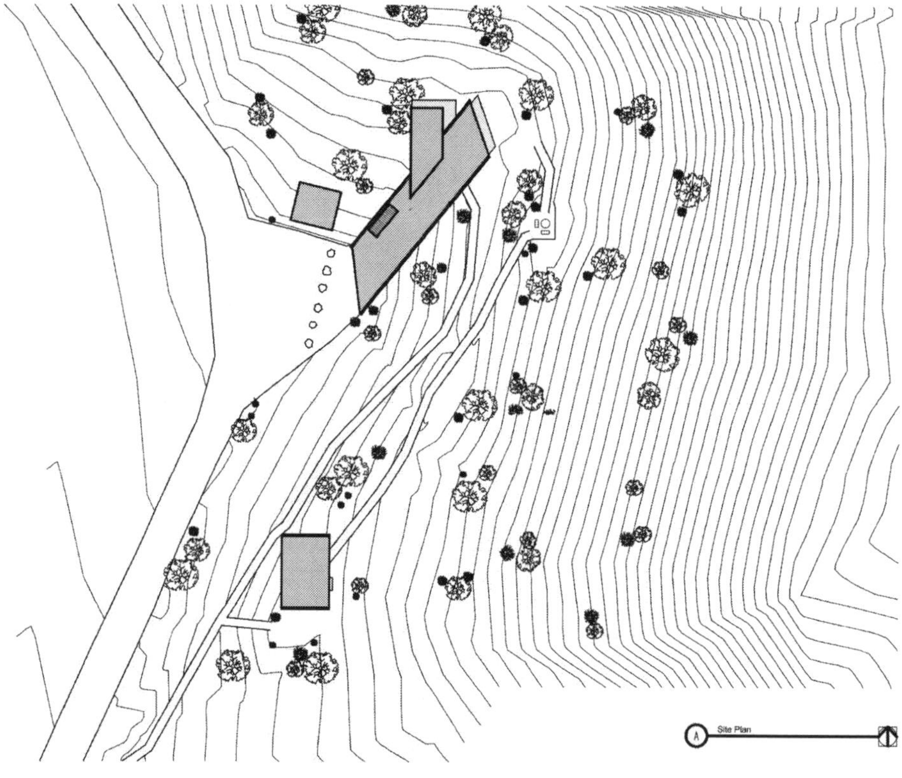
A
Site Plan

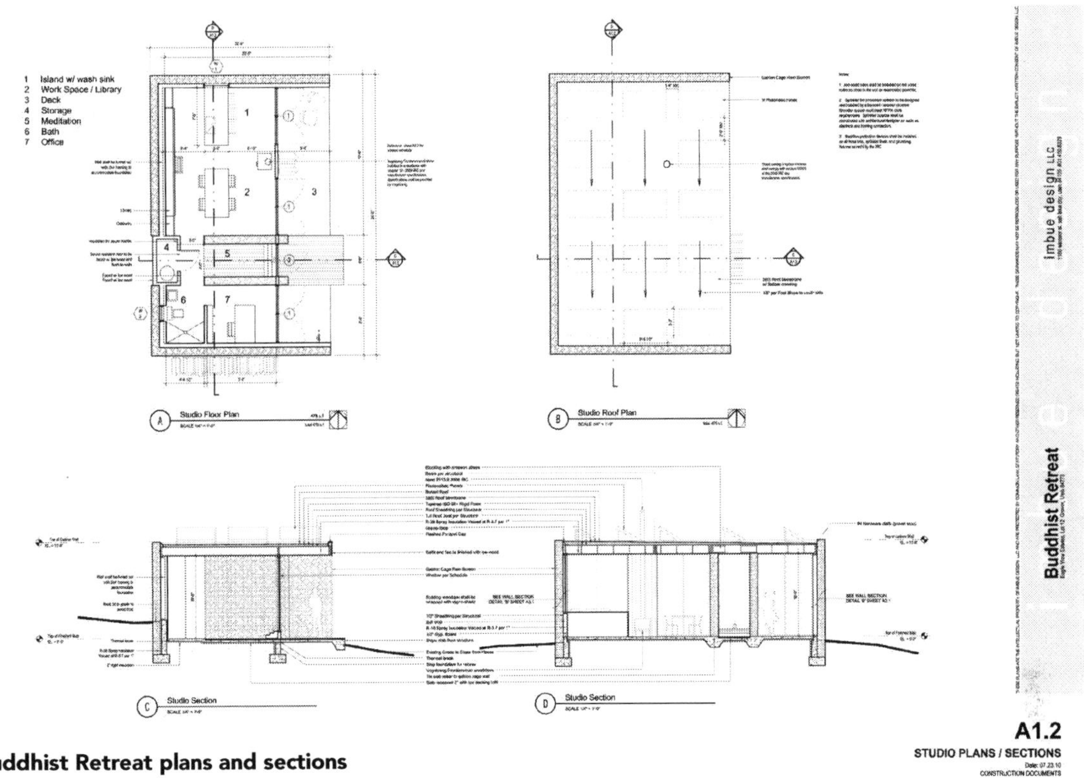
1 Island w/ wash sink
2 Work Space / Library
3 Deck
4 Storage
5 Meditation
6 Bath
7 Office
Studio Floor Plan
Studio Roof Plan
Studio Section
Studio Section
Buddhist Retreat
imbue design LLC
A1.2
STUDIO PLANS / SECTIONS
CONSTRUCTION DOCUMENTS

Buddhist Retreat plans and sections

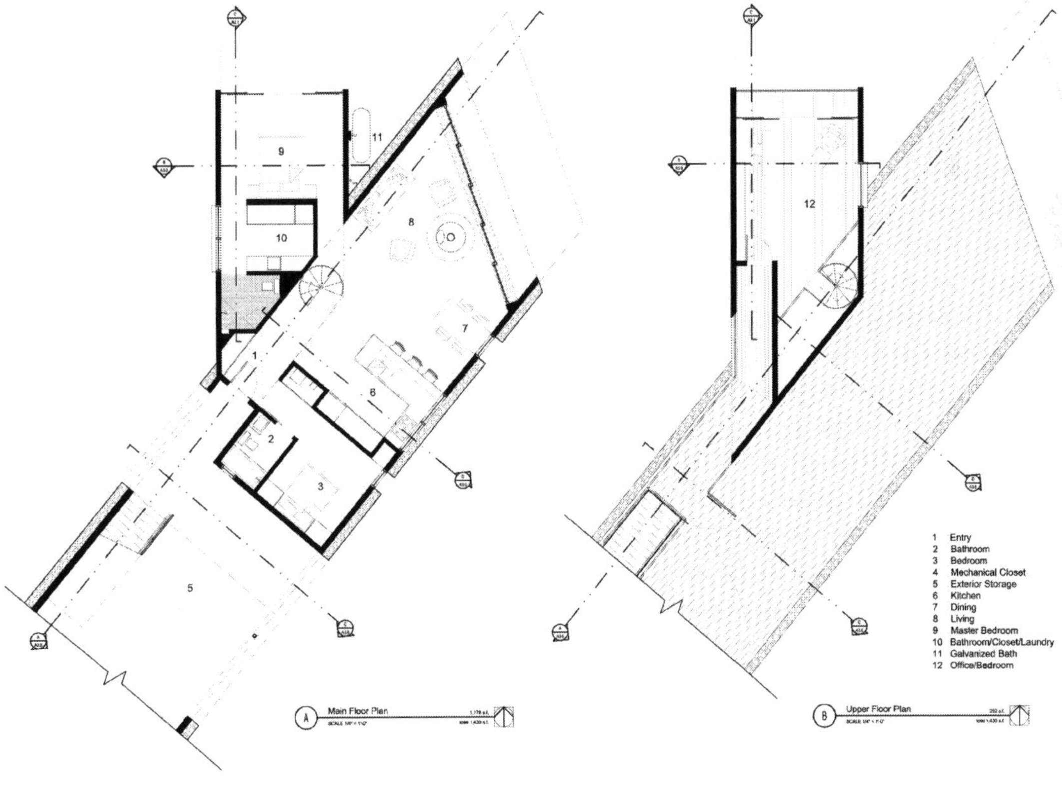
1 Entry
2 Bathroom
3 Bedroom
4 Mechanical Closet
5 Exterior Storage
6 Kitchen
7 Dining
8 Living
9 Master Bedroom
10 Bathroom/Closet/Laundry
11 Galvanized Bath
12 Office/Bedroom
Main Floor Plan
Upper Floor Plan

Buddhist Retreat floor plans

Mt. Olympus conservatory rendering

4486

Mt. Olympus front elevation

Mt. Olympus rear exterior

Mt. Olympus screen stairs interior rendering

Justin
Bieber

Mt. Olympus interior rendering

Chapter 20

Roto Architects[1]

Mr. Michael Rotondi, FAIA, Founder and Principal

On Reading, Religious Practice, and Design

For Mr. Rotondi, designing retreats has incorporated personal experience with his skills as an architect and his principles and beliefs about humanity. He says, "I started reading a lot about mostly American Indians and started making pilgrimages to Indian country and reading the creation stories in the places that were described. I do this when working on projects, to become embedded in the place that was being described. So I spent a lot of time with American Indians and that led to Eastern religion and philosophy. At the same time I began to think how to integrate it with the stuff I grew up with. So I read a lot of Thomas Merton. And then I began working with American Indians in South Dakota. I was going back and forth for six years working on projects and spending time sitting with the elders.

"After that," says Mr. Rotondi, "I worked with an American Buddhist group in Barre, Massachusetts for a couple of years. I would also practice," he says. "I practiced all through that period in a more formal way. But vipaśyanā is somewhere between formal and informal practice. It's really a meditation practice so I took to that. I also began spending time with Tibetan Buddhists for six to seven years.

"Taking projects like that on is also an opportunity to spend time with the lamas," Mr. Rotondi explains. "I was practicing so I could know in a more intimate way what needed to be designed." He continues, "There are things we can extrapolate from a number of other experiences and recombine them. As architects, to design things, design houses, I mean whatever we design, we're really good at recombining things. But there are some things you have to experience first hand, like religious practice.

"I was surprised," he admits. "The first time I did a retreat I spent two weeks with a hundred other people. It became really evident that I was in solitude while I was in community. I'd never had that experience before. I may know what it's like to move through a crowd and have nobody talk to you, but to consciously be in solitude and community at the same time was an unusual experience and a new thought for me."

Religious Experience and the Design Process

The insights garnered from personal religious practice changed Mr. Rotondi's approach to designing such spaces: "I began to understand that that's what meditation is really about. Going to a place to meditate is like going to the gym: you work out, you build your muscles, and you use your muscles in the world. You're supposed to get really good at meditation so you take it into the world and you reach high states of concentration when you're driving, when you're talking to another person, when you're giving a lecture, you're drawing, whatever it is, you can be in solitude and community wherever you are."

Mr. Rotondi clarifies further, "You don't have to go to the mountaintop to reach that state anymore. That was a big revelation. And the conversation I had afterwards, the guy I was working with was pleased that I figured that out so quickly, and that's exactly what the design problem is, which is also at the heart of spiritual practice. It's not that you turn it on and off, you try to stay in that state of being all of the time.

"I've focused on creating spaces that bring your mind to rest and invigorate your body. These trigger the deepest intelligence of all which allows you to make contact with everything that exists. And that can happen through meditation or prayer."

On People, Listening, and Design

"I love people," says Mr. Rotondi. "I love listening to their stories. You get a lot more information from people when you ask questions to listen and not turn everything into your own story. Like you listen and say oh, that reminds me of the time, and you're off talking about yourself. If you really want to learn, that's the last thing you want to do is talk about yourself. You want to listen to what other people to say. There's times you have to talk about yourself. But I find I learn a lot from listening to other people. A whole lot, actually.

"So you have the creation stories, the myth, which is a story, you have the ritual, and then the space. The myth is basically the big story, the ritual we can say is the program, and the space is the medium for the body, either moving or at rest. The practical problem to solve in meditation space is making it as quiet as possible, making the architecture as quiet as possible. The architecture has to come to rest if you want the mind to come to rest. And the architecture has to be, doesn't have to be, but it's best if it's holding you to the ground as opposed to ascension. Ascension is a Christian thing. In meditation, it's not about ascension, it's about groundedness.

You don't want compression, so then the question can be, how low can this space be and how high can this space be.

"When I was working with American Indians, the elders made it clear that I was there to listen to their stories and convert their stories into buildings. And the objective wasn't even the buildings, it was to help them rebuild their nation. That was kind of shocking to hear at first because it seemed too big a task. I was up there to do some building and didn't think there was anything that I could. That puts it into the biggest context."

This basic faith and respect for people directly informs Mr. Rotondi's philosophical approach. Quite simply, he says, "The first thing is to stop thinking about designing a signature architecture. Instead, I try to listen with my own body, with whomever I'm working with. Then I try to jump over my own shadow when I'm designing. So I don't repeat myself."

In a larger context, Mr. Rotondi believes that "the role of humans in the universe, because we can think about things and because of the consciousness that we have, is to push back against entropy. Which is where everything becomes the same. Humans are not only responsive and adaptive, we're also constructive. We make things. We're constructive, not just adaptive. Which means we have an effect on the environment we live in. We shouldn't apologize for reconstructing the world *if* we're doing it in a way that nurtures the world and how it grows. And that can be how we construct the artificial world for humans to inhabit as well as how the artificial world interfaces with the natural world. Instead of stopping nature in its tracks is there a way to enhance it or amplify it? In turn, it's not only just a nice thing to do for nature, it allows us to stay around a little bit longer."

Note

1 Michael Rotondi. Interviews with Sherin Wing via phone and Skype, respectively. Los Angeles, October 18, 2012 and November 22, 2014.

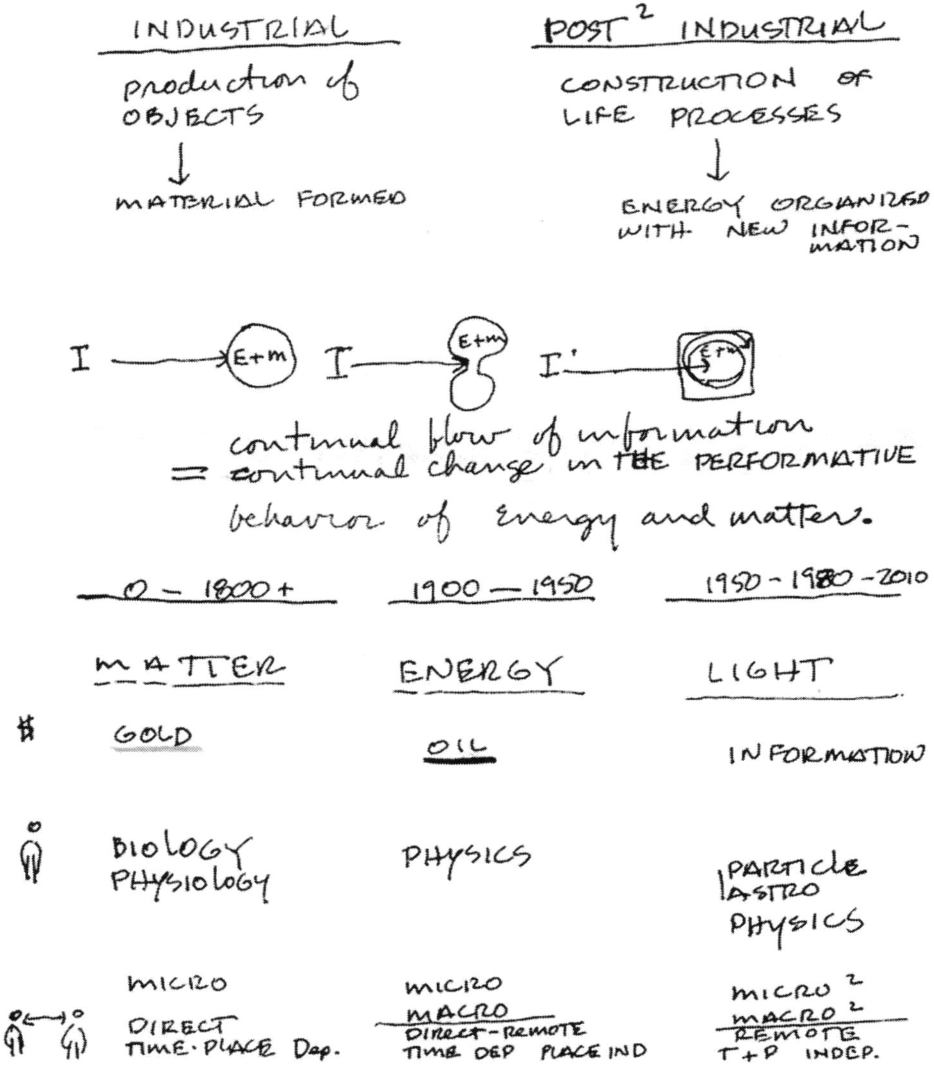
INDUSTRIAL
production of OBJECTS
MATERIAL FORMED
POST 2 INDUSTRIAL
CONSTRUCTION OF LIFE PROCESSES
ENERGY ORGANIZED WITH NEW INFORMATION
I
E+m
I
E+m
I'
E+m
continual flow of information
= continual change in THE PERFORMATIVE behavior of energy and matter.
0 – 1800+
1900 — 1950
1950 - 1980 - 2010
MATTER
ENERGY
LIGHT
$
GOLD
OIL
INFORMATION
BIOLOGY PHYSIOLOGY
PHYSICS
PARTICLE ASTRO PHYSICS
MICRO
DIRECT TIME·PLACE Dep.
MICRO MACRO
DIRECT-REMOTE TIME DEP PLACE IND
MICRO 2 MACRO 2
REMOTE T+P INDEP.

Conceptual thinking, love/fear

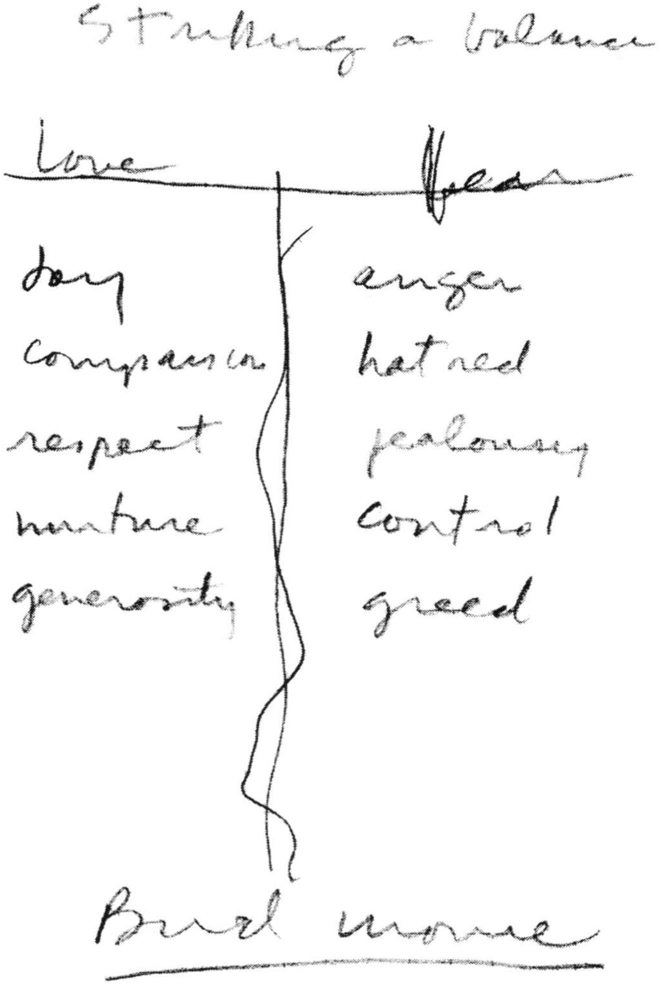
Striking a balance
love
fear
joy
compassion
respect
nurture
generosity
anger
hatred
jealousy
control
greed

Conceptual thinking, energy/currency

Meditation sketch 1

Meditation sketch 2

100000 Stūpas project

100000 Stūpas project

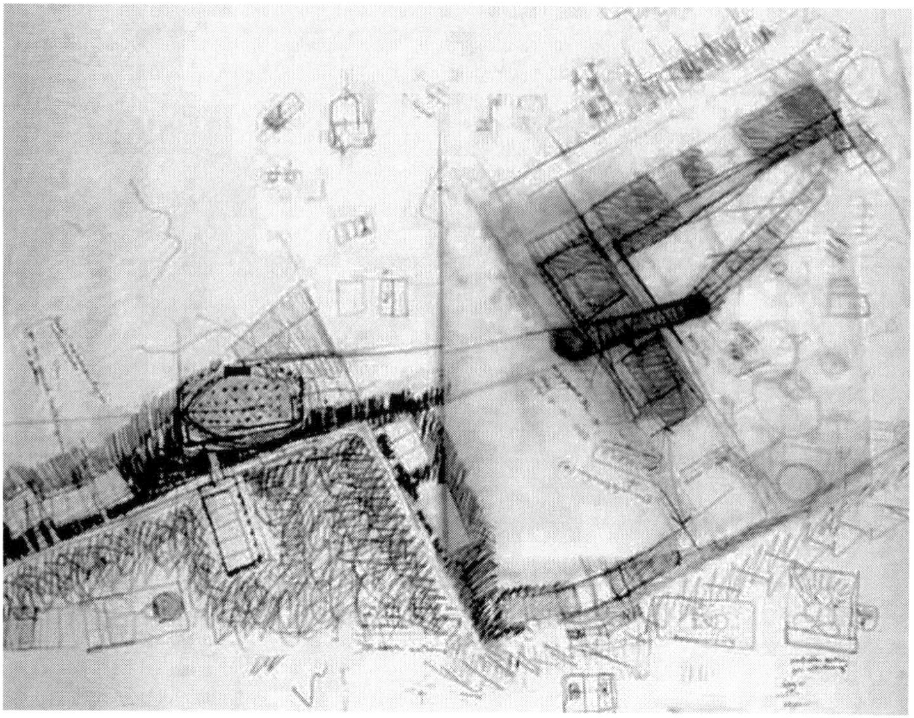

Forest Refuge barre ma sketch

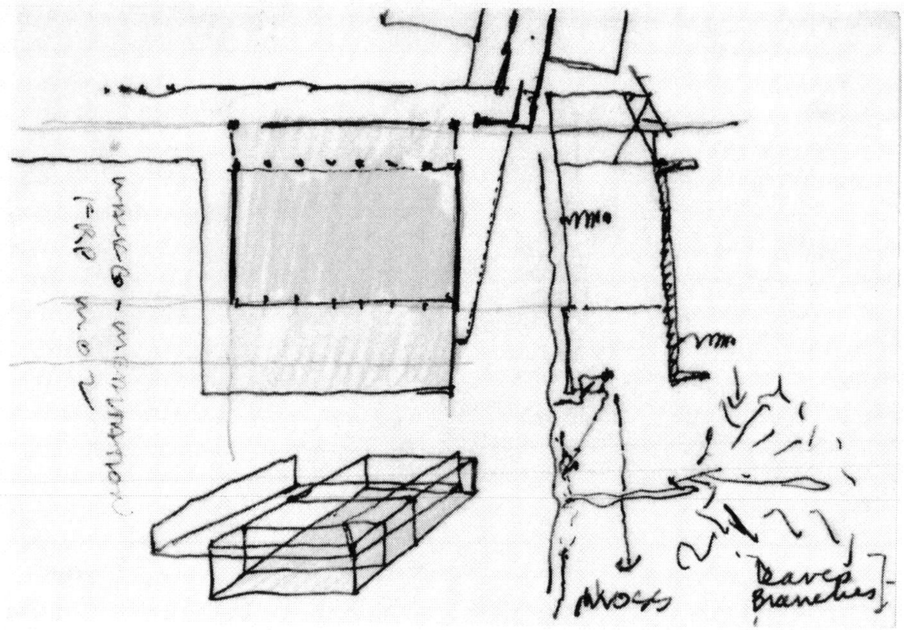
MOSS
Leaves
Branches

Forest Refuge project

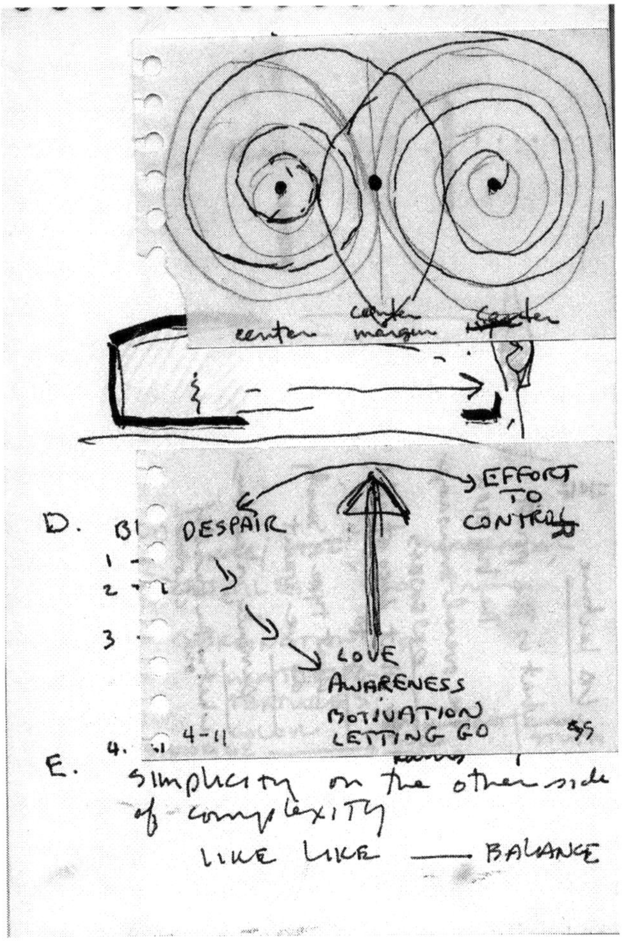
center
center margin
center
D.
DESPAIR
EFFORT TO CONTROL
LOVE
AWARENESS
MOTIVATION
LETTING GO
4-11
E.
simplicity on the other side of complexity
LIKE LIKE — BALANCE

Forest Refuge project, concept 2

meditation
Dining
DINING

Forest Refuge project barre ma

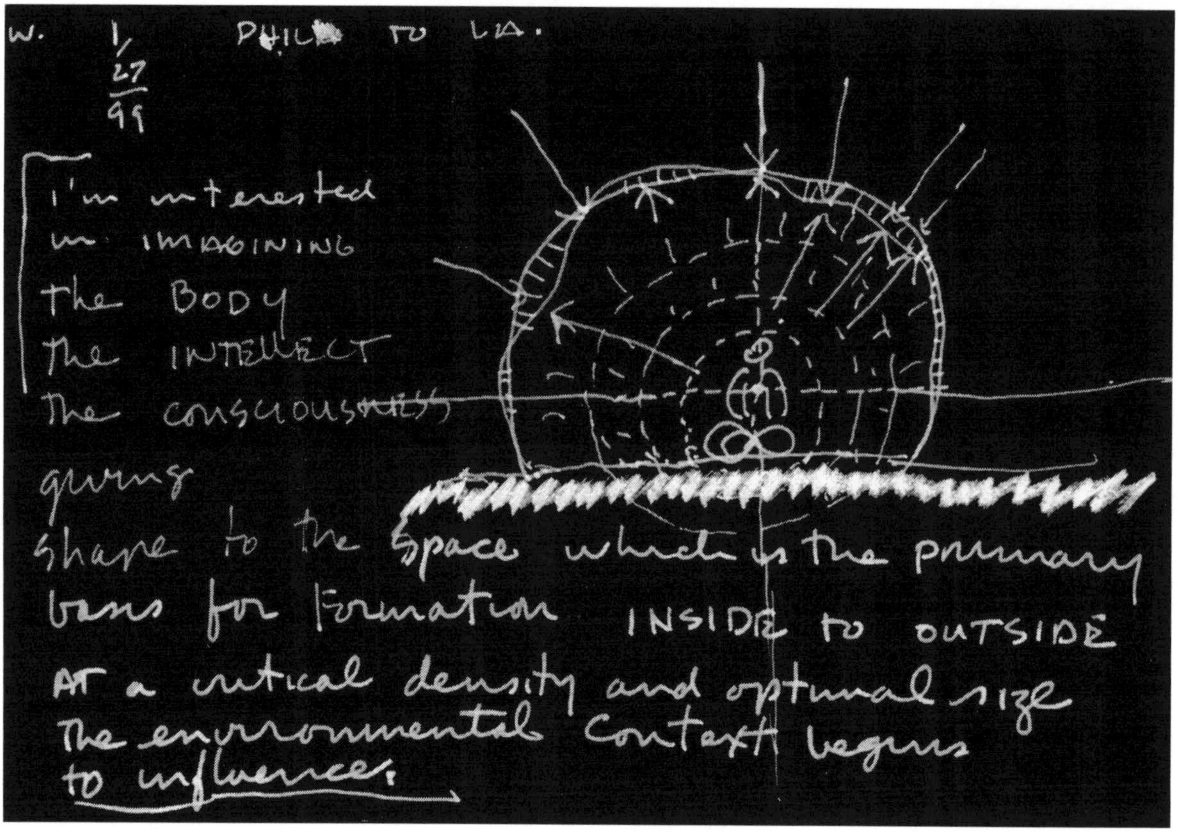
W. 1/27/99 PHIL TO LA.
I'm interested in IMAGINING
The BODY
The INTELLECT
The CONSCIOUSNESS
giving
shape to the space which is the primary basis for Formation
INSIDE TO OUTSIDE
At a critical density and optimal size The environmental context begins to influence.

Forest Refuge project barre ma concept

Miracle Manor Retreat, Color is Space 2

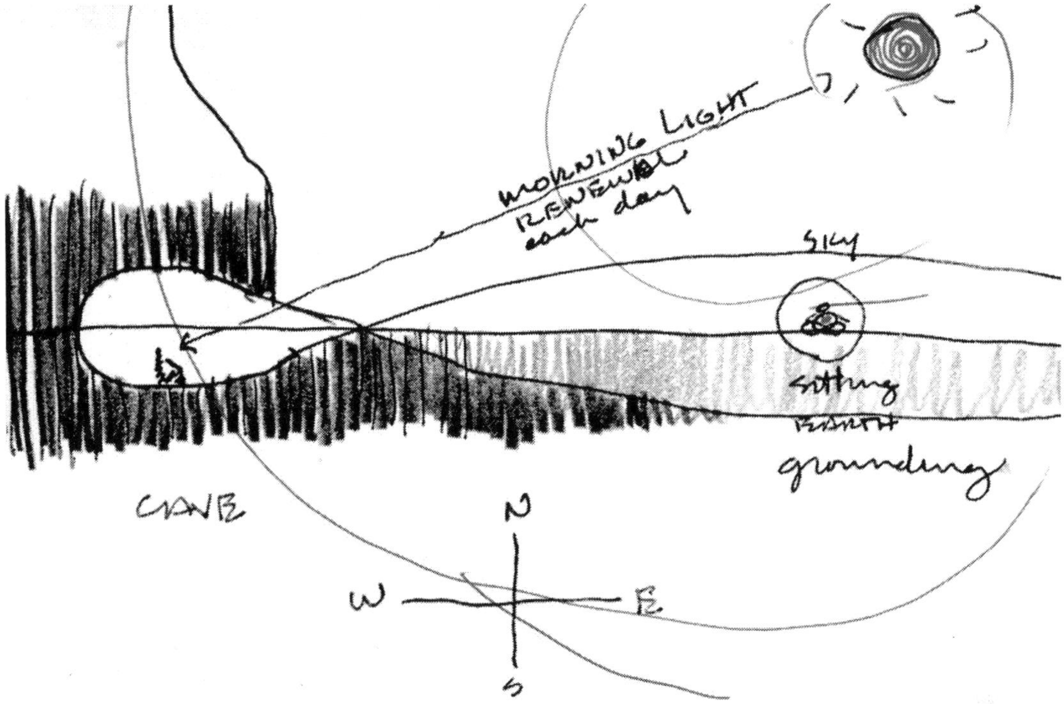
MORNING LIGHT
RENEWAL
each day
SKY
sitting
grounding
CAVE
N
W
E
S

Conceptual thinking mediation drawing

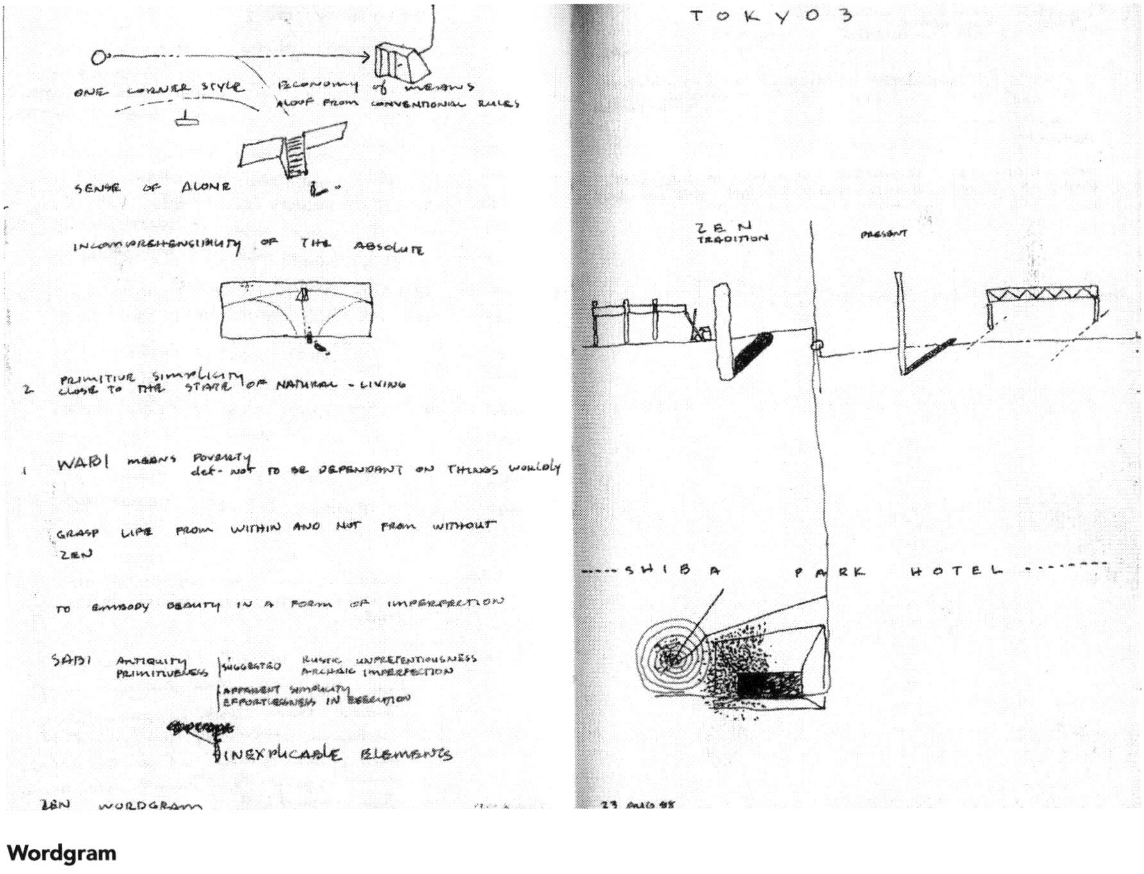
ONE CORNER STYLE
ECONOMY of MEANS
ALOOF FROM CONVENTIONAL RULES
SENSE OF ALONE
INCOMPREHENSIBILITY OF THE ABSOLUTE
2 PRIMITIVE SIMPLICITY
CLOSE TO THE STATE OF NATURAL - LIVING
1 WABI MEANS POVERTY
def- NOT TO BE DEPENDANT ON THINGS WORLDLY
GRASP LIFE FROM WITHIN AND NOT FROM WITHOUT
ZEN
TO EMBODY BEAUTY IN A FORM OF IMPERFECTION
SABI ANTIQUITY
PRIMITIVENESS
SUGGESTED
RUSTIC UNPRETENTIOUSNESS
ARCHAIC IMPERFECTION
APPARENT SIMPLICITY
EFFORTLESSNESS IN EXECUTION
INEXPLICABLE ELEMENTS
ZEN WORDGRAM
TOKYO 3
ZEN
TRADITION
PRESENT
SHIBA PARK HOTEL
23 AUG 98

Wordgram

PART 7

UNDERSTANDING RELIGIONS THROUGH ARCHITECTURE

Chapter 21

Religious Traditions, an Overview in Architecture

How does one design religious projects when one is unfamiliar with the religious culture? What is the approach? How does one perform research, and what sources should one rely on?

The answer is, in a sense, simple. Information for designs should rely on multiple, rigorous sources. Yet while innumerable academic research has been performed on the religions featured in this book, the web still offers people their first and most convenient source of information.

Convenience and ubiquity, however, do not guarantee accuracy or rigor. In fact, most web sources are biased opinions written by amateurs who merely repeat what they have found elsewhere on the web. Their main method of writing is to use personal realizations or biases or to copy other websites. Indeed, if one looks on the web for any content, from religions to medical conditions, one finds that long paragraphs are copied wholesale, without citation, from one site to another.

Many untrained in critical thinking assume, for example, that all cultures share the same basic "truths"—they just manifest differently.[1] In other words, universal religious "essences" exist, it is simply that they are expressed differently. The real truth is that generalizations make everything appear superficially similar.[2] Universalizations are specific to no one and are dismissive of the contours that make people and the cultures they produce unique by flattening all cultures.

Not coincidentally, this flattening often favors Euro/American cultures. In other words, Western intellectual and architectural narcissism views inherent cultural differences as only surface manifestations of a basic sameness, defined in Euro/American terminology.[3] At their core, universalities and metanarratives "dominate and repress; [they] impose the ethnocentric same on the different," in a way that privileges Euro-androcentricity as the standard against which all else is evaluated.[4] These perpetuated generalizations are too often based on colonialist or missionary agendas foregrounded by "Christian theological assumptions."[5]

Conflating modest religious structures with a "simple" religious system or tradition exemplifies the problem with universalizations. It is frequently assumed that uncomplicated, or even stark religious projects reflect simplistic, *indigenous,* religious traditions, no matter what region of the world is being discussed.

Foregrounding this assumption is often the unspoken comparison with a Christian church or monastery that is hundreds of years old. Conversely, the comparison may be with a recent religious project designed by a famous architect. Yet neither are representative of most religious architecture.

First, not all religious structures are designed by professional architects. What's more, streamlined, unadorned architecture may be an aesthetic choice, whether or not a professional architect is involved. Finally, straightforward projects can indicate the amount of disposable income a religious community has. For those with less money, less elaborate structures are simply a matter of financial practicality. Again, this may or may not involve a professional architect.

In fact, an overlooked factor is that more complex religious projects often accompany the accumulated wealth of a community.[6] It is a simple formula of construction and maintenance: communities with more disposable income have relatively high construction and maintenance costs for their buildings while those with less income have relatively lesser construction and maintenance costs.[7]

Perhaps one impulse toward universal theories stems from the need to relate to different peoples and cultures. Seeking shared commonalities presumably facilitates understanding. By rendering what appear to be fundamentally different and threatening conditions into non-threatening "realities," people are comforted and become less scared. And there are certain basic universalizations people accept, such as the rejection of torture and murder, even when they are presumably justified by war or in the name of national security.

Yet "we cannot assume a common human nature across which categories such as religion and experiences of the sacred are shared."[8] Catholic practitioners, for example, will doubtless assert that their doctrinal and liturgical traditions are fundamentally dissimilar to those practicing Mormonism or Hindi. Ultimately, ahistorical essences that scholars and professionals seek through comparison only illustrate the author's own values and agendas.

A better way of relating to different cultures and peoples is understanding that difference is inherent in humanity. Difference—not to be confused with endless relativity, which is actually a form of comparative universalizing—is no less valuable than similarity.[9] Contextualizing lies at the heart of understanding differences. Toward that end, scholars and architects must be meticulous in their research to avoid romanticized cultural generalizations and to produce religious projects that are meaningful.[10]

The following pages are therefore not generalizations, but specific insights on the interaction between religious traditions and architecture. We will examine how "different sets of values and ideals, customs and ethical values" construct sacred spaces.[11] Interestingly, although historians and architects consider doctrine and rituals as prediscursive for designing religious spaces, neither are the most important nor sole method for inscribing them.[12] It is people who animate a space and it is their engagement that embeds space with sacrality and meaning.

Notes

1 William E. Paden, "Comparative Religion," in *The Routledge Companion to the Study of Religion*, edited by John R. Hinnells (London and New York: Routledge, 2005): 211.

2 Heelas, 2005: 267.

3 Paden calls these "false analogies" and "misleading associations" that are seen as "charged with political arrogance: appropriating 'others' to one's [own] worldview and depriving them of their own voices" (2005: 216–217).

4 Heelas, 2005: 265.

5 Richard King, "Orientalism and the Study of Religions," in *The Routledge Companion to the Study of Religion*, edited by John R. Hinnells (London and New York: Routledge, 2005): 284.

6 Lawrence and Low, 1990: 463.

7 Lawrence and Low, 1990: 463.

8 Knott, 2005: 245.

9 In Heelas' summary of Postmodernism, this view of difference as valuable is explained thusly: "People have the right to be different: the importance attached to 'respect' is bound up with the importance attached to people having the freedom to live—at least within limits—different forms of life" (2005: 264).

10 Lawrence and Low, 1990: 458.

11 Hinnells, 2005: 9.

12 Chidester and Linenthal, 1995: 9.

Chapter 22

Buddhism

The earliest, most well-known Western European encounter with Buddhism occurred during the 16th century with Matteo Ricci. His engagement comprised the first exposure of anyone outside of South and East Asia with Buddhism. Yet this presumed patriarch of Western Sinology misinterpreted, circumscribed, and excluded entire areas of Chinese intellectual and religious life to suit his own biases.[1] For one, Ricci's Sinology was responsible for Latinizing the name KongFuzi to Confucius. He misconstrued it as a religion, and completely ignored Buddhism, Daoism, and Folk religions.[2]

What many do not know is that, prior to Ricci, *missionaries* were the earliest European explorers of China, with Jesuits and Christian missionaries seeking new venues for proselytization.[3] Missionaries dismissed "native" cultures and concepts, justifying their own impositions in ways that continue today.[4]

Collectively, their engagements and understandings of Buddhism were rife with philosophical biases. First, they misunderstood the terminology because their linguistic skills were imperfect at best. Even worse, they completely ignored the intellectual context in which Buddhist religious concepts were formed.

All these encounters assumed that religious concepts and practices in East Asia including Buddhism were mere corruptions of Western European traditions, a habit that revived during the Industrialization and the Enlightenment when justifying material and cultural colonialism.

More recent scholars such as Marcel Granet (1884–1940) ignored the importance of Daoism and Buddhism, just as did Max Weber's sociological interpretations of Chinese religion.[5] Their *mis*understandings of Chinese religions were then subsequently transferred to Japan, Korea, and Tibet.

Enlightenment and Buddhism in East and South Asia

By the Enlightenment, European Orientalists began favoring Buddhism over Confucianism and Daoism. Several simultaneous developments caused this. First, European Enlightenment intellectuals began an intense period of cataloguing non-Christian religions based on the European cultural shortcomings that they fulfilled.[6] Confucianism was now valued for its ethics, Hinduism for its mysticism, while Buddhism was upheld for its rationality.[7]

Coincident with this project were intellectuals who began identifying "with the Aryans, a fair-skinned race of conquerors whose exploits were now being repeated by their European descendants; and some were attracted to the Indian's special philosophy of reason and restraining, 'classical' Buddhism. . .constructed by Europeans. . .[which] deified texts."[8]

These people sought Buddhism's "origins" located in South Asia, India to be specific, not the "corrupted" version they had known for the previous two hundred years. Thus in Enlightenment renderings, Buddhism now became "'Classical' Buddhism" that originated in India. This "original" Buddhism fed the "Oriental Renaissance in Europe, with its fantasies of lost wisdom, its search for the languages of Eden, and its construction of classical ages long past, coupled with the denigration of contemporary 'Oriental.'"[9]

Why were Enlightenment individuals seeking Buddhism's "origins"? Quite simply, "European Romantics sought their own lack in the East":[10] specifically, they perceived a deficiency that resulted from a life devoid of connection and deeper meaning. Their resultant understanding of Buddhism was therefore prompted by their own desire for cultural and spiritual conquests, a desire that is often seen not as an ascetic pursuit but an attempt to consume and gain "inner-worldly satisfaction."[11] Buddhism provided them with a "spiritual rationality" without the trappings of a Christian religion.

As a result, Buddhism was no longer associated with those initial encounters with it in China, but with its "origins" in India. Yet despite seeking an antidote for Protestant, religious-based knowledge, Enlightenment intellectuals privileged aspects of Buddhism that resonated with European Christianity. Those aspects included text because European intellectuals privileged texts. In so doing, they reflected "specifically Western concerns, interests, and agendas," completely ignoring the importance of practice to Buddhist monkish life.[12]

Not surprisingly, these intellectuals reduced community, practice-based religious belief to a *personal* belief because post-Enlightenment "rationalism" only had space for individual belief.[13] In fact, their version of "Buddhism" became a personal intellectual pursuit for personal convenience.

Compounding this was the intellectual projection that religious practice could be seen "in terms of a unified theory. . .which assumed that all religions, as all cultures, could be traced to and from the survivors of the Great Flood."[14] That projection meant that it was correct to view non-Christian religions such as Buddhism as misconstructions of Christianity, and moreover that their tenets were equivalent to Christian truths.[15] Later years saw scholars and practitioners applying a theory of universalism to their work, relying on the assumption that all cultures share the same "truths" that simply manifest differently.[16] Not coincidentally, this thinking also excuses Western projections, whether they are intellectual or architectural, in the name of everyone being "one" in a way that does not respect differences inherent in different secular and religious cultures.[17]

As to China, numerous misconceptions have also remained entrenched. Amongst them, the Western rendering of KongFuZi to Confucius stuck, even in East Asia, as well as the idea that Chinese Buddhism was not a "court"-sanctioned religion while Confucianism was—this is wrong. In fact, Confucian philosophy, Buddhism, and Daoism often vied for primacy within the court and for the emperor's ear in influencing policy that, much like today's religious lobbyists, tilted favor toward their own institutions. Another misconception is that Buddhism was practiced by all people. In reality, it was practiced by monastic elites.[18]

The Euro/American Gaze on Buddhism

The result skewed understandings of Buddhism itself. Today, Euro/Americans are still trying to divest themselves of the initial Chinese "taint" on Buddhism, preferring instead the more politically acceptable "Tibetan" or "Zen" Buddhisms (incidentally, "Zen" is merely the Japanese translation of the Chinese word "Chan" which refers to meditation in Buddhism).

These conceptualizations of Buddhism have influenced subsequent scholars, and more importantly and detrimentally, legions of the general populace. Observes Richard King, the "study of religion. . .has had a seminal role to play in the development of Western conceptions of and attitudes."[19] While currently Westerners continue to "consume" Buddhism, this time Tibetan Buddhism which again mimics the needs of Western consumers in exotic, ritualistic, individual spirituality and mysticism, to the detriment of actual Buddhist communal practice.[20]

People, whether they are seeking general information, or seeing knowledge upon which to make informed decisions—such as designing a Buddhist temple—need proper understanding, not biased opinions based on missionary agendas or romantic universalizing notions foregrounded by "Christian theological assumptions," which unfortunately endure.[21] I believe the key is to avoid romanticized cultural generalizations that, like early colonialism itself, grow out of a fatigue with contemporary architecture forms.[22]

One explanation asserts that as communities accumulate more disposable income, their structures become more complex.[23] It is a simple formula of construction and maintenance, in which communities with more disposable income have relatively high construction costs in relation to maintenance.[24]

Constructions of Chinese and Buddhist Architecture

This background directly informs Euro/American concepts of Buddhist architecture. For most, the idea of Buddhist architecture raises the specter of buildings with gabled, multi-inclined, upturned roofs.[25] In truth, this is merely one style—imperial architecture dating from the Ming dynasty. This style was used in the national capitols during the Ming dynasty, first in Nanjing and later in Beijing.[26] Much like the White House is replicated throughout state capitols, the Ming dynasty capitols were replicated in the provincial capitols around the country. One can also see this in the early Indian vihāras, which were simple forms with domed wooden roofs.[27]

How did this one typology become a proxy for all of Chinese architecture in the minds of Westerners? Scholars who wrote official dynastic histories lived in capitols, both national and provincial. Anything less was considered a hardship that was to be avoided at all costs.[28] That means their scholarly gaze was limited to imperial architecture.[29] Hence, so were their writings, official and otherwise. This writing was passed on to future generations, who memorized them to pass their own civil service exams and attain the position of scholar.

Not coincidentally, when Westerners began traveling to China and paying tribute to the court, their exposure was similarly limited to capitols, which means that their exposure to Chinese architecture was likewise narrow. This effect was further compounded by their access to official writings, which again were all focused on the imperial architecture—when it addressed the subject of architecture at all—scholars themselves were exposed to.

Clearly, this specific secular, imperial model should not be generalized as either "Chinese" or "Buddhist" architecture.[30] Yet the imperial architecture trope has persisted throughout the non-East Asian world, especially in architecture circles: "these notions are consistent with a perennial cultural construct of Chinese civilization as one with supreme reverence for its past and that defines itself [solely] according to descriptions in classical writings."[31] In other words, contemporary architects and historians are committing a type of cultural imperialism.

Reconstructing Chinese Buddhist Architecture

By relying solely on official texts as a complete record,[32] architects and historians ignored that these were 1) ideals based on, 2) specific imperial models reserved for, 3) high-ranking buildings, that is, buildings used by high-ranking officials for official business.[33] Put simply, official texts represented elite thinking that was the exception, not the rule.[34] Moreover, this methodology was a unique outgrowth of the Enlightenment, focused on indigenous, Western European peoples, yet these analytical modes were then used to "study" non-Western European, non-Christian religions.[35] As one study observes, "European modernity is set to prejudge truth-claims by the criterion of Enlightenment. While privileging and valorizing the authority and autonomy of reason for allegedly human (material) progress and emancipation, it marginalizes, disenfranchises, and denigrates the (reason's) Other whether it be 1) body, 2) woman, 3) nature, or 4) non-West.[36] The privileging of elite texts, which were often *prescriptive* rather than descriptive, often misconstrued non-Christian religions, freezing them as static "traditions" that did not respond to changing politics, economics, or other social and environmental vicissitudes.

Says one study, "restricting the study. . .[of] architecture to buildings of superior status combined with paintings and line drawings of architecture. . .has led to the creation of an idealized, or iconic, image of a hall," a trend that continues in contemporary historiography.[37] While imperial architecture symbolized legitimacy and power, it is erroneous and inapplicable to apply these tropes to designs to render a structure that is distinctly "Chinese."[38] In fact, what most people identify as "archetypal" Chinese architecture is a specific style meant to self-aggrandize through visual spectacle.[39] US state capitols offer a similar example in that they often replicate the White House dome to legitimize themselves. But for architectural historians to consider them emblematic of "US architecture" is as egregious as equating imperial architecture with either "Chinese" or "Buddhist" architecture.

Historical conflation in the sacred sphere provides a lesson for architecture studies which must be "suspicious of the traditional qualitative link between the aesthetic and the holy. . .associations that allow architectural qualities to generate feelings of awe, mystery, humility, comfort and other emotional responses are *culturally constructed*."[40] Architectural historiography that reads sacred architecture as "a spiritual communication with another realm," or some equally subjective characterization of its functions and meanings adds little to the discourse.[41] There are no objective, pre-originary facts. As Heelas observes, "which scholar could object to widening the frame of an increasingly political inquiry. . .[through an] awareness of their own 'situated' position."[42]

Chinese religious spaces function on religious and secular levels. In secular terms, they reassert cultural identity, reform power relationships and reaffirm social and economic values.[43] They provide a site of "common cultural and historical value [while] it privileges ecological preservation and sustainable development over religion."[44] In fact, in recent years, building and reconstructing sacred sites and structures has been to recover individual and collective status and identity.[45] An added benefit, as is the case for all religious buildings, is the economic gain of promoting tourism.[46]

Notes

1 Bernard Faure, *Chan Insights and Oversights: an Epistemological Critique of the Chan Tradition* (Princeton: Princeton University Press, 1993): 19.

2 Faure, 1993: 22–24.

3 Faure, 1993: 19.

4 Elizabeth Graham, for example, argues that Christian missionary encounters with Native American tribal peoples were not merely an exercise in domination, but that they "restructured the native conceptual universe and helped underpin the new order" (1998: 28). She continues, "Resistance and protest occur alongside active reexamination of former values, together with the development of new concepts about the world that indeed receive European input, but are the product of indigenous minds" (29). This apologia for the active domination and imposition of Eurocentric ideology and behaviors onto the tribal peoples completely ignores the fact that there was no *choice* offered to the tribal peoples and that Eurocentric ideology was violently forced upon them. This contemporary argument unfortunately typifies how agenda-laden missionary justifications continue to replicate.

5 Faure, 1993: 20–21.

6 Horsley, 2003: 18.

7 Horsley, 2003: 18. He continues to explain that basic criteria to be included in this list required a religious founder, an organized clergy, a canon of sacred texts, and a set of defining beliefs (ibid.).

8 Horsley, 2003: 15.

9 Horsley, 2003: 15, 37.

10 Horsley, 2003: 15, 37.

11 Horsley, 2003: 18, 36.

12 Horsley, 2003: 16.

13 Horsley, 2003: 16–17.

14 Paden, 2005: 210.

15 Paden, 2005: 210.
16 Paden, 2005: 211.
17 Paden calls these "false analogies" and "misleading associations" that are seen as "charged with political arrogance: appropriating 'others' to one's [own] worldview and depriving them of their own voices" (2005: 216–217).
18 Horsley, 2003: 15.
19 King, 2005: 276.
20 Horsley, 2003: 17.
21 King, 2005: 284.
22 Lawrence and Low, 1990: 458.
23 Lawrence and Low, 1990: 463.
24 Lawrence and Low, 1990: 463.
25 Nancy Shatzman Steinhardt, "Toward the Definition of a Yuan Dynasty Hall," *Journal of the Society of Architectural Historians*, Vol. 47, No. 1 (Mar., 1988): 57–73.
26 Nancy Shatzman Steinhardt, "The Tang Architectural Icon and the Politics of Chinese Architectural History," *The Art Bulletin*, Vol. 86, No. 2 (June, 2004): 229.
27 Michael W. Meister and Ananda K. Coomaraswamy, "Early Indian Architecture: IV. Huts and Related Temple Types," *RES: Anthropology and Aesthetics*, No. 14 (Spring, 1988): 16.
28 Shatzman Steinhardt, 2004: 229.
29 Shatzman Steinhardt, 2004: 230–231.
30 Shatzman Steinhardt, 2004: 230.
31 Shatzman Steinhardt, 2004: 230.
32 Which were, as Hinnells notes, the primary domain of intellectuals, *not* of the general populace, we skew what is supposedly historical to privilege literate elites (2005: 9).
33 Shatzman Steinhardt, 2004: 239.
34 Horton, 2004: 68.
35 Segal, 2005: 49.
36 Jung, 2002: 298.
37 Shatzman Steinhardt, 2004: 240.
38 Shatzman Steinhardt, 1988: 72.
39 Nancy Shatzman Steinhardt. "A Jin Hall at Jingtusi: Architecture in Search of Identity," *Ars Orientalis*, Vol. 33 (2003): 98.
40 Ivey, 2008: 456 (italics mine).
41 See, for example, McGahan, 2004: 3; Simmins, 2008: 47.
42 Heelas, 2005: 270.
43 Kang, 2009: 229
44 Kang, 2009: 229.
45 Chan, 2005: 65.
46 Chan, 2005: 76.

Chapter 23

Christianity

Books on sacred spaces often focus on Christian churches and what's even more interesting is that those tomes privilege the issue of light. Why? Quite simply, light symbolizes divinity and God himself.[1] For example, the halo in Christian iconography represented not only Divine Light but also the divinity Himself.[2] Manifesting that light physically through architecture therefore became a focus not just of architects but also of their historians.

Yet light is clearly not the only important element in Christian architecture. Nor should it dominate the historical narrative of architecture's development. Topography is another key factor in the construction of Christian architectural spaces. In fact, in early Christianity "sanctity was embedded in the topography."[3] That fact meant certain sites were sacred, or in certain cases, potentially sacred, while others were not. Architecture, then, did not simply house relics, it also marked sacred sites, based on the belief in sanctified topography.[4] This belief was tightly woven with the conviction that sacred sites and the buildings on them were invested with practical, secular political power.[5]

Given that older religious spaces were established in their sanctity, appropriation became a common architectural tactic. Specifically, Christian architecture would appropriate both iconography and plans from older Christian structures, or even from other indigenous religions. In essence, older built religious spaces provided a map to new sacred spaces, so that practitioners could "understand" the meaning of the new space:[6] in "medieval conceptions of architecture, a structure had not only form and function, but also a symbolical dimension, which often was conveyed by imitating a venerated prototype."[7]

Not only was iconography copied, but so were other physical components such as the number of aisles, piers,[8] and even columns,[9] along with architectural plans. Together, these elements proscribed ritual procession through the spaces. As with Buddhist temples, Christian churches contained a "vocabulary of religious architecture in which the ritual progression through buildings is consistent."[10] This kind of mimesis was replicated during the height of British Colonialism, when the goal of strengthening "imperial unity" manifested in symbolic architecture abroad.[11] The secular goal, much like the religious goal, was to link earlier and later structures through symbolic architectural "moves,"[12] thereby proving legitimacy for later structures or outposts.

The cosmos as conceived by Christian theology also exerted its influence on architecture. Medieval Christian monasteries were viewed as "representative of the cosmic mountain on whose summit paradise was believed to be situated."[13] Even medieval cities were inscribed with a religiously conceived cosmos.[14]

Of course, these generalities, like all, must be focused by historical specificities. For example, during the 1800s, "competing ideas and therefore tensions [emerged] about the function of the meetinghouse as public hall or special worship place."[15]

Coincident with this was different strands of Christianity also vying for ascendancy. This power struggle manifested through their architecture. For example, Protestantism was initially suspicious of using specialized architecture or images, but the rivalry between it and Catholicism drove the cross-pollination of architectural and icongraphic forms.[16] As a result, subsequent Protestant churches appropriated several elements from Catholic structures that survive today, including stained glass and candles, and even Gothic architecture could provide legitimate, acceptable access to God.[17]

Indeed, these appropriations of both architecture and iconographic imagery "inspired changes that revitalized Protestant worship."[18] Protestants were not alone in their adoption of Catholic imagery: Anglicans, Baptists, Methodists, Congregationalists, and Presbyterians in the United States also engaged in this borrowing.[19] Ironically, after Vatican II, the influence reversed, with Protestantism influencing the Catholic Church's ideas of architecture.[20]

Notes

1 Slobodan Ćurčić, "Divine Light, Constructing the Immaterial in Byzantine Art and Architecture," in *Architecture of the Sacred: Space, Ritual, and Experience from Classical Greece to Byzantium*, edited by Bonna D. Wescoat and Robert G. Ousterhout (Cambridge: Cambridge University Press, 2012): 308.

2 Ćurčić, 2012: 308.

3 Robert G. Ousterhout, "The Sanctity of Place and the Sanctity of Buildings: Jerusalem Versus Constantinople," in *Architecture of the Sacred: Space, Ritual, and Experience from Classical Greece to Byzantium*, edited by Wescoat and Ousterhout (2012): 281.

4 Ousterhout, 2012: 300.

5 Ousterhout, 2012: 281.

6 Branham, 2012: 212.

7 Heldman, 1992: 224.

8 Heldman, 1992: 224.

9 John Alexander, "Shaping Sacred Space in the Sixteenth Century: Design Criteria for the collegio Borromeo's Chapel," *Journal of the Society of Architectural Historians*, Vol. 63, No. 2 (June, 2004): 170.

10 Tracy G. Miller, "Water Sprites and Ancestor Spirits: Reading the Architecture of Jinci," *The Art Bulletin*, Vol. 86, No. 1 (March, 2004): 21.

11 Brenner, 2003: 50–52.
12 Brenner, 2003: 55.
13 Mary W. Helms, "Sacred Landscape and the Early Medieval Cloister. Unity, Paradise, and the Cosmic Mountain," *Anthropos*, Vol. 97, No. 2 (2002): 435.
14 Lilley, 2004: 296.
15 Ivey, 2008: 456.
16 Ivey, 2008: 454.
17 Ivey, 2008: 454–455.
18 Ryan K. Smith, as cited by Ivey, 2008: 455.
19 This applies particularly to Gothic style, religious symbolism, and sacramental art, according to Smith, as cited in Ivey, 2008: 455.
20 Ivey, 2008: 456.

Chapter 24

Islam

Cultural Colonialism

Examining religion through architecture must account for the ways in which iconography and liturgy, ideology and text are materially represented. This task has been especially problematic when confronting Islam through the lens of Euro/American popular and academic writings. Most taxonomies for exploring Islam and its architectures do not reflect the cultures, ideologies, or material expressions; rather, they reflect Euro/American cultures, ideologies, and material expressions that are then projected upon other religions.[1]

How historians and architects construct non-Christian religions in Western Europe and the United States is too often an exercise in privileged individual expressions. They ignore historical and current "operations of political-economic power uncontested and acquiesces in the commodification of religious expressions."[2] Put differently, I am suspicious of any attempt to coalesce non-Euro/American architectural traditions into a summary category whose inclusion is based on the very fact that they are neither "Western" or "modern."[3]

Without a proper historical context, intellectual forays into Islamic architectural heritage have used Eurocentric terms such as "Mohammedan" and "oriental."[4] In fact, it has only been recently that "religious studies has begun to take seriously the political implications and issues involved when Western scholars and institutions claim the authority to represent and speak about the religions and cultures of others."[5]

Cultural colonialism is not new: "Eastern cultural content was salvageable, with the help of the West," but only when it is re-contextualized and rescripted to suit the cultural and political needs of those located in Western Europe and the United States.[6] Those needs were primarily economic, from the corporations seeking cheaper sources for luxury goods to those younger sons for whom primogeniture denied an inheritance. Early and many contemporary scholars and dilettantes are part of a long lineage of, "architects, artists, and draughtsmen who travelled to the 'Orient' in the wake of the first European [colonizations]. . .in search of adventure, employment, and the thrill of fantasy associated with that mysterious land."[7] Both designers and historians were reductive in their understanding because their methodologies and biases reaffirmed a historical determinism that held Western architecture at its apex.[8] The underlying assumption is one in which "Western history has an overriding importance—for good or ill—in the making of the modern world, and that explorations of that history should be a major anthropological concern."[9]

These impulses reflect an intellectual narcissism that all other historical occurrences and phenomena should only be understood in terms that reference the "self," defined by the Euro/American nation performing the analysis. Therefore categories and methodologies of analysis used for Euro/American nations are transferred wholesale to the "other."

Islamic Architecture

The most obvious problem foregrounding most of these works is, as stated above, the abiding trust in Western history's central importance in shaping all other nations' histories.[10] Whether people do or do not agree with this stance is irrelevant; what *is* relevant is that this belief has produced a single narrative about not just Islam, but Islamic architecture.

That narrative on Islamic architecture was originally constructed by "aesthetes" or people who viewed it as an "exotic, mysterious, and aesthetically curious, carrying the whiff of far-distant lands."[11] Their legacy was formalized by Western art historians who regarded Islamic architecture as their scholarly purview. In fact, art and architecture are often combined in university academic departments because presumably they share aesthetic, symbolic, and theoretical characteristics.

Because their emphasis focused on the symbolic and aesthetic, art historians failed to understand the other dimensions that architecture operated on, namely physical, political, economic, and social.[12] Architecture contains practical and functional dimensions that organize human interaction. These conditions are not applicable to either art history or literature. By reducing Islamic architecture to an aesthetic discourse, professionals and scholars alike ignore the fundamental power relations that structure built religious spaces:[13] three-dimensional space that not only fosters human interaction but organizes and hierarchizes it.[14]

Yet because the initial, aesthetically-dominated foray into Islamic architecture—the first of many non-Euro/American architectures—was performed by art historians, it and other cultures have become typologically fixed.[15] Architecture, in this view, whether categorized by religion (e.g. Islamic) or region (e.g. South Asian, Indian, Chinese), is admired for its "traditional" or "ancient" elements. Its function is reduced to a unitary, "pre-modern" expression that commingles politics with religion indistinctly.

In contemporary renderings, certain "ancient" elements are used to evoke what are considered static, fixed architectural styles. These styles are then assigned to an entire region. Hence, "historically dynamic attributes [are] frequently portrayed as specific to Western architecture,"[16] unless it is China, in which case its supposed "hyper" dynamism is seen as simply a sad mimicry of "true" modernism which occurs in Euro/American regions. In the case of Islamic architecture, favored characteristics included "sensual" and "ornamental."[17] In short, using terminology, typologies, and frameworks meant for Euro/American nations prevents designers and historians from understanding the architecture in the Arab states, East Asia, South Asia, and Africa.[18]

The intellectual narcissism has been compounded by an overarching colonial category termed "Islam" which "became the explanatory framework for European imperialism to understand the 'Arab mind.'"[19] That mind was an amalgam, a singular "thing" that could be studied precisely because it was a homogenous entity that transcended history. In other words, textual information could be pieced together to form a single, monolithic narrative. Location was essential to this single history, so that the Middle East became the center for orthopraxy against which all other Islamic praxis was measured.[20] This explains why it is still surprising for many in the general populace to realize that many African nations also practice Islam, just as it is surprising for many that Chinese nationals are not "automatically" Buddhist.

Today, historians and designers are still applying Eurocentric models of typology and terminology[21] to cultural and architectural traditions that demand evaluation on their own terms.[22] Yet, "because of its institutional power, the authoritative historiography of western architecture. . .[views] Islamic architecture. . .as the opposite of western architecture: conservative vs. progressive, formal categories static vs. self-evolving ones, and reflecting cultural imperatives vs. creative individual subjectivity."[23]

Unsurprisingly, this stationary past does not require proper research. A few taps on the computer keyboard in a short afternoon will certainly suffice any designer working in an Islamic country, or so the assumption goes.

In truth, each regional architectural tradition is unique, heterogeneous, and reflective of the particular social, political, and economic forces that have historically been in play.[24] That fact is why the static "art history" typologies are inappropriate at best, and at worst, erroneous.

This is especially true in the decontextualization of sacred geometries, or geometrical shapes that contain particular religious meanings. Too often, when students or neophytes of religious design approach a new project, they decontextualize certain signs to "represent" or hearken the religion without understanding its meaning. For example, in Anglican history, the barrel vaults "constructed a space where the thin veil separating earth from heaven was parted, a space where. . .mortals met the divine."[25] Similarly, certain sacred geometries found in Islam contain specific meanings and cannot be abstracted as mere decorative patterns. Rather, they must be understood for what they invoke in order to be used thoughtfully.

Another aspect of Islam that many misunderstand is that it functions as a "structuring agent" for all facets of life,[26] which is why prayer occurs not just in the mosque, but also throughout the day wherever the person is.[27] In fact, as both scholarly and popular writers have emphasized, Islam "emphasizes unity and community, valuating individualism far less than Christianity."[28]

Recently, scholars and architects have begun dismantling these entrenched problems of viewing and understanding. It is important for historians and architects to be aware of the "imperial power relations [that produced Euro/American knowledge] as well as of their own social location and role."[29]

Notes

1 Labelle Prussin, "Non-Western Sacred Sites: African Models," *Journal of the Society of Architectural Historians*, Vol. 58, No. 3 (September, 1999): 424.

2 Horsley, 2003: 39.

3 Ask Memmot and Davidson, "Why the realm of Euro-American architectural discourse has been so reticent to share its epistemological domain with non-Western and indigenous building tradition. . .[it] is easier to place such traditions out of the way, in the realm of the 'vernacular' a term which originated in the Western linguistic tradition to signify the language of the 'common'" (quote marks mine) (Paul Memmott and James Davidson, "Exploring a Cross-Cultural Theory of Architecture," *Traditional Dwellings and Settlements Review*, Vol. 19, No. 2 [Spring, 2008]: 52).

4 Nasser Rabbat, "What is Islamic Architecture Anyway?" *Journal of Art Historiography*, No. 6 (June, 2012): 2.

5 King, 2005: 277.

6 Horsley, 2003: 25.

7 Rabbat, 2012: 1–2.

8 Rabbat, 2008: 2.

9 Talal Asad, *Genealogies of Religion: Discipline and Reasons of Power in Christianity and Islam* (Baltimore: Johns Hopkins University Press, 1993): 7.

10 Asad, 1993: 7.
11 Rabbat, 2012: 1.
12 Whyte, 2006: 163.
13 Asad, 1993: 15.
14 Ratansky, 1995: 10.
15 Rabbat, 2008: 3.
16 Rabbat, 2008: 3.
17 Rabbat, 2008: 3.
18 Says Rabbat, "categorizing Islamic architecture after Western stylistic sequence—i.e., Classical, Medieval, or Baroque—has subjected the development of Islamic architecture to the rhythm of another architectural tradition" (Rabbat, 2008: 3).
19 Desplat, 2012: 13.
20 Desplat, 2012: 13.
21 Rabbat, 2012: 4.
22 Burgess, 2004: 313.
23 Rabbat, 2012: 13–14.
24 Memmot and Davidson, 2008: 52.
25 Nelson, 2007: 207.
26 Insoll, 2004: 89.
27 Kadri M.G. Elaraby, "Neo-Islamic Architecture and Urban Design in the Middle East: From Threshold to Adaptive Design," *Built Environment (1978–)*, Vol. 22, No. 22 (1996): 138.
28 Burgess, 2004: 314; Reza Aslan, *No God But God: the Origins, Evolution, and Future of Islam* (New York: Random House, 2011): 195.
29 Horsley, 2003: 18.

Chapter 25

Judaism

As with any other religion, the architectural history of synagogues is varied and contested, by its "users" as well as by those who write about it. For past scholars and architects, contrast has been a key aspect of identifying and defining Judaism.[1] Specifically, they routinely compared and contrasted Judaic and Christian typologies in a Yin/Yang manner, a complementary relationship that means "activation/completion" (not "man/woman" as many Westerners translate). These contrastive definitions have consistently favored Christianity because many of the scholars were trained in Christian theology. Therefore Judaism is seen as "a unitary but overly parochial and political 'religion' that was succeeded historically by the more spiritual and universalistic religion 'Christianity.'"[2]

The same compare/contrast methodology was used for Judaic architecture, which produced severely limited spatial narratives. As argued previously, identifying similarities across different cultures is a risky proposition. Unacknowledged biases are the most frequent result of comparisons. However, there is one similarity that Judaic spaces share with other religions' spaces: they are intertwined with secular space.[3] In fact, beginning in medieval times, synagogues were marked and defined by their distinction from secular buildings.[4] What's more, they often incorporated secular spaces within their walls.

Even more interestingly, synagogues were not only interwoven with secular buildings, they were also linked to Christian architectural developments. One reason is that early in their histories, Judaism and Christianity developed in the same regions.[5] Proximity exerts mutual influence, which in architecture produces stylistic cross-pollination.

For synagogues, coexistence and mutual influence began with early Roman secular architecture. It not only shaped Jewish synagogues but also Christian churches, "the synagogue derived its main form from the same source as did the Christian Church. . .the Roman basilicas [which] existed in all parts of the Empire and were the most convenient structures then existing for purposes of congregational worship."[6] Mutual inspiration continued through medieval times, with synagogues containing Byzantine elements,[7] as well as Renaissance–Baroque influences.[8]

There are two interrelated reasons for it. One is that religious dominance was often established through physical means: imposing edifices and buildings appeared more commanding and authoritative.[9] Competing with other religious traditions manifested in building more grandiose or imposing physical projects. So for religious institutions to successfully compete with each other, they had to incorporate and adapt to dominant religious architectural trends of their time.[10]

They also competed for legitimacy and authority by mimicking each other's architectural tropes such as site location, height of the structure, as well as visible adornments.[11] By establishing their religious authority through such physical displays, institutions hoped to amass more followers and practitioners, which in turn strengthened the institution itself.

Regional stylistic trends also swayed individuals significantly, whether they were professional architects or not.[12] That in turn exerted influence over their design decisions, especially in the case of those spaces not designed by professional architects or designers. It is therefore unsurprising that synagogues often included Christian church tropes and vice versa.[13]

Despite the fact that they contained stylistic elements that were either secular or Christian, synagogues through the 18th century were primarily designed by Jewish architects who understood Judaic religious programmatic requirements.[14] But by the 1800s, synagogues were also being designed by architects unfamiliar with Judaism.[15] They made liberal use of Christian architectural tropes in designs called "cathedral synagogues."[16] Such mimicry was unlike medieval times since the goal was not to gain more penitents by incorporating certain "foreign" elements. Instead, "cathedral synagogues" provided a clear example of architectural ignorance and religious projection.[17]

The 1800s witnessed another architectural synagogue style: the Moorish synagogue.[18] The trend began in Germany and its popularity lasted until World War I.[19] At that time, the style grew out of disfavor as Jewish communities in Europe began to perceive Moorish-style synagogues as a marker for their "otherness"; that dissatisfaction was echoed by architects.[20] It was, interestingly, replaced by a "National Romanticism" in Eastern and Northern Europe that incorporated local architectural features into synagogues as a way of expressing national identity.[21] These architectural movements in synagogue architecture can be viewed as exchanges of cultural, hence architectural, influences.[22]

Cultural and architectural reciprocation in the early 20th century was heavily shaped by the International Modernist movement, whose influence could be detected through simplified volumes.[23] In countries where Islam dominates, domed synagogues became common.[24] Moreover, synagogue architecture is also shaped by historic periods of dislocation and interference, not least of which occurred during the mid-20th century.[25] In view of this, contemporary synagogues can be seen as an assertion of identity formed in the absence of potentially oppositional social and political forces.[26]

Notes

1 Horsley, 2003: 26.
2 Horsley, 2003: 26.
3 Burgess, 2004: 312.
4 Burgess, 2004: 312.
5 Mauro, Bertagnin, Ilham Khuri-Makdis, and Susan Gilson Miller, "A Mediterranean Jewish Quarter and Its Architectural Legacy: the *Giudecca* of Trani, Italy (1000–1550)," *Traditional Dwellings and Settlements Review*, Vol. 14, No. 2 (2003): 34.
6 William G. Tachau, "The Architecture of the Synagogue," *American Jewish Year Book*, Vol. 28 (1972): 167.
7 Bertagnin, Ilham Khuri-Makdis, and Miller, 2003: 38.
8 Oksana Boyko, "The Synagogue in Zhovkva: History and Architectural Development, *Ukrainian Journal of Physical Optics*, Supp. 2 (2011): 42.
9 Kravtsov, 2010: 81.
10 Kravtsov, 2010: 81.
11 Kravtsov, 2010: 81.
12 Bertagnin, Ilham Khuri-Makdis, and Miller, 2003: 34.
13 Bertagnin, Ilham Khuri-Makdis, and Miller, 2003: 34.
14 Sharman Kadish, "Constructing Identity: Anglo-Jewry and Synagogue Architecture," *Architectural History*, Vol. 45 (2002): 393.
15 Kadish, 2002: 393.
16 Kadish, 2002: 393.
17 Kadish, 2002: 393.
18 Ivan Davidson Kalmar, "Moorish Style: Orientalism, the Jews, and Synagogue Architecture," *Jewish Social Studies*, Vol. 7, No. 3 (Spring/Summer, 2001): 69.
19 Kalmar, 2001: 69.
20 Kravtsov, 2010: 97.
21 Kravtsov, 2010: 99.
22 Bertagnin, Ilham Khuri-Makdis, and Miller, 2003: 34.
23 G.M. Goodwin, "The Design of a Modern Synagogue – Goodman, Percival Temple Beth-El in Providence, Rhode Island (1947–1952), " *American Jewish Archives*, Vol. 45, No. 1 (1993): 62; also Kadish, 2002: 398.
24 Kadish, 2002: 398.
25 Kadish, 2002: 386.
26 Kadish, 2002: 387.

PART 8

BIOGRAPHIES AND OBSERVATIONS

Chapter 26

Arcario+Iovino Architects

Mr. Edward Arcari, AIA, Founder and Principal

Mr. Anthony Iovino, AIA, LEED, Founder and Principal

Background

"All I ever wanted to do was architecture! There was never any question," says Mr. Arcari. Yet aspiration alone, he acknowledges, is not always sufficient. Serendipity, too, has its role: "I was lucky enough to have teachers early on, even in junior high and high school who nurtured me and brought me along." In fact, Mr. Arcari's emphasis is not just on his own hard work, but also on the timing and generosity of those who nurtured both his talents and his goals. "In college, I was able to get into a good school in New York, and there I was able to work for one of my professors."

Mr. Iovino felt similarly about pursuing architecture from a young age, "Like Ed, it was something I knew I wanted to do early on. I grew up around putting things together, enjoying creating things and then everything came together in architecture school. I went to Pratt."

Like so many firms, theirs is one that began under the nurturance of a larger environment, whether it is a school or another firm.Says Mr. Arcari, "I worked for a couple of different firms and then I landed a job with a firm in New York and Tony happened to be there at the same time."

"I did internships which landed me at the firm where Ed was," says Mr. Iovino.

"I was there for three years," says Mr. Arcari, "and at a certain point we decided to go out on our own. It felt right, we were both single, no family attachments, so no responsibilities other than for ourselves. I had some leads; like anybody does, they get their first lead and they decide to take the leap and it's been non-stop ever since."

Mr. Iovino affirms, "Architecture is a passion for both of us. And we work well together and we run the business well together. After all, twenty-one years is a long time for a partnership."

Observations and Advice

With such a fount of long and varied experience, both partners offer interesting perspectives on approaching religious projects. "It's about connecting with people on a one-to-one level," says Mr. Arcari, "Listening to people and not coming in to a client meeting thinking that you know everything."

Mr. Iovino continues, "We ask a lot of questions to understand what the answer they're looking for is. A lot of times you give them something they didn't anticipate. But you have to get out of them what their needs are. And then you give them something rooted in reality but beyond what they imagined."

In other words, "Get to know your client as best you can. Visit their current spaces and understand what's important to them in terms of before and after, especially in terms of the services. Really get to know them on a personal level."

Mr. Arcari agrees, "Especially since I do most of it, I usually take one of my kids and go visit them during their religious worship." The purpose is not to announce his presence, but to understand the cultural context: "I'm there just to kind of blend in and see what's going on. I've been to fairs, different dinners, Sunday services, to sit on the sidelines and see what's going on and to understand how they use the space for worship to other things." Those other things, he says, like, "How do they hold a dinner? How is their kitchen working?"

Mr. Iovino adds, "It's also really important during the design process to keep your clients' eyes on reality and the overall process."

He continues, "The more we work with different religious groups, the more we learn how to deal with them more easily and effectively. We know what to expect. Oftentimes, in a church project, you have a committee, and people on the committee, one's a builder, one's an electrician, a plumber, so on and so forth, and they all of course know better than you. So we're learning, in a practical way, to let them speak. Listen to them like we listen to their other needs, and they do have valid ideas a lot of the time. However, I also tell people early on I'm just not going to do what you want. If we really disagree with something, we're going to let you know and we'll work through it. So we've learned to push back, as well, when we need to. Whether it be something technical with the building or if it's a design issue."

Even more interesting is to realize that one's own religious beliefs are ultimately unimportant. Mr. Iovino explains that, "It's almost good that we're secular. In fact, our bigger religious projects have nothing to do with our own religions. We said for the Teaneck Synagogue, they hired these two Italian guys to design their facility. But I think it benefits them as well as us. They're going to get something different than something pro forma."

Chapter 27

hMa (Hanrahan Meyers Architects)

Victoria Meyers, M.Arch, Founder and Principal

Background

"I always wanted to be an architect from the time I could talk," says Ms. Meyers. "I read most of Frank Lloyd Wright's writings before I even got to high school. I worked from about thirteen or fourteen just doing odd errands in the office of an architect in this small town where I grew up, East Salzburg, Pennsylvania. I worked in their office in college and in graduate school.

"When I went to college I didn't want to go far from home and I wanted to get the same degree that Frank Lloyd Wright got, which was in Civil Engineering. He never got an architecture degree. So I got my joint degree in Civil Engineering and in Art History, which was great. I had to do a thesis for the Art History major. The first half of the thesis was an investigation of the Cluniac Order. The second part was a comparison of Ronchamp. Then I went to work as a Civil Engineer."

The next step was to pursue a graduate degree in Architecture, which Ms. Meyers did at Harvard. Out of that grew her partnership with Thomas Hanrahan. In fact, the firm "was a meeting of minds. My partner and I were from the same Harvard class. There were skills that he had that I didn't have and vice versa. So we were complementary. And there was a desire on both of our parts to create a pretty contemporary language of form. So we went after projects together immediately after school. We landed our first project a year or two after graduation. And then kept producing stuff.

"A lot of projects were us projecting the future of New York, before the Westside of Manhattan was completely abandoned. It was abandoned and trashed, and a lot of homeless people lived there. We created this whole series of proposals of creating an entire Westside development of parks. Which is what we have in New York now. And it was really on the basis of that project that we were selected by the Architectural League of NY as Young Architects, which is their young architects award program.

"Then we were hired by Battery Park to take over the master planning of the north neighborhood park. In that capacity, we wrote all of the guidelines for all of the buildings and all the parks, and all the pathways in the north neighborhood. We wrote guidelines to do green infrastructure which had not yet been developed or thought or certified by programs such as LEED."

Ms. Meyers' commitment to art has also influenced her own work: "I think my involvement with visual and sound artists has challenged the way I look at other things and has challenged the way I look at my own work, and also the way I operate with elements of sound, space, and light and other factors."

Observations and Advice

Given Ms. Meyers' experience as an architect, author, and professor, she has some interesting insights about the profession which begin with the educational process: "Everyone I know who's in architecture knows that we're in a crisis throughout the United States in the educational field. Most of the students I know can barely read. And they can't write. Most of them don't know who any of the great architects in history are.

"Students are not learning qualitatively," she says. "They don't get a course where they go through every single significant architecture treatise and look at the works simultaneously. They may get a course where they read the treatises, but they never look at any of the work. That doesn't work.

"We're discussing context, so that they can get a comprehensive picture. When they can see the entire picture, they can acquire the critical thinking skills to see when their own work is finished." This is because "the art of architecture has such a strong continuum with other things that if you don't understand that history, you cannot participate as a colleague in the architecture forum. Because this forum operates at a high level that demands a lot of knowledge."

The deficiencies in architecture education are also reflected in the practical skills emerging professionals lack. Says Ms. Meyers, "If you hand a contractor a set of documents where you've drawn a structure which has absolutely no relationship with the building you want to build, your result is going to be a disaster."

Part of these weaknesses stem from the instructors themselves: "There is a tendency on the part of people teaching school recently to become less practitioner-based. I see people teaching who don't understand the difference between a good and bad drawing. A good drawing is one where you can see someone who sees spatial relationships. It's like looking at a really good anatomical drawing by a medical draftsman, where they're cutting through the arm and showing all the major arteries and bones. When I look at an architectural drawing, I can see that that person knows how that building works."

The consequences are that "students have much less sense of understanding about the intellectual power of drawings and models. They think that's just the fluffy stuff anyone can do. But you have to have an incredible intellect to make a model that is an intelligent model and to make a drawing which is an intelligent drawing where every line has significance and demonstrates skill."

Another aspect of education that is important is understanding the financial practicalities of running an architecture firm. Specifically, there is an interconnectedness between the art and business of architecture. She says, "The lack of understanding about the interconnectedness of things is worrisome. Architecture students aren't taught that it is more competitive to get a job in an office than it has ever been. Also the profit margin is lower than it's ever been. All you need is one employee to go bankrupt. I don't think the kids are taught that." The dichotomy between the continued pressure for students to produce "signature" projects and the crushing student debt means students are "so pressured financially today that they are often frantic they aren't learning anything anyway."

Ms. Meyers' thoughts on the state of the profession institutionally and individually result from her work not just as a professional but also as a professor and a writer. In terms of the educational system, she says, "It's a funny time. It's a difficult time in education because when I talk about some of the key twentieth-century themes like Duchamp's Large Glass or John Cage's Silence, students will have no idea who they are. But they are basic to understanding architecture. And I say, 'if you don't believe me, you should look up the work of Diller Scofidio because Diller talked at length about the fact that Duchamp's Large Glass is the basis of their body of work.' At which point the kids will look at me quizzically like, is she telling the truth or is she making this up?"

In sum, Ms. Meyers finds that there is a disconnect in the field: "I think there are people who are building really fantastic things today, but I also think there's been this incredible separation in the field. Either you're in an office that has at least three hundred people and you're cranking over a hundred buildings a year or you're in a smaller office and you're getting by but you're not getting projects that have the program that can support the kind of thinking I'm talking about. And yet if you're in one of the bigger projects, it's also doubtful that you're going to get much attention either." By highlighting these issues, Ms. Meyers hopes to effect some change in the field.

Whether one is a student, architect, or writer, there is one central factor to remember: critical thinking has both practical and design elements. One cannot focus solely on one aspect. She offers one example of the practicalities that directly impact the business of architecture: "Elevators are a consideration when you're doing a church because generally you're on more than one level. If you have a public assembly and you have a public space, you have to have handicap access and you have to have an elevator." These issues are not insignificant, as Ms. Meyers points out, "Once you have one or two small elevators, you're in a situation because elevators are very difficult companies to deal with. If you are doing a high rise and you're a developer and you're doing one or two high rises a year, you have power with elevator companies. They will install your elevators in a timely manner and they'll do it correctly because you work with them frequently. But if you're a smaller office, you're architects, you've done a church only once or twice and you don't constantly use elevators, then you're not going to be giving them a lot of return business. That means you don't have any leverage. Nor does the client."

The implications are that it can be very difficult to get these subcontractors to work with architects and clients effectively and in a timely manner: "For one project, it took us almost five years to get the elevators signed off. For example, they keyed in the first floor as the basement and the basement as the first floor. And we spent two years having them come back at the Infinity Chapel because they just didn't have quality employees capable of typing in 'one' for the first floor and 'b' for the basement. This went on for years.

"That alone held up the certificate of occupancy. Which meant that while the church could be open, they had to hire a person who has a certain kind of sign-off from the city and you have to pay them to be there as a guard whenever you have people in the building for liability reasons. If the city finds out you had a public assembly without that person there, they can shut you down."

Then there are the strategies for critical thinking in developing the design: "I think the place you're in is really good architecture if it puts you into a new place. When you're in that place, it frees and liberates you from your daily life. And it also gives you a different perspective. and I think that's extremely liberating." She continues, "You're altering the space and perspective by altering the space materially, as in material culture. It can be an amazing way of giving people an alternative reality, that's good architecture. That is certainly true in a religious building."

From a personal standpoint, "I'm looking for some way the project is going to be quirky and going to confront somebody with an interpretation of reality that they may have never thought of or may not be ready for. The clients may not even talk about it," she admits, "But they'll go in and they'll realize it's there. It's a funny thing, every time I've done a residential project, about six months after it's completed, I get a phone call. They're kind of shocked or annoyed about some elements but at the end of the day it's why they like the project. Because they cherish these things that put this in this other place, psychologically."

The process also requires critical analysis: "The process is more about working on the design until the design is found. So when the design is done, I know it because I see it. I don't change it. And that process is an unknowable quantity of time. I've gone through and experienced, with the Infinity Chapel for example, where that model was made the first week after we met the client. And I didn't change a line. Because it was perfect and I knew it was perfect. And once I've got a perfect design, I'm very unwilling to drop it.

"I think it's unquantifiable, which is something I teach my students in the studios. I have great sympathy because there are some semesters where you can work as hard as you possibly can and it's a disaster. If I have someone who has experienced that and I see that they're working really hard, if they have a disaster at the end, I will still give them an A because they worked really hard."

On the other hand, as with her own experience with Infinity Chapel, "There can also be freaky accidents where you build a single model, and you look at it and say, this is perfect and you freeze it. I think that for every architect, you have to know when the cake is baked. And when that cake is baked, I don't really touch it.

"I had this one student who wouldn't leave her project alone and I kept saying, this cake is baked. And she kept getting hysterical and I said I don't care if you're hysterical, you've got this thing which most architects would kill for. And why would you keep messing with it." This is where critical analytical skills come into play: "When someone does that, I really have to question their ability to judge critically. You also see this in various architects. They'll come up with beautiful ideas and they can't recognize the good stuff and they'll just toss them in the can. Or just keep making the project worse and worse. So it is a skill set to be able to look at it and recognize when it's finished.

"It's a shock," she admits, "when you get it done really quickly like we did with Infinity Chapel. And my partner kept looking at it and saying we have to change this and I said, I'm not changing a line and you're not touching this. This thing is perfect. And it was a fluke. And my students are very confused about that. I just say it may take you one week, it may take you one year. But you have to keep working until you get a thing which is really perfect."

That perfection relies on the ability to judge, which is developed through proper education, "That is an education that teaches students about other, related subjects that are written and visual, not an approach in disjunctive cherry-picking that only highlights a few 'famous' models of each subject. What's more, those subjects should extend beyond architecture to include cultural and material history such as Intellectual History, Cultural Anthropology, and contemporary disciplines like Engineering to properly contextualize visual disciplines like Art History, too often decontextualized as merely a visual catalogue, much the way that Architectural History is. It is only through a proper context that students will become architects who can critically judge their own work the way that Lee Krasner and the European Modernists could: they were classically trained first. It was only *then* that they could advance to the abstractions they created. What's more, their understanding was intellectual, not just visual. And so it should be with current architects."

Chapter 28

Imbue Design

Hunter Gunderson, Founder and Principal

Matthew Swindel, Founder and Principal

Christopher Talvy, Founder and Principal

Background

Mr. Talvy beings, "Architecture was for me a really simple path. I come from a family that's entrenched in contracting. My dad's a contractor and he came from a family that has been working jobsites forever. So when I was 12 years old, I was working on a jobsite." He pauses and laughs, "I don't know what the child labor laws think about that but I was swinging a hammer and wiring houses at a very young age. So the work ethic was instilled in me very young and did that throughout my life."

Those parental influences came from both sides, "My mom was an artist, which, combined with my father's influence, made architecture seem like a perfect fit. After I took a couple classes and fell in love with it, I have been pursuing it ever since. I'm super passionate about it. Zero regrets and I can't imagine doing anything else. When I enrolled in Utah University, I felt it was one of the best moves I ever made because I was blown away by the environment and the opportunity to get a solid education that I'm really proud of. Of course, that's where I met these fine gentlemen," he laughs again, "when we enrolled in the Design Build Bluff program. It was a house we built in the dessert for a Navajo family. We developed a bond through working together. And watching their skills in design and fabrication gave me a lot of confidence in them."

Mr. Gunderson interjects, "I think that's where our love for residential came from. And if you look at the house we worked on for Design Build Bluff, that house is full of sacred symbolism, and actual culture. The house is circular and big massive walls, they point out to the four sacred mountains the Navajo believe the gods use to prescribe the land that they were given. If you see the firepit, that is usually the hearth of the home, but the clients wanted to live outside as much as they could so the firepit was put on the outside of the home rather than inside. So there is a lot of spirituality there. And that's probably where we kind of made the roots in what we do now."

From there, he describes his background, "I'm from Salt Lake and pretty much my entire life. A little bit in Mexico and little bit in Hawaii."

Says Mr. Talvy, "Hunter's our token Mormon!"

"Yes," Mr. Gunderson agrees, "I'm the token Mormon. I'm the only religious one but by no means the only spiritual one. These guys are spiritual giants which I think is expressed through their design and their passion."

He continues, "My dad was a general contractor and I was always on jobsites, swinging a hammer and seeing jobsites with just framing and no finishes and for me, it's very magical. It was time spent with my dad so that meant a lot to me. But when I got to school, I didn't know what I wanted to be so I took all the generals I could. At one point, you have to choose a major or the school's going to kick you out. I happened to be taking an architecture class at that time. It wasn't even really architecture, it was actually a design course in the architecture program."

Mr. Gunderson pauses, "It was a language I had never seen before and an idea I had never thought of before. It seemed like in other classes, there was always just one answer but suddenly I get to this class, and I'm trying to figure out what their answer is and they have no answer for me. And to realize I could create my own answer that is a meaningful and rigorous answer was so intriguing to me. That is when I decided to pursue more architecture classes and I realized that that is where everything comes together for me. I loved the business, I love art, I loved psychology, physics, and it all seemed to come together in architecture and so that's how I finally decided after thousands of dollars and many years to do architecture."

Mr. Swindel's story begins slightly differently. "I grew up outside of Portland," he says, "but my family moved to Utah and we grew up skiing. So I've always just loved being around here and being outdoors. I didn't know what I wanted to do either and I had a design class. I had done art in school, and I'd always been pretty interested in that but I wasn't sure I wanted to pursue art as an artist. When I took the design class, the design studio, I became interested in the idea that you come up with a concept, you put that on the paper, and then you try to build something from it. The process from conceptualization to actualization, the tangibility of it was really interesting to me and that was architecture. So when I did the Design Build Bluff course, I became really interested because it was a full-scale project and it changed my perception on what architecture was and what I wanted to do."

In fact, the Design Build Bluff program at Utah University inspired the entire group to continue with residential projects. Says Hunter, "We were so high on architecture and life and thinking everything was amazing that when we got back to school and they had a work fair where they try to hire the students, we were utterly disappointed. So that was when I jokingly said to Talvy, 'You know, let's just start our own thing.' And he said, 'Okay.' And I said, it's just a joke and he said, 'No, we should do it.' So little by little we actually started and we designed while we were still at school."

As the two began receiving more commissions, they realized they needed help: "After about a year of working, we found that we were way in over our heads because we had way too much work and so we called Matt, and said, 'Matt, we need your help.' At the time he was in San Diego, kind of doing a similar thing on his own. He said, 'Well, I have to think about it.' And about five minutes later, he called us back up, and said, 'I'm in,' and he came back to Salt Lake!"

Despite having worked for several years at a firm, the partners have decided to remain a three-man firm. Mr. Talvy says, "We really enjoy this smaller scale. We all work at one desk. We have this long, linear desk, and all three computers are sitting right next to each other so it's a very collaborative process. We like having a lot of control over the projects." Mr. Swindel laughs, "Typical, right?" But in seriousness, Mr. Talvy observes that, "When you take on employees, you start losing aspects of the projects that are dear to us and there's a reason why we get these clients."

Their shared experiences give them an interesting perspective on how to work. It begins with basic steps like research, says Mr. Talvy, "Everyone needs to do basic research, whether it's reading up is an obvious solution. But you also have to get entrenched in the client and explore how they experience the religion and how they respond to it. You build a project around it. And it will be that much stronger because it will be both religiously and client-tied. So you need to refer to the client."

Observations and Advice

Their observations are straightforward. Using the client as a constant base also prevents the design from becoming mired in "signature" moves. "It does go back to the process of talking to the client," says Mr. Gunderson, "and then for us, offering the three different options. If you show clients the spectrum of what is possible, each client will choose a different path. So we offer diverse buildings for them to choose from."

Chapter 29

Kris Yao Artech

Mr. Kris Yao, FAIA, Founder, Principal

Kris Yao is the Founding Principal of Kris Yao Artech, located in Taipei, Taiwan. He describes how even as a young boy, he was drawn to artistic pursuits: "When I was younger, I was interested in art and painting." He elaborates, "Thanks to an organization which was next to our school, the New Center or Agency of the United States, we were exposed to a lot of different magazines. I remember I saw two buildings that inspired me. One was Ronchamp Chapel by Le Corbusier, the other was Falling Water by Frank Lloyd Wright. I thought, 'Wow, it is so impressive that these buildings can be done this way.' Those two buildings made quite an impression on me."

"When I was in high school in Taiwan," he continues, "it was a very quiet time. Nothing much was happening to me academically or otherwise. We were separated into four groups. Either you were going into engineering and science, or you would study literature, or become a doctor, or a business person. Basically you were separated into these four groups. Remember, this was a sleepy, lazy time and most of the boys were in the first group, engineering. And like everyone else, I was in that group, until at the very last moment when I had to choose departments for a university before the big entrance examination. And the results found nothing in that category that interested me except architecture." Mr. Yao laughs, "Luckily, architecture was put together with engineering and science!"

Mr. Yao then attended Tunghai University where he obtained his B.Arch. After that he continued his studies at University of California, Berkeley where he received an M.Arch. "Berkeley is great," Mr. Yao says. "It deconstructed everything and that's very good."

Philosophical Outlook

"Religion is definitely a culture or what you might call micro-culture," says Mr. Yao. "Being a Chinese person, you might be more familiar with Buddhism, and being a German, you might be more familiar with Catholicism. But that doesn't really mean that you really know the *essence* of the religion. I think that's no doubt because everybody grows out of their cultures, surroundings and all that. So for example there are lot of misunderstandings in Buddhism, by regular people in Taiwan, even though Taiwanese people are living in a predominately Buddhist country."

Mr. Yao explains further, "I grew up in a quasi-Buddhist family, but until I really studied it more, I didn't really know what Buddhism was, what its quintessence was. When people are from a culture where a religion predominates, they tend to assume they know more about it."

"The truth is, you might have some inkling, but you don't really know anything substantive until you study it or research it." That includes scripture as well as scholarly exposition: "I find that if one studies Buddhist philosophy instead of approaching it as a religious belief, one will encounter useful documents or studies where all kinds of theories are discussed." This understanding has aided his architectural approach to Buddhist projects. "It has helped on the Buddhist projects I worked on because I am now, as an adult, more familiar with Buddhism."

Advice

Mr. Yao's advice begins simply: "Work hard."

Then he elaborates on the role of symbolism in architecture, "On religious projects, I think the advice is be careful about symbolism. These days, for some peculiar reason, architects like to use symbolism in a very crude way. For example, you always see western architects working in China, and the first thing they say, is 'dragon!' For all these symbols, it is only people who are not familiar with the culture who think they are important symbols."

He pauses and the continues, "It almost becomes funny. I guess if we go to the west, we might do the same thing. Because you can Google it very easily. Symbolism becomes a very shallow and pathetic excuse for doing architecture."

In the end, Mr. Yao says, "I think architects still have to go back to the basics: the space, the materials, the light, the emotions of the people. All these basic things are what is important. Trying to borrow cheap symbolism doesn't go too far." He pauses, "And it's very regrettable."

"The other thing is that most students should try to think more about time. In other words, longevity. The permanence of things. These days we build all these corporate buildings or even cultural buildings, all these fancy, flashy exotic forms. But are we thinking only about the newborn moment of the building. In Buddhism, they talk about the birth, the middle, and then cessation. The beginning, the middle, the end.

"Architects often only think about the birth of a building. Some people get scolded because they don't think how to sustain the building beyond its inception.

But people need to think about how buildings decay. And especially in religious buildings, people should think about the permanence of a building." Mr. Yao reminds us, "We appreciate the longevity of those old churches in southern Europe, all these ruin-like monasteries in Tibet and wherever. There is this thing that goes on, continues, beyond the immediacy of the initial building of a project. And this is especially true for religious buildings."

In fact, time is a theme that can be applied not just to a specific building's design, but in one's overall approach to work, "I think it's important to take the long view and consider things beyond the present. There is a term in Japanese, *wabi-sabi*. *Wabi-sabi* is aesthetics or the attitude towards beauty after accepting the impermanence of all phenomenon. From that one develops a different set of aesthetic values."

Mr. Yao pauses and then says, "I love that story of a Buddhist monk, that there are all these beautiful sand and rock gardens in Kyoto, but how does a monk clean a garden filled with fallen leaves? Basically he goes out and carefully picks out all the leaves, cleans whatever is untidy, and uses a bamboo broom and sweep the stones into a circular wave-like patterns. And after everything is done, he goes to the tree in the corner and shakes the leaves down and then it's done."

Chapter 30

Makespace Architects

Mr. Shahed Saleem, Dip. Arch., MA RIBA, Founder and Director

Background

Mr. Saleem began working after training first in architecture and then archaeology. He says, "I studied architecture in Kingston University in southwest London. Always drawing, and making stuff, it seemed to make the most sense to me. I was probably thinking of graphic design or some kind of other arts at the time."

But architecture school in London, according to Mr. Saleem, takes a different approach than what most associate with the education. "The thing with London architecture schools is that they are different from schools outside London. Their approach is very cultural. In other words, it's taught as a cultural subject more than a technical, skill-based subject. So when I was at Kingston I looked at issues of post-colonial identities and social relationships to architecture." In other words, explains Mr. Saleem, "the way that we were taught crossed over quite a lot with cultural studies. We examined wider debates about how architecture fits into processes of society. It was very much about architecture as a subject through which society and culture is made. That's the emphasis I took away from school."

With this background, Mr. Saleem decided to explore the workings of architecture in conflict zones: "After I did work in London and went to Bosnia over a number of years from 1996 to 2000, in Sarajevo. This is after the war there. I went with an aid convoy in architecture." He continues, "What fascinated me was the way society was completely deconstructed and being completely reconstructed, and how identity, religion, and ethnicity were being negotiated as this process of making culture and space. That led me to looking at the possibility of development and construction and I was looking at mosques at the time."

Mr. Saleem decided that his experiences needed more context, so he pursued a degree in a different academic discipline: "I then got an MA in Anthropology and Development Studies at SOAS, which involved two years of coursework. We focused on the processes through which social groups are made and formed. I studied anthropology and learned the basics of a discipline that wasn't architecture. So I learned to interrogate the world in another, non-architectural way. And the kind of issues anthropologists are interested in resonated with me because it enabled me to gather tools to unpack social trauma and the issues that go along with it."

Observations and Advice

"Having done that schooling and work made me able to do the book project I'm working on now, about the history of mosques in the UK. I had this fieldwork-based training that included an interrogation of social factors. That enabled me to take the book project. That was a project that brought together all these strands of thought and inspiration."

In fact, his educational and work background has been, "an exploration of contemporary identity within built contexts and what that might be and how it might manifest through architecture, which for me is multilayered and fluid."

Therefore, he says, "I would suggest that people think a good few times before putting any proposal together. Really think about the lateral issues and about what they're doing. I might also advise to not make things too complicated so the building or mosque is only one aspect in a wider complicated, multi-layered narrative. It's not going to do everything or be everything. So don't take it too seriously."

Chapter 31

OOPEAA (Office for Peripheral Architecture)

Mr. Anssi Lassila, M.Arch, Founder and Director

Background

Mr. Lassilla studied at the University of Oulu where, as a graduate student at the age of 24, he entered a competition. "That was in 1998," he says. "I was a fifth-year student and I wanted to participate in the competition. In Finland we have a tradition that if you want make your own career or open your own office, you must have won a couple of competitions. And of course I had some friends with a dream to have my own office someday so I entered the competition!"

Observations and Advice

Mr. Lassila's observations are very succinct. Successful communication with clients must include listening. But that extends beyond simply the client. With the strong tradition of working closely with artisan-level construction workers in Finland, Mr. Lassila finds that communication is more about listening than talking. In the end, the best advice is short: "I think it is a very important thing to learn, to communicate and listen well to clients. It's also important to communicate well with carpenters who really make the project."

Chapter 32

Roto Architects

Mr. Michael Rotondi, FAIA, Founder and Principal

Observations and Advice

Mr. Rotondi's outlook is guided by an unending curiosity: "I want to know everything about everything before I die and it's not possible. So I see any project that comes along as a potential research project as well as whatever the practical things I have to solve. So I'm always trying to think about the things I think about often and in different ways. It would be nice if I could see the world as if for the first time like children do, where you have no basis for knowing something because it's the first time you've seen it, it's the first time you've experienced it. And so you see it with great wonder. When you see things over and over again, you see them like an expert. You come to conclusions that aren't too dissimilar from the conclusions you came to before. So you're not enchanted by the world anymore."

He offers an example: "If I were shining a flashlight on a sphere, a big sphere, I'd see only that part that the light hits. I don't see the rest of it. That's the way I imagine everything in the world is. So there have to be other people standing around with their own flashlights telling you what they say, and then when they tell you see, you're able to construct it into a greater, holistic vision.

"So that's why I keep reading," he says. "That's why I'm always, I rarely talk on a plane, but sometimes I do if I'm sitting next to a nano-technologist or something like that. Which I actually did coming from China recently, a nano-biotechnologist. That was interesting!"

That reading, Mr. Rotondi explains, is directly related to spiritual practice: "I came back to spiritual practice but not religious practice. I started working with, reading a lot about any society that had figured out how to integrate matters of the mind and matters of the heart because in our world they're really separated out which is really Cartesian. I don't think it so much of Descartes' doing, well it was, but it was also he had to separate the body from the mind so that the church didn't burn him at the cross. The soul is in the body, you know, the mind was age of reason, the church was okay with that.

"I did a good job at pretending to be angry at the world even though I was, my life wasn't a crisis but a shift back into the youth. But my default is back to the inherent goodness in everything and if anything transgresses, it almost wasn't their fault. It's about limits. And the better I know limits, the less I complain about other people's limits. For example, if you complain about people who are too shy or overweight or too talkative, it's a projection because you're talking about yourself."

"Work is prayer. If you're doing the right thing and you really like what you're doing. I don't have any hobbies. People say what do you do and I say I'm working. There's a mystic master Eckhart who wrote volumes about the passion for creation. And work is creative therefore work is prayer. And you do it in a way that you're focused in such an intense manner that it begins to dissolve time. The Shakers were like that. The extraordinary things they made, it was made that way because they saw it as prayer. You get the least amount of material, the greatest proportions, elegant systems, beautiful shapes. They're not making units to be moved. The endgame isn't selling to Google.

BIBLIOGRAPHY

Abu-Lughod, Janet. "On the Remaking of History: How to Reinvent the Past," in *Remaking History: Discussions in Contemporary Culture*, edited by Barbara Kruger and Phil Mariani (Seattle: Dia Art Foundation, 1989): 111–129.

A China Missionary. "First Thoughts on the Débâcle of Christian Missions in China," *African Affairs*, Vol. 51, No. 202 (Janaury, 1952): 33–41.

Alexander, John. "Shaping Sacred Space in the Sixteenth Century: Design Criteria for the collegio Borromeo's Chapel," *Journal of the Society of Architectural Historians*, Vol. 63, No. 2 (June, 2004): 164–179.

Al-Jami, Abdulluh and Michael H. Mitias. "Does an Islamic Architecture Exist?" *Revista Portuguesa de Filosofia*, T. 60, Fasc. 1 (January–March, 2004): 197–214.

Allen, Douglas. "Phenomenology of Religion," in *The Routledge Companion to the Study of Religion*, edited by John R. Hinnells (London and New York: Routledge, 2005): 182–207.

Asad, Talal. *Genealogies of Religion: Discipline and Reasons of Power in Christianity and Islam*. (Baltimore: Johns Hopkins University Press, 1993).

Asad, Talal. *The Idea of An Anthropology of Islam* (District of Columbia: Center for Contemporary Arab Studies, 1986).

Aslan, Reza. *No God But God: the Origins, Evolution, and Future of Islam* (New York: Random House, 2011).

Awkward, Michael. "Race, Gender, and the Politics of Reading," *Black American Literature Forum*, Vol. 22, No. 1 (1988): 5–27.

Baan, Iwan. *Brasilia – Chadnigarh Living With Modernity* (Zurich: Lars Müller Publishers, 2010).

Bakker, Hans. "Construction and Reconstruction of Sacred Space in Vārāṇasī," *Numen*, Vol. 43, Fasc. 1 (January, 1996): 32–55.

Barrett, Mark. "The Monastery as Sacred Space," in *Sacred Space: Interdisciplinary Perspectives within Contemporary Contexts*, edited by Steve Brie, Jenny Daggers and David Torevell (Newcastle upon Tyne: Cambridge Scholars Publishing, 2010): 9–22.

Bell, Catherine. *Ritual Theory, Ritual Practice* (Oxford: Oxford University Press, 1992).

Bermudez, Julian and Brandon Ro. "Extraordinary Architectural Experiences: Comparative Study of Three Paradigmatic Cases of Sacred Spaces, The Pantheon, the Chartres Cathedral and the Chapel of Ronchamp," 2nd International Congress on Ambiances (Montreal 2012): 689–694.

Bertagnin, Mauro, Ilham Khuri-Makdis, and Susan Gilson Miller. "A Mediterranean Jewish Quarter and Its Architectural Legacy: the *Giudecca* of Trani, Italy (1000–1550)," *Traditional Dwellings and Settlements Review*, Vol. 14, No. 2 (2003): 33–46.

Bhatt, Ritu. "Indianizing Indian Architecture: A Postmodern Tradition," *Traditional Dwellings and Settlements Review*, Vol. 13, No. 1 (Fall, 2001): 43–51.

Biddick, Kathleen. "Becoming Collection: The Spatial Afterlife of Medieval Universal Histories in Late Medieval Italian Cities," in *Medieval Practices of Space*, edited by Barbara A. Hanawalt and Michal Kobialka (Berkeley and Los Angeles: University of California Press, 2000): 223–241.

Blake, Kevin. "Sacred and Secular Landscape Symbolism at Mount Taylor, New Mexico," *Journal of the Southwest*, Vol. 41, No. 4 (Winter, 1999): 487–509.

Blight, David W. *Race and Reunion: the Civil War in American History* (Cambridge, MA: Belknap Press of Harvard University Press, 2001).

Boyko, Oksana. "The Synagogue in Zhovkva: History and Architectural Development, *Ukrainian Journal of Physical Optics*, Supp. 2 (2011): 18–46.

Bradford, Amory H. "The Missionary Outlook," *The Biblical World*, Vol. 13, No. 2 (February, 1899): 79–87.

Branham, Joan R. "Mapping Sacrifice on Bodies and Spaces in Late-antique Judaism and Early Christianity," in *Architecture of the Sacred: Space, Ritual, and Experience from Classical Greece to Byzantium*, edited by Bonna D. Wescoat and Robert G. Ousterhout (Cambridge: Cambridge University Press, 2012): 200–230.

Brenner, Alex. "'Some Imperial Institute': Architecture, Symbolism, and the Ideal of Empire in Late Victoria Britain," *Journal of the Society of Architectural Historians*, Vol. 62, No. 1 (March, 2003): 50–73.

Brie, Steve, Jenny Daggers, and David Torevell. "Introduction," in *Sacred Space: Interdisciplinary Perspectives within Contemporary Contexts*, edited by Steve Brie, Jenny Daggers, and David Torevell (Newcastle upon Tyne: Cambridge Scholars Publishing, 2010): 1–8.

Brown, Linda A. "Dangerous Places and Wild Spaces: Creating Meaning with Materials and Space at Contemporary Maya Shrines on El Duende Mountain," *Journal of Archaeological Method and Theory*, Vol. 11, No. 1 (March, 2004): 31–58.

Burgess, J. Peter. "The Sacred Site in Civil Space: Meaning and Status of the Temple Mount/al-Haram al-Sharif," *Social Identities*, Vol. 10, No. 3 (2004): 311–325.

Burroughs, Charles. "Spaces of Arbitration and the Organization of Space," in *Medieval Practices of Space*, edited by Barbara A. Hanawalt and Michal Kobialka (Berkeley and Los Angeles: University of California Press, 2000): 64–100.

Bynum, Caroline Walker, "The Mysticism and Asceticism of Medieval Women: Some Comments on the Typologies of Max Weber and Ernst Troeltsch," in *Fragmentation and Redemption: Essays on Gender and the Human Body in Medieval Religion* (New York: Urzone, Inc. 1992): 53–78.

Casey, Edward S. *The Fate of Place: A Philosophical History* (Berkeley and Los Angeles: University of California Press. 1997).

Chan, Selina Ching. "Temple-Building and Heritage in China," *Ethnology*, Vol. 44, No. 1 (Winter, 2005): 65–79.

Chidester, David and Edward T. Linenthal. "Introduction," in *American Sacred Space*, edited by David Chidester and Edward T. Linenthal (Bloomington and Indianapolis: Indiana University Press, 1995): 1–42.

Corrigan, John. "Spatiality and Religion," in *The Spatial Turn: Interdisciplinary Perspectives*, edited by Barney Warf and Santa Arias (New York: Routledge, 2009): 157–172.

Cosgrove, Denis "Landscape and Landschaft," *German Historical Institute Bulletin*, No. 35 (Fall, 2004): 1–15.

Crossley, James G. and Christian Karner, "Introduction: Writing History, Constructing Religion," in *Writing History, Constructing Religion*, edited by James G. Crossley and Christian Karner (Burlington and Hampshire: Ashgate, 2005): 3–8.

Ćurčić, Slobodan. "Divine Light, Constructing the Immaterial in Byzantine Art and Architecture," in *Architecture of the Sacred: Space, Ritual, and Experience from Classical Greece to Byzantium*, edited by Bonna D. Wescoat and Robert G. Ousterhout (Cambridge: Cambridge University Press, 2012): 307–337.

Desplat, Patrick A. "Introduction: Representations of Space, Place-making and Urban Life in Muslim Societies," in *Prayer in the City: The Making of Muslim Sacred Places and Urban Life*, edited by Patrick A. Desplat and Dorothea E. Shulz (Bielefeld: Transcript Verlag, 2012): 9–34.

Donaldson, Laura E. and Pui-lan Kwok. "Introduction," in *Postcolonialism, Feminism and Religious Discourse*, edited by Laura E. Donaldson and Kwok Pui-lan (New York: Routledge, 2002): 1–40.

Dox, Donnalee. "Theatrical Space, Mutable Space, and the Space of Imagination: Three Readings of the Croxton *Play of the Sacrament*," in *Medieval Practices of Space*, edited by Barbara A. Hanawalt and Michal Kobialka (Berkeley and Los Angeles: University of California Press, 2000): 167–198.

Elaraby, Kadri M.G. "Neo-Islamic Architecture and Urban Design in the Middle East: From Threshold to Adaptive Design," *Built Environment (1978-)*, Vol. 22, No. 22 (1996): 138–150.

Eliade, Mircea. *Myths, Rites, Symbols: A Mircea Eliade Reader, Vol. 2*, edited by Wendell C. Beane and William G. Doty (New York: Harper and Row Publishers, 1975).

Eliade, Mircea. *The Sacred and the Profane*. New York: Harcourt, 1957, reprint 1987. Translated by William Trask.

Elsner, Jaś. "Material Culture and Ritual: State of the Question," in *Architecture of the Sacred: Space, Ritual, and Experience from Classical Greece to Byzantium*, edited by Bonna D. Wescoat and Robert G. Ousterhout (Cambridge: Cambridge University Press, 2012): 1–26.

Faure, Bernard. *Chan Insights and Oversights: an Epistemological Critique of the Chan Tradition* (Princeton: Princeton University Press, 1993).

Faure, Bernard. "Relics and Flesh Bodies: the Creation of Ch'an Pilgrimage Sites," in *Pilgrims and Sacred Sites in China*, edited by Susan Naquin and Chün-fang Yü (Berkeley and California: University of California Press, 1992): 150–189.

Faure, Bernard. "Space and Place in Chinese Religious Traditions," *History of Religions*, Vol. 26, No. 4 (May, 1987): 337–356.

Gazin-Schwartz, Amy. "Archaeology and Folklore of Material Culture, Ritual, and Everyday Life," *International Journal of Historical Archaeology*, Vol. 5, No. 4 (2001): 263–280.

Gimello, Robert M. "Chang Shang-ying on Wu-t'ai Shan," in *Pilgrims and Sacred Sites in China*, edited by Susan Naquin and Chün-fang Yü (Berkeley and California: University of California Press, 1992): 89–149.

Goodwin, G.M. "The Design of a Modern Synagogue – Goodman, Percival Temple Beth-El in Proidence, Rhode Island (1947–1952)," *American Jewish Archives*, Vol. 45, No. 1 (1993): 31–71.

Graham, Elizabeth. "Mission Archaeology," *Annual Review of Anthropology*, Vol. 27 (1998): 25–62.

Grimes, Ronald L. "Ritual, Performance, and the Sequestering of Sacred Space," Dunbarton Oaks Bynzantine Symposium, (2003): 1–18.

Guisso, Richard W. "Thunder Over the Lake: The Five Classics and the Perception of Woman in Early China," in *Woman in China: Current Directions in Historical Scholarship*, edited by Richard W. Guisso and Stanley Johannsen (Youngstown: Philo Press, 1981): 47–62.

Hackett, Rosalind I.J. "Anthropology of Religion," in *The Routledge Companion to the Study of Religion*, edited by John R. Hinnells (London and New York: Routledge, 2005): 144–163.

Hamilton, Sarah and Andrew Spicer. "Defining the Holy: the Delineation of Sacred Space," in *Defining the Holy: Sacred Space in Medieval and Early Modern Europe*, edited by Andrew Spicer and Sarah Hamilton (Aldershot: Ashgate, 2005): 1–10.

Hans Bakker. "Construction and Reconstruction of Sacred Space in Vārāṇasī," *Numen*, Vol. 43, No. 1 (January, 1996): 32–55.

Harkin, Michael E. "Sacred Places, Scarred Spaces," *Wicazo Sa Review*, Vol. 15, No. 1 (2000): 49–70.

Hauser-Schäublin, Brigitta "The Politics of Sacred Space: Using Conceptual Models of Space for Socio-Political Transformations in Bali," *Bijdragen tot de Taal-, Land-en Volkenkunde*, Vol. 160, No. 2/3 (2004): 283–314.

Hayden, Dolores. *The Power of Place: Urban Landscapes as Public History* (Cambridge, MA: MIT Press, 1994).

Heelas, Paul, "Postmodernism," in *The Routledge Companion to the Study of Religion*, edited by John R. Hinnells (London and New York: Routledge, 2005): 259–274.

Heldman, Marilyn E. "Architectural Symbolism, Sacred Geography and the Ethiopian Church," *Journal of Religion in Africa*, Vol. 22, Fasc. 3 (August, 1992): 222–241.

Helms, Mary W. "Sacred Landscape and the Early Medieval Cloister. Unity, Paradise, and the Cosmic Mountain," *Anthropos*, Vol. 97, No. 2 (2002): 435–453.

Hinnells, John R. "Introduction," in *The Routledge Companion to the Study of Religion*, edited by John R. Hinnells (London and New York: Routledge, 2005): 1–5.

Hinnells, John R. "Why Study Religions?" in *The Routledge Companion to the Study of Religion*, edited by John R. Hinnells (London and New York: Routledge, 2005): 5–20.

Horsley, Richard A. "Religion and Other Products of Empire," *Journal of the American Academy of Religion*, Vol. 71, No. 1 (March, 2003): 13–44.

Horton, Mark C. "Islam, Archaeology, and Swahili Identity," in *Changing Social Identity with the Spread of Islam: Archaeological Perspectives*, edited by D. Whitcomb (Chicago: University of Chicago, 2004): 67–88.

Howarth, David. "Space, Subjectivity, and Politics", *Alternatives: Global, Local, Political*, Vol. 31, No. 2 (April–June 2006): 105–134.

Insoll, Timothy. "Introduction," in *The Oxford Handbook of the Archaeology of Ritual and Religion*, edited by Timothy Insoll (New York: Oxford University Press, 2011): 1–5.

Insoll, Timothy. "Syncretism, Time, and Identity: Islamic Archaeology in West Africa," in *Changing Social Identity with the Spread of Islam: Archaeological Perspectives*, edited by Donald Whitcomb (Chicago: Oriental Institute of the University of Chicago, 2004): 89–101.

Ivey, Paul Eli. Review of *Gothic Arches, Latin Crosses: Anti-Catholicism and American Church Designs in the Nineteenth Century* by Ryan K. Smith; *American Sanctuary: Understanding Sacred Spaces* by Louis P. Nelson. *Journal of the Society of Architectural Historians*, Vol. 6, No. 3 (September 2008): 454–457.

Joyce, Arthur A. "Sacred Space and Social Relations in the Valley of Oaxaca," in *Mesoamerican Archaeology*, edited by J. Hendon and R. Joyce (Oxford: Blackwell, 2004): 192–216.

Jung, Hwa Yol. "Enlightenment and the Question of the Other: A Postmodern Audition," *Human Studies*, Vol. 25, No. 3 (2002): 297–306.

Kadish, Sharman. "Constructing Identity: Anglo-Jewry and Synagogue Architecture," *Architectural History*, Vol. 45 (2002): 386–408.

Kalmar, Ivan Davidson. "Moorish Style: Orientalism, the Jews, and Synagogue Architecture," *Jewish Social Studies*, Vol. 7, No. 3 (Spring/Summer, 2001): 68–100.

Kang, Xiaofei. "Two Temples, Three Religions, and a Tourist Attraction: Contesting Sacred Space on China's Ethnic Frontier," *Modern China*, Vol. 35, No. 3 (May, 2009): 227–255.

Karner, Christian. "Postmodernism and the Study of Religions," in *Writing History, Constructing Religion*, edited by James G. Crossley and Christian Karner (Burlington: Ashgate, 2005): 31–47.

King, Richard. "Orientalism and the Study of Religions," in *The Routledge*

Companion to the Study of Religion, edited by John R. Hinnells (London and New York: Routledge, 2005): 275–290.

Knott, Kim. "Insider/Outsider Perspectives," in *The Routledge Companion to the Study of Religion*, edited by John R. Hinnells (London and New York: Routledge, 2005): 243–258.

Kobialka, Michael. "Staging Place/Space in the Eleventh-Century Monastic Practices," in *Medieval Practices of Space*, edited by Barbara A. Hanawalt and Michael Kobialka (Minneapolis: University of Minnesota Press, 2000): 128–148.

Kravtsov, Sergey R. "Jewish Identities in Synagogue Architecture of Galicia and Bukovina," *Ars Judaica: The Bar-Ilan Journal of Jewish Art*, No. 6 (2010): 81–100.

Kreuz, Eva-Maria. "Light in Sacred Buildings," *Design Manuals*, Part 5 (2008): 60–67.

Lawrence, Denise L. and Setha M. Low. "The Built Environment and Spatial Form," *Annual Review of Anthropology*, Vol. 19 (1990): 453–505.

Lefebvre, Henri. *The Production of Space*, trans. Donald Nicholson-Smith (Oxford: Blackwell, 1991).

Levine, Gregory J. "On the Geography of Religion," *Transactions of the Institute of British Geographers*, Vol. 11, No. 4 (1986): 428–440.

Li, Shiqiao. "Reconstituting Chinese Building Tradition: The Yingzao Fashion in the Early Twentieth Century," *Journal of the Society of Architectural Historians*, Vol. 62, No. 4 (December, 2003): 470–489.

Lilley, Keith D. "Cities of God? Medieval Urban Forms and their Christian Symbolism," *Transactions of the Institute of British Geographers*, Vol. 29, No. 3 (September, 2004): 296–313.

Luz, Nimrod. "The Politics of Sacred Places: Palestinian Identity, Collective Memory, and Resistance in the Hassan Bek Mosque Conflict," *Environment and Planning D: Society and Space*, No. 26, Vol. 6 (2008): 1036–1052.

McClintock, Anne. *Imperial Leather: Race, Gender and Sexuality* (New York: Routledge, 1995).

McGahan, Michelle Lee. "Architecture as Transition: Creating Sacred Space" (Master's thesis, University of Cincinnati, 2004).

Meister, Michael W. and Ananda K. Coomaraswamy. "Early Indian Architecture: IV. Huts and Related Temple Types," *RES: Anthropology and Aesthetics*, No. 14 (Spring, 1988): 5–26.

Memmott, Paul and James Davidson. "Exploring a Cross-Cultural Theory of Architecture," *Traditional Dwellings and Settlements Review*, Vol. 19, No. 2 (Spring, 2008): 57–68.

Miller, Tracy G. "Water Sprites and Ancestor Spirits: Reading the Architecture of Jinci," *The Art Bulletin*, Vol. 86, No. 1 (March, 2004): 6–30.

Naquin, Susan and Chün-fang Yü. "Introduction," in *Pilgrims and Sacred Sites in China*, edited by Susan Naquin and Chün-fang Yü (Berkeley and California: University of California Press, 1992): 1–38.

Nelson, Louis P. "Sensing the Sacred: Anglican Material Religion in Early South Carolina," *Winterthur Portfolio*, Vol. 41, No. 4 (Winter, 2007): 203–238.

Ousterhout, Robert G. "The Sanctity of Place and the Sanctity of Buildings: Jerusalem Versus Constantinople," in *Architecture of the Sacred: Space, Ritual, and Experience from Classical Greece to Byzantium*, edited by Bonna D. Wescoat and Robert G. Ousterhout (Cambridge: Cambridge University Press, 2012): 281–306.

Paden, William E. "Comparative Religion," in *The Routledge Companion to the Study of Religion*, edited by John R. Hinnells (London and New York: Routledge, 2005): 208–225.

Park, Chris. "Religion and Geography," in *The Routledge Companion to the Study of Religion*, edited by John R. Hinnells (London and New York: Routledge, 2004): 439–456.

Piotrowski, Andrezej. "Architecture and the Iconoclastic Controversy in Late Medieval Italian Cities," in *Medieval Practices of Space*, edited by Barbara A. Hanawalt and Michal Kobialka (Berkeley and Los Angeles: University of California Press, 2000): 101–127.

Prakash, Gyan. "Who's Afraid of Postcoloniality," *Social Text*, Vol. 14, No. 4 (1996): 187–203.

Prussin, Labelle. "Non-Western Sacred Sites: African Models," *Journal of the Society of Architectural Historians*, Vol. 58, No. 3 (September, 1999): 424–433.

Rabbat, Nasser. "Toward a Critical Historiography of Islamic Architecture," *Repenser les limites: l'architecture à travers l'espace, le temps et les disciplines*, Paris, INHA, 2005, http://inha.revues.org/642 (October 28, 2008): 1–6.

Rabbat, Nasser. "What is Islamic Architecture Anyway?" *Journal of Art Historiography*, No. 6 (June, 2012): 1–15

Rakatansky, Mark. "Identity and the Discourse of Politics in Contemporary Architecture," *Assemblage*, No. 27 (August 1995): 8–18.

Riesebrodt, Martin and Mary Ellen Knoeczny. "Sociology of Religion," in *The Routledge Companion to the Study of Religion*, edited by John R. Hinnells (London and New York: Routledge, 2005): 125–143.

Said, Edward. *Culture and Imperialism* (New York: Random House, 1994).

Segal, Robert A. "Theories of Religion," in *The Routledge Companion to the Study of Religion*, edited by John R. Hinnells (London and New York: Routledge, 2005): 49–60.

Sharpe, Eric J. "The Study of Religion in Historical Perspective," in *Routledge Companion to the Study of Religion*, edited by J. Hinnells (London: Routledge, 2004): 21–38.

Shatzman Steinhardt, Nancy. "A Jin Hall at Jingtusi: Architecture in Search of Identity," in *Ars Orientalis*, Vol. 33 (2003): 76–119.

Shatzman Steinhardt, Nancy. "The Mizong Hall of Qinglong Si: Space, Ritual, and Classicism in Tang Architecture," *Archives of Asian Art*, Vol. 44 (1991): 27–50.

Shatzman Steinhardt, Nancy. "The Tang Architectural Icon and the Politics of Chinese Architectural History," *The Art Bulletin*, Vol. 86, No. 2 (June, 2004): 228–254.

Shatzman Steinhardt, Nancy. "Toward the Definition of a Yuan Dynasty Hall," *Journal of the Society of Architectural Historians*, Vol. 47, No. 1 (March, 1988): 57–73.

Simmins, Geoffrey. *Sacred Spaces and Sacred Places* (Saarbrücken: VDM Publishing, 2008).

Soja, Edward W. "Taking Space Personally," in *The Spatial Turn: Interdisciplinary Perspectives*, edited by Barney Warf and Santa Arias (New York: Routledge, 2009): 11–37.

Stoddard, Robert H. "Perceptions About the Geography of Religious Sites in the Kathmandu Valley," *Contributions to Nepalese Studies*, Vol. VII, No. 1–2 (December, 1979- June, 1980): 97–119.

Stoddard, Robert H. "Pilgrimage Places and Sacred Geometries," in *Pilgrimate: Sacred Landscapes and Self-Organized Complexity*, edited by John McKim Malville and Baidyanath Saraswati (New Delhi: Indira Gandhi National Centre for the Arts, 2009): 163–177.

Stoddard, Robert and Alan Morinis. "Introduction: The Geographic Contribution to Studies of Pilgrimage," in *Sacred Places, Sacred Spaces: The Geography of Pilgrimages*, edited by Robert H. Stoddard and

Alan Morinis (Baton Rouge: Louisiana State University Department of Geography and Anthropology, 1997): 2–4.

Tachau, William G. "The Architecture of the Synagogue," *American Jewish Year Book*, Vol. 28 (1972): 155–192.

Walsh, Michael J. "Efficacious Surroundings: Temple Space and Buddhist Well-being," *Journal of Religion and Health*, Vol. 46, No. 4 (Dec., 2007): 471–479.

Warf, Barney and Santa Arias. "Introduction: the Reinsertion of Space in the Humanities and Social Sciences," in *The Spatial Turn: Interdisciplinary Perspectives*, edited by Barney Warf and Santa Arias (New York: Routledge, 2009): 1–10.

Weightman, Barbara A. "Sacred Landscapes and the Phenomenon of Light," *American Geographical Society*, Vol. 86, No. 1 (January, 1996): 59–71.

Wescoat, Bonna D., and Robert G. Ousterhout. "Afterword," in *Architecture of the Sacred: Space, Ritual, and Experience from Classical Greece to Byzantium*, edited by Bonna D. Wescoat and Robert G. Ousterhout (Cambridge: Cambridge University Press, 2012b): 365–375.

Wescoat, Bonna D. and Robert G. Ousterhout, "Preface," in *Architecture of the Sacred: Space, Ritual, and Experience from Classical Greece to Byzantium*, edited by Bonna D. Wescoat and Robert G. Ousterhout (Cambridge: Cambridge University Press, 2012a): xxiii.

Whitcomb, Donald. "Introduction," in *Changing Social Identity with the Spread of Islam: Archaeological Perspectives*, edited by Donald Whitcomb (Chicago: Oriental Institute of the University of Chicago, 2004): 1–10.

Whyte, William. "How do Buildings Mean? Some Issues of Interpretation in the History of Architecture," *History and Theory*, Vol. 45, No. 2 (May, 2006): 153–177.

Wing, Sherin. "Re-Gendering Buddhism: Postcolonialism, Gender, and the Princess Miaoshan Legend (PhD diss., University of California, Los Angeles, 2010).

Wing, Sherin. "Gendering Buddhism: The Miaoshan Legend Reconsidered," *Journal of Feminist Studies in Religion*, Vol. 27, No. 1 (Spring 2011): 5–31.

Wolniewicz, Richard. "Ethnic Church Architecture," *Polish American Studies*, Vol. 54, No. 1 (Spring, 1997): 53–73.

Wu, Pei-yi. "An Ambivalent Pilgrim to T'ai Shan in the 17th Century," in *Pilgrims and Sacred Sites in China*, edited by Susan Naquin and Chün-fang Yü (Berkeley and California: University of California Press, 1992): 65–88.

Yü, Chün-fang. "P'u-t'o Shan: Pilgrimage and the Creation of the Chinese Potalaka," in *Pilgrims and Sacred Sites in China*, edited by Susan Naquin and Chün-fang Yü (Berkeley and California: University of California Press, 1992): 190–245.

Zelinsky, Wilbur. "The Uniqueness of the American Religious Landscape," *Geographical Review*, Vol. 91, No. 3 (July, 2001): 565–585.

ACKNOWLEDGMENTS

There are several people who deserve recognition and gratitude for helping me with this book. Special thanks goes to Guy Horton, whose suggestion began this journey, first as an article and then as a book. His love, as well as his ideas and help with communication, made this book possible. Thank you to Susan Szenasy, editor in chief at *Metropolis Magazine*, who agreed to publish an article on Michael Rotondi's—and thanks to him for agreeing to be interviewed—work in sacred spaces and which became a future guide for this book. Wendy Fuller, editor at Taylor & Francis, took a chance on my proposal, went to bat for me, and then agreed to sign me on. Grace Harrison, at Taylor & Francis, has been kind in putting up with my writer's difficulties as I wrote the book and then was so encouraging with her compliments. Many thanks to Kathy Chun for her friendship and the legal advice over great drinks and Nick Chun for all those good times to get me through. Gerhard Hellemann and Junghee Lee deserve thanks for constant jokes and reminders of my writing duties. Gratitude to Jennifer Jung Kim, who helped me gain access to the journal databases at UCLA to ensure that my research was not completely outdated or irrelevant. Definite thanks to the participants, who include Edward Arcari, Hunter Gunderson, Anthony Iovino, Anssi Lassila, Victoria Meyers, Michael Rotondi, Shahed Saleem, Matthew Swindel, and Kris Yao, as well as their employees Katie Branham, Dariusz Bona, Kathy Chiao, Teresa Frausin, and Angie Kim, for all their help. Finally, thank you to Jianling and Kailing, Wanda, Wilson, Charmeen and Darlene for their constant love and encouragement.

CREDITS

Chapter 5
Korean Presbyterian Church Sections A, courtesy Arcari+Iovino.
Korean Presbyterian Church Section B, courtesy Arcari+Iovino.
Korean Presbyterian Church plans 1–3, courtesy Arcari+Iovino.
Teaneck synagogue exterior, courtesy Jim Shive.
Teaneck synagogue exterior, courtesy Jim Shive.
Teaneck synagogue interior, courtesy Jim Shive.
Teaneck synagogue interior, courtesy Jim Shive.

Chapter 6
Infinity Chapel interior, courtesy Victoria Meyers.
Infinity Chapel interior, courtesy Victoria Meyers.
Infinity shapes diagram, courtesy hMa.
Infinity Chapel development diagram, courtesy hMa.
Infinity light sequence diagrams, courtesy hMa.
Infinity Chapel interior, courtesy Victoria Meyers.
Infinity Chapel interior, courtesy Victoria Meyers.
Chapel of the Light stage rendering, courtesy hMa.
Chapel of the Light side wall rendering, courtesy hMa.
Chapel of the Light stage, courtesy Victoria Meyers.
Chapel of the Light interior, courtesy Victoria Meyers.
Chapel of the Light exterior, courtesy Victoria Meyers.

Chapter 7
Peitou Catholic Church plans 1–3, courtesy Kris Yao Artech.
Peitou Catholic Church elevations, courtesy Kris Yao Artech.
Peitou Catholic Church models, courtesy Kris Yao Artech.

Chapter 8
Hackney exterior 1–4, courtesy Makespace Architects.
Hackney panorama, courtesy Makespace Architects.
Hackney interior, courtesy Makespace Architects.
Aaberdeen exterior 1–2, courtesy Makespace Architects.
Aberdeen cutaway, courtesy Makespace Architect.

Chapter 9
Kärsämäki floor plan, courtesy OOPEAA.
Kärsämäki sections 1–2, courtesy OOPEAA.
Kärsämäki sketches 1–2, courtesy OOPEAA.
Kärsämäki exterior 1–4, courtesy Jussi Tiainen.
Kärsämäki interior 1–3, courtesy Jussi Tiainen.
Kuokkala interior sketch, courtesy OOPEAA.
Kuokkala plans, courtesy OOPEAA.
Kuokkala façade rendering, courtesy OOPEAA.
Kuokkala sections 1–2, courtesy OOPEAA.
Kuokkala exterior 1–5, courtesy Jussi Tiainen.
Kuokkala interior 1–7, courtesy Jussi Tiainen.
Klaukkala plan cellar, courtesy OOPEAA.
Klaukkala plans 1–2, courtesy OOPEAA.
Klaukkala southwest elevation, courtesy OOPEAA.
Klaukkala northwest elevation, courtesy OOPEAA.
Klaukkala sections 1–4, courtesy OOPEAA.
Klaukkala sketch exterior axonometric view, courtesy OOPEAA.
Klaukkala sketch interior, courtesy OOPEAA.
Klaukkala exterior 1–11, courtesy Jussi Tiainen.
Klaukkala interior 1–6, courtesy Jussi Tiainen.

Chapter 13
All images courtesy of Roto Architects.

Chapter 14
Fo Guang Shan Monastery, second floor, courtesy Kris Yao Artech.
Fo Guang Shan, ground floor, courtesy Kris Yao Artech.
Fo Guang Shan rendering, courtesy Kris Yao Artech.
Fo Guang Shan, courtesy Xavier Benony.
Fo Guang Shan, courtesy Willy Berre.
Fo Guang Shan North Carolina site, courtesy Kris Yao Artech.
Fo Guang Shan North Carolina site, first floor plan, courtesy Kris Yao Artech.
Fo Guang Shan North Carolina site, second floor plan, courtesy Kris Yao Artech.
Fo Guang Shan North Carolina, sections, courtesy Kris Yao Artech.
Fo Guang Shan North Carolina, elevation, courtesy Kris Yao Artech.
Fo Guang Shan, North Carolina, courtesy Kris Yao Artech.
Fo Guang Shan, North Carolina, courtesy Kris Yao Artech.
Fo Guang Shan, North Carolina, courtesy Bob Andron.
Water Moon Monastery, courtesy Jeffrey Cheng.
Water Moon Monastery, courtesy Jeffrey Cheng.
Water Moon site, courtesy Kris Yao Artech.
Water Moon south elevation, courtesy Kris Yao Artech.
Water Moon first floor plan, courtesy Kris Yao Artech.
Water Moon second floor plan, courtesy Kris Yao Artech.
Water Moon, courtesy Deng Po Jen.
Water Moon, courtesy Kris Yao Artech.
Water Moon, courtesy Jeffrey Cheng.
Water Moon, courtesy Jeffrey Cheng.
Water Moon, courtesy Jeffrey Cheng.
Water Moon, courtesy Deng Po Jen.
Water Moon, courtesy Jeffrey Cheng.

Chapter 18
Won Dharma exterior 1–4, courtesy Debra Bilow.
Won Dharma exterior 1–5, courtesy hMa.
Won Dharma landscape planting, courtesy hMa.
Won Dharma infinite bleed edge diagram, courtesy hMa.
Won Dharma void diagram, courtesy hMa.
Won Dharma ecology diagram, courtesy hMa.
Won Dharma plans 1–2, courtesy hMa.

Chapter 19
Buddhist Retreat breezeway, courtesy Imbue Design.
Buddhist Retreat north side, night, courtesy Imbue Design.
Buddhist Retreat entry stairs, courtesy Imbue Design.
Buddhist Retreat north volume, courtesy Imbue Design.
Buddhist Retreat pre-dawn deck, courtesy Imbue Design.
Buddhist Retreat site plan, courtesy Imbue Design.
Buddhist Retreat plans and sections, courtesy Imbue Design.
Buddhist Retreat floor plans, courtesy Imbue Design.
Mt. Olympus conservatory rendering, courtesy Imbue Design.
Mt. Olympus front elevation, courtesy Imbue Design.
Mt. Olympus rear exterior, courtesy Imbue Design.
Mt. Olympus screen stairs interior rendering, courtesy Imbue Design.
Mt. Olympus interior rendering, courtesy Imbue Design.

INDEX

Made in the USA
San Bernardino, CA
08 December 2019

61089128R00180